The Schlager Anthology of Women's History

A Student's Guide to Essential Primary Sources

The Schlager Anthology of Women's History

A Student's Guide to Essential Primary Sources

Kelli McCoy
Editor in Chief

Dallas, TX

The Schlager Anthology of Women's History:
A Student's Guide to Essential Primary Sources

Copyright © 2023 by Schlager Group Inc.

All rights reserved. No part of this book may be reproduced or utilized in any form or by any means, electronic or mechanical, including photocopying, recording, or by any information storage or retrieval systems, without permission in writing from the publisher. For information, contact:

Schlager Group Inc.
10228 E. Northwest HWY, STE 1151
Dallas, TX 75238
USA
(888) 416-5727
info@schlagergroup.com

You can find Schlager Group online at https://www.schlagergroup.com

For Schlager Group:
Vice President, Editorial: Sarah Robertson
Vice President, Operations and Strategy: Benjamin Painter
Founder and President: Neil Schlager

Printed in the United States of America 10 9 8 7 6 5 4 3 2 1
Print ISBN: 9781961844018
eBook: 9781961844025

Library of Congress Control Number: 2023947236

Contents

Reader's Guide..xii
Contributors..xiv
Acknowledgments...xv
Introduction...xvii

Volume 1

Chapter 1: Women and Gender in the Ancient World..3
Enheduanna: *Hymns to Inana*...7
Code of Assura...11
Sappho: Poems and Fragments...14
Herodotus: *The History of the Persian Wars*...18
Ban Zhao: *Lessons for a Woman*...21
Plutarch: *Moralia*: "On the Bravery of Women"..25
Soranus: *Gynaecology*..29
Juvenal: *The Satires*...33
Vibia Perpetua: *The Passion of Saints Perpetua and Felicity*..37
St. Jerome: Letter CVII to Laeta..41

Chapter 2: Women in the Early Modern Era...45
Julian of Norwich: *Revelations of Divine Love*..48
Geoffrey Chaucer: "The Wife of Bath"...51
Christine de Pisan: *The Treasure of the City of Ladies*...55
Joan of Arc: Letter to King Henry VI of England...59
Margery Kempe: *The Book of Margery Kempe*..62
Henrich Kramer: *Malleus Maleficarum*..66
Veronica Franco: A Warning to a Mother Considering Turning Her Daughter into a Courtesan...................70
Queen Elizabeth I: Speech to the Troops at Tilbury..73
Ursula de Jesus: "Visions of the World to Come"...76
Juana Inés de la Cruz: "The Poet's Answer to Sor Filotea de la Cruz"...79
Mary Astell: *A Serious Proposal to the Ladies for the Advancement of Their True and Greatest Interest*..............83
Lady Mary Wortley Montagu: Smallpox Vaccination in Turkey..87
Lady Hong: "Diary of Lady Hong, Queen of Korea"..90
William Blackstone: *Commentaries on the Laws of England*: "Of Husband and Wife"...........93

Chapter 3: Women in Colonial and Revolutionary America..97
Massachusetts Bay Colony Trial against Anne Hutchinson...100
Margaret Brent's Request for Voting Rights..104
Virginia's Act XII: Negro Women's Children to Serve according to the Condition of the Mother..................106

Anne Bradstreet: "Before the Birth of One of Her Children"..108
Deodat Lawson: "A Further Account of the Tryals of the New England Witches,
Sent in a Letter from Thence, to a Gentleman in London"...111
Letter from Elizabeth Sprigs to Her Father...115
Phillis Wheatley: "His Excellency General Washington"...117
Abigail Adams: "Remember the Ladies" Letter to John Adams...120
Cherokee Women: Letter to Governor Benjamin Franklin..122
Benjamin Rush: "Thoughts upon Female Education"...125

Chapter 4: Women's Rights in the Late Modern Era..131
Catherine Sawbridge Macaulay Graham: *Letters on Education*..135
Olympe de Gouges: *Declaration of the Rights of Woman and of the Female Citizen* 139
Mary Wollstonecraft: *A Vindication of the Rights of Woman*..142
Mary Hays: Appeal to the Men of Great Britain in Behalf of Women....................................147
Priscilla Bell Wakefield: *Reflections on the Present Condition of the Female Sex;
with Suggestions for Its Improvement*...150
Savitribai Phule: "Go, Get Education"...154
Caroline Norton: *Letter to the Queen on Lord Chancellor Cranworth's Marriage and Divorce Bill*............................157
Maria Eugenia Echenique: "The Emancipation of Women"...162
Emmeline Pankhurst: "Freedom or Death"...165
Virginia Woolf: *A Room of One's Own*..170

Chapter 5: American Women's Lives in the Nineteenth Century.........................175
Catherine E. Beecher: *Treatise on Domestic Economy*...178
Margaret Fuller: *Woman in the Nineteenth Century*...182
Frances Anne Kemble: *Journal of a Residence on a Georgian Plantation in 1838–1839*.........187
Amelia Jenks Bloomer: "Alas! Poor Adam" Speech..191
Victoria Woodhull: *Lecture on Constitutional Equality*..196
Page Act of 1875..200
Sarah Winnemucca Hopkins: *Life among the Piutes*...203
Susan B. Anthony: "The Status of Woman, Past, Present, and Future"..................................206
Elinore Pruitt Stewart: *Letters of a Woman Homesteader*...210

Chapter 6: Votes for Women: Suffrage in the United States.................................213
Sarah M. Grimké: Reply to the Pastoral Letter the General Association
of Congregational Ministers of Massachusetts..216
Elizabeth Cady Stanton: Seneca Falls Convention Declaration of Sentiments.....................220
Lucretia Mott: "Discourse on Women" 224
Sojourner Truth: "Ain't I a Woman?" 228
Elizabeth Cady Stanton: Address to the New York Legislature...231
Minor v. Happersett..235
Francis Parkman: *Some of the Reasons against Woman Suffrage*..239
Josephine St. Pierre Ruffin: "Address to the First National Conference of Colored Women" 243

Mary Church Terrell: "The Progress of Colored Women" 246
Anna Howard Shaw: Address on the Place of Women in Society 249
Ida Husted Harper: Statement before the U.S. Senate Select Committee on Woman Suffrage 252
Charlotte Perkins Gilman: "The Humanness of Women" 256
Jane Addams: "Why Women Should Vote" 260
Alice Paul: Testimony before the House Judiciary Committee 264
Mabel Ping-Hua Lee: "The Submerged Half" 268
Carrie Chapman Catt: "Equal Suffrage" 272
Nineteenth Amendment to the U.S. Constitution 275
William Pickens: "The Woman Voter Hits the Color Line" 278
Alice Moore Dunbar-Nelson: "The Negro Woman and the Ballot" 281
Eleanor Roosevelt: "Women Must Learn to Play the Game as Men Do" 284

Volume 2

Chapter 7: Women's Reform and Justice Movements in the United States..289
Frances Wright: "Of Free Enquiry" 293
Lydia Maria Child: *An Appeal in Favor of That Class of Americans Called Africans* 297
Harriet Jacobs: *Incidents in the Life of a Slave Girl* 300
Nellie Bly: *Ten Days in a Mad-House* 303
Jane Addams: "The Subjective Necessity for Social Settlements" 307
Ida B. Wells: *Southern Horrors* 310
Frances Willard: Address before the Woman's Christian Temperance Union 313
Clara Barton: *The Red Cross in Peace and War* 316
Ida B. Wells: "Lynching: Our National Crime" 319
Rachel Carson: *Silent Spring* 322

Chatper 8: Women's Work and Labor Movements..326
Mary S. Paul: Letters from Lowell Mills 330
Isabella Beeton: *Mrs. Beeton's Book of Household Management* 334
Bradwell v. the State of Illinois 338
Lucy Parsons: "The Negro: Let Him Leave Politics to the Politician and Prayers to the Preacher" 342
Clara Zetkin: "Women's Work and the Trade Unions" 345
Jack London: *The People of the Abyss* 348
Florence Kelley: "Child Labor and Women's Suffrage" 352
Kelly Miller: "The Economic Handicap of the Negro in the North" 355
Muller v. Oregon 358
Clara Lemlich: "Life in the Shop" 362
Rose Schneiderman: Speech on the Triangle Shirtwaist Fire 365
Leonora O'Reilly: Statement to the U.S. House Judiciary Committee 368
Elizabeth Gurley Flynn: "The Truth about the Paterson Strike" 371
Helena Swanwick: *The War in Its Effect upon Women* 375

National Women's Trade Union League: Women's Work and War..378
Equal Pay Act..381
Executive Order 11246: Equal Employment Opportunity...384
Dolores Huerta: Statement to the Senate Subcommittee on Migratory Labor..388
Pauline Newman: A Worker Recalls Her Time at the Triangle Shirtwaist Factory 392

Chapter 9: Feminism and Equal Rights in the United States..396
Edith M. Stern: "Women Are Household Slaves"..400
Hoyt v. Florida...404
Betty Friedan: *The Feminine Mystique*..408
President's Commission on the Status of Women: "American Women"..412
Fannie Lou Hamer: Testimony at the Democratic National Convention..416
Title VII of the Civil Rights Act of 1964...419
Pauli Murray and Mary O. Eastwood: "Jane Crow and the Law: Sex Discrimination and Title VII".......423
Casey Hayden and Mary King: "Sex and Caste"..427
National Organization for Women Statement of Purpose..431
Loving v. Virginia..435
Robin Morgan: "No More Miss America!"..439
Segregated Employment Ads..443
Ella Baker: "The Black Woman in the Civil Rights Struggle"..447
Gloria Steinem: "Living the Revolution"...450
Shirley Chisholm: "For the Equal Rights Amendment"...454
Phyllis Schlafly: "What's Wrong with 'Equal Rights' for Women?"...458
Equal Rights Amendment..462
Title IX Education Act of 1972...464
Frontiero v. Richardson...468
Shirley Chisholm: "The Black Woman in Contemporary America"..472
Taylor v. Louisiana..476
Audre Lorde: "Poetry Is Not a Luxury"...479
Meritor Savings Bank v. Vinson..483
Jo Ann Gibson Robinson: *The Montgomery Bus Boycott and the Women Who Started It*......................487
Bella Abzug: "Women and the Fate of the Earth"...491
Sandra Day O'Connor: "Portia's Progress"..495
Violence Against Women Act..499
United States v. Virginia...503
Patsy Mink: Speech on the 25th Anniversary of Title IX...507
Billie Jean King: Commencement Address for University of Massachusetts, Amherst...........................511

Chapter 10: Reproductive Rights in the United States..514
Comstock Act..517
Margaret Sanger: "Birth Control and Racial Betterment"..520
Buck v. Bell..524

Griswold v. Connecticut..528
Roe v. Wade..532
Relf v. Weinberger..536
International Campaign for Abortion Rights: International Day of Action...............................540
Webster v. Reproductive Health Services..544
Margaret Cerullo: "Hidden History: An Illegal Abortion in 1968"..548
Planned Parenthood v. Casey...551
Ruth Bader Ginsburg: Concurrence in *Stenberg, Attorney General of Nebraska, et al. v. Carhart*.............555
Dobbs v. Jackson Women's Health Organization..558

Volume 3

Chapter 11: Gender, Sexuality, and Marriage in the United States..........................**565**
Emma Goldman: "Marriage and Love"...569
Mann Act...573
Mackenzie v. Hare..577
Christine Jorgensen: "The Story of My Life"..580
Denise Harmon: "Stonewall Means Fight Back!"...584
Sylvia Rivera: "Y'All Better Quiet Down"..587
Adrienne Rich: "Compulsory Heterosexuality and Lesbian Experience"......................................590
June Jordan: "A New Politics of Sexuality"...595
Lawrence v. Texas...598
Obergefell v. Hodges...602

Chapter 12: Modern, Postmodern, and Postcolonial Feminisms............................**607**
Simone de Beauvoir: *The Second Sex*...610
Luce Irigaray: "Women on the Market"..613
Hazel V. Carby: "White Woman Listen! Black Feminism and the Boundaries of Sisterhood"...616
Chandra Talpade Mohanty: "Under Western Eyes"...620
Xiao Lu: "China: Feudal Attitudes, Party Control, and Half the Sky"..623
Ama Ata Aidoo: "Ghana: To Be a Woman"..627
Audre Lorde: "The Master's Tools Will Never Dismantle the Master's House".........................630
Gloria Anzaldúa: *Borderlands/La Frontera: The New Mestiza*..634
María Lugones: "Toward a Decolonial Feminism"..638

Chapter 13: Intersectionality in the United States...**643**
Zitkala-Ša: "The Cutting of My Long Hair"...646
Jessie Redmon Fauset: "Some Notes on Color"...649
Marita O. Bonner: "On Being Young—A Woman—And Colored"..652
Zora Neale Hurston: "How It Feels to Be Colored Me"...655
Mary McLeod Bethune: "What Does American Democracy Mean to Me?"..............................658
Combahee River Collective Statement..661

bell hooks: *Feminist Theory: From Margin to Center*..664
Anita Hill: Opening Statement at the Senate Confirmation Hearing of Clarence Thomas......................668
"African American Women in Defense of Ourselves"..672
Alicia Garza: "A Herstory of the #BlackLivesMatter Movement"..675
Say Her Name: Resisting Police Brutality against Black Women..678
Kimberlé Williams Crenshaw: "Say Her Name" Speech..682
Judith Heumann: "Our Fight for Disability Rights—And Why We're Not Done Yet"...........................687
Oprah Winfrey: Cecil B. DeMille Award Acceptance Speech...691
Tarana Burke: "Full Power of Women"..695

Chapter 14: Women's Rights Are Human Rights..**699**
Indira Gandhi: "What Educated Women Can Do"..702
"A Mother's Life in Rural Pernambuco, Brazil"..706
Rigoberta Menchú Tum: Nobel Peace Prize Lecture..709
Hillary Rodham Clinton: "Women's Rights Are Human Rights"...713
Benazir Bhutto: Address at the Fourth World Conference on Women..718
Charlotte Bunch: "Through Women's Eyes: Global Forces Facing Women in the 21st Century"..........722
Queen Noor of Jordan: Remarks at the National Organization
  for Arab-American Women Banquet..726
Wangari Maathai: Nobel Peace Prize Acceptance Speech..730
Betty Williams: "Peace in the World Is Everybody's Business"..734
"Elena's Story"..738
"Fabienne's Story"...742

Chapter 15: Justice Movements in the Twenty-first Century...**746**
Shirin Ebadi: "Iran Awakening: Human Rights, Women, and Islam"..749
Luisa D. Diogo: "Women for a Better World"..753
Ellen Johnson Sirleaf: "A Voice for Freedom"..757
Michelle Bachelet: "Time to Make the Promise of Equality a Reality"...760
Chimamanda Ngozi Adichie: "We Should All Be Feminists"..764
Michelle Obama: Remarks at the 2012 International Women of Courage Awards................................768
Malala Yousafzai: Nobel Peace Prize Acceptance Speech..772
Emma Watson: "HeForShe" Speech to the United Nations...776
Atifete Jahjaga: Support of Women's Property Rights in Kosovo..780
Joyce Banda: Wheelock College Commencement Address...784
Carmen Perez: Address at the Women's March on Washington..788
X González: "We Call BS"..792
Autumn Peltier: Address at the UN World Water Day...796
Greta Thunberg: "Our House Is on Fire"..799
Josina Machel: "Male Violence against Women: The Next Frontier in Humanity"..............................803
Kamala Harris: "The Status of Women Is the Status of Democracy"..806
Sustainable Development Goal 5: Achieve Gender Equality and Empower All Women and Girls.........809

List of Documents by Category 813
Index 819

The Schlager Anthology of Women's History

A Student's Guide to Essential Primary Sources

Chapter 11

Gender, Sexuality, and Marriage in the United States

Marriage in the United States was traditionally viewed as a union, based on love, between a man and a woman. This union was sanctioned by either the church or by civil authorities. Societal standards of the 1700s and 1800s reinforced the notion of marriage as a partnership in which each gender had fairly defined roles. Both the law and customs were based on patriarchy, the idea that the male, or father, was head of the household and leader of the family.

Early Feminists Challenge the Traditional Concept of Marriage

Feminists increasingly challenged this concept of marriage in the 1900s. Some women's rights leaders saw marriage as an inherently discriminatory structure that devalued women and made them subservient to men. Others believed the institution constrained women's relationships and limited their life choices. Finally, others highlighted the potential negative effects of marriage on children who were raised with negative gender stereotypes because of the inequalities between husband and wife. The radical anarchist Emma Goldman wrote a highly critical essay on marriage in 1910. In "Marriage and Love," Goldman argued that while some marriages were based on love and consideration, the majority were simply an "economic arrangement" between a man and a woman. This agreement generally put women at a disadvantage since it forced them to surrender their autonomy to their husband in exchange for financial support. Laws at the time made it difficult, and often very expensive, to seek a divorce, which essentially trapped women who were in unhappy or abusive marriages. It was not until the 1950s that divorce began to become more common in the United States.

While some Americans increasingly questioned traditional views of marriage and sexuality, the government responded with legislation designed to strengthen the customary views of matrimony, gender, and sexuality. Under the Extradition Act of 1907, U.S. women who married foreign nationals lost their citizenship. They could not regain their American citizenship unless their husbands became U.S. citizens. However, American males who married females who were not citizens retained their citizenship. The Supreme Court upheld the Extradition Act in the 1915 case *Mackenzie v. Hare*. In 1910 Congress enacted the Mann Act. The new law was designed to stop human trafficking for "immoral purposes," mainly prostitution. However, the new measure was quickly expanded to include prohibitions on premarital sex, polygamy (marriage with multiple spouses), and interracial relationships. Through the years, the Mann Act was used to prosecute unmarried couples and those in mixed-race relationships.

Christine Jorgensen and Transgender Rights

Meanwhile, by the 1950s a growing number of Americans had begun to question traditional gender roles and sexuality. In 1953 George William Jorgensen underwent a series of surgeries and hormone treatments in Denmark to transition from a biological male to a female, becoming Christine Jorgensen. In *The Story of My Life*, published in 1953, Jorgensen described her experiences as a transgendered person. Jorgensen was not the first person to transition. However, because her story became public first through a story in the *New York Daily News*, and then through her publication, Jorgensen became an early symbol of the transgender movement. She also emerged as a minor celebrity who used her fame to promote tolerance and acceptance.

At the same time, through the 1950s and into the 1960s, many states increased enforcement of laws against homosexuality. Other states, however, decriminalized same-sex acts. In 1962 Illinois became the first state to repeal laws against homosexual activity. Connecticut followed in 1971, and for the remainder of that decade a growing number of states also ended bans on same sex intercourse. Part of the impetus for change was the Stonewall Riots in New York City. In June 1969 police raided several gay and lesbian bars in New York, including the Stonewall Inn. In response patrons rioted and launched street protests. The riots ignited widespread homosexual rights demonstrations and led to the first gay pride parade in 1970. Denise Harmon's "Stonewall Means Fight Back!" described the events that led to the Stonewall Riots and called for the homosexual community to band together to fight for equality. Three years later, transvestite Sylvia Rivera issued a more strident call for action in a passionate address that became known as the "Y'all Better Quiet Down" speech.

The rise of the lesbian, gay, bisexual, transgender, and queer (LGBTQ+) movement was met by a backlash among social conservatives in the 1980s and 1990s. For instance, in 1996 Congress passed the Defense of Marriage Act, which denied federal recognition of same-sex marriages by defining matrimony as the union of a heterosexual (someone attracted to a member of the opposite sex) male and female. The tensions between the traditional view of sexuality (known as heteronormative) and the LGBTQ+ community were explored by June Jordan in her 1991 essay "A New Politics of Sexuality." Jordan argued that sexuality defined one's place in society. Those that were heteronormative had privileges and power denied to members of the LGBTQ+ community. In addition, oppression by the dominant heteronormative culture created internal strife among the LGBTQ+ community and prevented unity of action.

A Wave of Victories for the LGBTQ+ Movement

The LGBTQ+ community began to secure major victories in the early 2000s. In 2003, in the case *Lawrence v. Texas,* the Supreme Court ruled that state laws against consensual same-sex activity were unconstitutional. Instead, people had a right to privacy in their personal sex lives. The groundbreaking decision was a significant success for the LGBTQ+ community. It was followed by a series of other triumphs. In 2011 Congress repealed the so-called "Don't Ask, Don't Tell" policy in which LGBTQ+ service members could continue as part of the military as long as they did not divulge their sexual orientation. Most importantly, by 2015 more than thirty states had legalized same-sex marriage. That year, the Supreme Court legalized same-sex marriage in the remaining states in the case *Obergefell v. Hodges*. Nonetheless, the LGBTQ+ community continued to face a variety of challenges in the United States as their struggle for full equality continued.

Further Reading

Books

Carpenter, Dale. *Flagrant Conduct: The Story of Lawrence v. Texas*. New York: W. W. Norton & Company, 2012.

Deitcher, David, ed. *The Question of Equality: Lesbian and Gay Politics in America since Stonewall*. New York: Scribner, 1995.

Docter, Richard F. *Becoming a Woman: A Biography of Christine Jorgensen*. New York: Routledge, 2013.

Duberman, Martin. *Stonewall: The Definitive Story of the LGBTQ Rights Uprising That Changed America*. New York: Penguin, 2019.

Dynes, Wayne R., and Stephen Donaldson. *Homosexuality: Discrimination, Criminology, and the Law*. New York: Garland, 1992.

Faderman, Lillian. *Odd Girls and Twilight Lovers: A History of Lesbian Life in Twentieth Century America*. New York: Penguin Books, 1991.

Frank, Nathaniel. *Awakening: How Gays and Lesbians Brought Marriage Equality to America*. Cambridge, MA: Harvard University Press, 2017.

Langum, David J. *Crossing Over the Line: Legislating Morality and the Mann Act*. Chicago: University of Chicago Press, 1994.

Meyerowitz, Joanne J. *How Sex Changed: A History of Transsexuality in the United States*. Cambridge, MA: Harvard University Press, 2009.

Pitman, Gayle E. *The Stonewall Riots: Coming Out in the Streets*. New York: Abrams Books, 2019.

Vaid, Urvashi. *Virtual Equality: The Mainstreaming of Gay & Lesbian Liberation*. New York: Anchor Books, 1995.

Weiss, Penny A., and Loretta Kensinger, eds. *Feminist Interpretations of Emma Goldman*. University Park: Pennsylvania State University Press, 2007.

Articles

Hildebrandt, Achim. "Routes to Decriminalization: A Comparative Analysis of the Legalization of Same-Sex Sexual Acts." *Sexualities* 17 (February 2014).

Yoshino, Kenji. "A New Birth of Freedom? Obergefell v. Hodges." *Harvard Law Review* 129, no. 1 (2015).

Further Reading

Websites

"LGBT Heritage." National Park Service website, accessed September 1, 2023, https://www.nps.gov/subjects/tellingallamericansstories/lgbtqheritage.htm.

"LGBT Rights." Human Rights Watch website, accessed September 1, 2023, https://www.hrw.org/topic/lgbt-rights.

Obergefell v. Hodges. National Constitution Center website, accessed September 1, 2023, https://constitutioncenter.org/the-constitution/supreme-court-case-library/obergefell-v-hodges.

"The Pill and the Sexual Revolution." PBS American Experience website, accessed September 5, 2023, https://www.pbs.org/wgbh/americanexperience/features/pill-and-sexual-revolution/.

Emma Goldman: "Marriage and Love"

Author
Emma Goldman

Date
1910

Document Type
Essays, Reports, Manifestos

Significance
Early proponent of sexual liberation and freedom for women

Overview

Born in the Russian Federation in 1869, Emma Goldman emigrated to the United States in 1885 and became an influential political activist and anarchist in the first decades of the twentieth century. From 1893 to 1917, Emma Goldman delivered numerous and controversial lectures regarding anarchism, women's rights, patriotism, and labor conditions. In addition to her efforts on the lecture circuit, in 1906 Goldman established the anarchist journal *Mother Earth*, which she edited in New York City's bohemian center of Greenwich Village. In 1910 several of Goldman's *Mother Earth* pieces were collected in the anthology *Anarchism and Other Essays*.

In one essay from the collection, "Marriage and Love," Goldman focuses on the possibilities of anarchism to provide liberation for women. Influenced by her mother's experiences as well as her own, she advocates for freedom, sexual liberation, and female agency. The exploitation of women within such capitalist institutions as marriage earned the ire of Goldman, who advocates the creative power of love beyond the sanctions of the state or the church. The influential anthology of Goldman's political writings *Anarchism and Other Essays* was republished in 1917. Although mostly forgotten in the decades following her death in 1940, her writings proved inspirational for second-wave feminists in the 1960s and 1970s.

Emma Goldman
(Library of Congress)

Document Text

The popular notion about marriage and love is that they are synonymous, that they spring from the same motives, and cover the same human needs. Like most popular notions this also rests not on actual facts, but on superstition.

Marriage and love have nothing in common; they are as far apart as the poles; are, in fact, antagonistic to each other. No doubt some marriages have been the result of love. Not, however, because love could assert itself only in marriage; much rather is it because few people can completely outgrow a convention. There are to-day large numbers of men and women to whom marriage is naught but a farce, but who submit to it for the sake of public opinion. At any rate, while it is true that some marriages are based on love, and while it is equally true that in some cases love continues in married life, I maintain that it does so regardless of marriage, and not because of it. . . .

Marriage is primarily an economic arrangement, an insurance pact. It differs from the ordinary life insurance agreement only in that it is more binding, more exacting. Its returns are insignificantly small compared with the investments. In taking out an insurance policy one pays for it in dollars and cents, always at liberty to discontinue payments. If, however, woman's premium is a husband, she pays for it with her name, her privacy, her self-respect, her very life, "until death doth part." Moreover, the marriage insurance condemns her to life-long dependency, to parasitism, to complete uselessness, individual as well as social. Man, too, pays his toll, but as his sphere is wider, marriage does not limit him as much as woman. He feels his chains more in an economic sense. . . .

From infancy, almost, the average girl is told that marriage is her ultimate goal; therefore her training and education must be directed towards that end. Like the mute beast fattened for slaughter, she is prepared for that. Yet, strange to say, she is allowed to know much less about her function as wife and mother than the ordinary artisan of his trade. It is indecent and filthy for a respectable girl to know anything of the marital relation. Oh, for the inconsistency of respectability, that needs the marriage vow to turn something which is filthy into the purest and most sacred arrangement that none dare question or criticize. Yet that is exactly the attitude of the average upholder of marriage. The prospective wife and mother is kept in complete ignorance of her only asset in the competitive field—sex. Thus she enters into life-long relations with a man only to find herself shocked, repelled, outraged beyond measure by the most natural and healthy instinct, sex. It is safe to say that a large percentage of the unhappiness, misery, distress, and physical suffering of matrimony is due to the criminal ignorance in sex matters that is being extolled as a great virtue. Nor is it at all an exaggeration when I say that more than one home has been broken up because of this deplorable fact.

If, however, woman is free and big enough to learn the mystery of sex without the sanction of State or Church, she will stand condemned as utterly unfit to become the wife of a "good" man, his goodness consisting of an empty head and plenty of money. Can there be anything more outrageous than the idea that a healthy, grown woman, full of life and passion, must deny nature's demand, must subdue her most intense craving, undermine her health and break her spirit, must stunt her vision, abstain from the depth and glory of sex experience until a "good" man comes along to take her unto himself as a wife? That is precisely what marriage means. . . .

The woman considers her position as worker transitory, to be thrown aside for the first bidder. That is why it is infinitely harder to organize women than men. "Why should I join a union? I am going to get married, to have a home." Has she not been taught from infancy to look upon that as her ultimate calling? She learns soon enough that the home, though not so large a prison as the factory, has more solid doors and bars. It has a keeper so faithful that naught can escape him. . . .

But the child, how is it to be protected, if not for marriage? After all, is not that the most important consideration? The sham, the hypocrisy of it! Marriage protecting the child, yet thousands of children destitute and homeless. Marriage protecting the child, yet orphan asylums and reformatories over crowded, the Society for the Prevention of Cruelty to Children keeping busy in rescuing the little victims from "loving" parents, to place them under more loving care, the Gerry Society. Oh, the mockery of it! . . .

It is like that other paternal arrangement—capitalism. It robs man of his birthright, stunts his growth, poisons his body, keeps him in ignorance, in poverty and dependence, and then institutes charities that thrive on the last vestige of man's self-respect. . . .

Love, the strongest and deepest element in all life, the harbinger of hope, of joy, of ecstasy; love, the defier of all laws, of all conventions; love, the freest, the most powerful moulder of human destiny; how can such an all-compelling force be synonymous with that poor little State and Church-begotten weed, marriage? . . .

Some day, some day men and women will rise, they will reach the mountain peak, they will meet big and strong and free, ready to receive, to partake, and to bask in the golden rays of love. What fancy, what imagination, what poetic genius can foresee even approximately the potentialities of such a force in the life of men and women. If the world is ever to give birth to true companionship and oneness, not marriage, but love will be the parent.

Glossary

Gerry Society: the New York Society for the Prevention of Cruelty to Children, the world's first child protective agency, founded in 1875 by Elbridge Thomas Gerry and Henry Bergh

parasitism: the practice of living as a parasite in or on another organism

sanction: blessing

Short-Answer Questions

1. How does Goldman argue against the popular notion that marriage and love are synonymous?

2. How are the economic aspects of marriage portrayed, and what are the differences for men and women?

3. According to the document, how does society perpetuate the misconceptions about sex within the institution of marriage, and how does this contribute to unhappiness or dissatisfaction in relationships?

Mann Act

Author
James Robert Mann

Date
1910

Document Type
Legislative

Significance
Criminalized many types of sexual activity

Overview

As urban centers industrialized, cities grew, and women found new forms of independence and agency, the attention of some Progressive Era reformers turned toward enforcing morality, specifically that of sex workers. For some, a new, chaotic urban environment threatened female virtue, which therefore had to be protected. Cities in the nineteenth century generally had been accommodating toward brothels or red-light districts, but increased immigration, heightened numbers of women in the workforce, and challenges to traditionally rigid forms of the family fed a moral panic. Reformers mainly focused on white women, who were portrayed as being coerced into prostitution, as opposed to African American or Asian women in similar circumstances, who were considered morally inferior.

Guided through Congress by Representative James R. Mann (R-IL) and signed by President William Howard Taft on June 25, 1910, the Mann Act, formally known as the White-Slave Traffic Act, is a federal law that criminalizes the transportation of individuals across state lines for immoral purposes, specifically sex work or "debauchery." The act defines "transportation" broadly, including any means of transportation, including car, train, airplane, or even walking. The act's reach extends to both voluntary and coerced transportation. Aimed at preventing human trafficking and the exploitation of women and children, penalties include imprisonment for up to ten years and fines.

Due to the legislation's ambiguous language, consensual sexual activity was oftentimes criminalized. African American men bore the brunt of this focus, most famously in the case of world heavyweight boxing champion Jack Johnson, an African American, who was charged with violation of the Mann Act due to crossing state lines with his girlfriend, who was white. Additionally, charges that the Mann Act was abused as a form of blackmail against cheating husbands were frequent.

The Mann Act has undergone several amendments and modifications since its inception. In 1978, Congress passed an amendment that exempted consensual adult relationships from the act's provisions, addressing some of the concerns raised by its critics. Additional alterations in 1986 reduced ambiguity, but the act remains in effect.

James Robert Mann
(Library of Congress)

Document Text

An Act to further regulate interstate commerce and foreign commerce by prohibiting the transportation therein for immoral purposes of women and girls, and for other purposes. . . .

SEC. 2. That any person who shall knowingly transport or cause to be transported, or aid or assist in obtaining transportation for, or in transporting, in interstate or foreign commerce, or in any Territory or in the District of Columbia, any woman or girl for the purpose of prostitution or debauchery, or for any other immoral purpose, or with the intent and purpose to induce, entice, or compel such woman or girl to become a prostitute or to give herself up to debauchery, or to engage in any other immoral practice; or who shall knowingly procure or obtain, or cause to be procured or obtained, or aid or assist in procuring or obtaining, any ticket or tickets, or any form of transportation or evidence of the right thereto, to be used by any woman or girl in interstate or foreign commerce, or in any Territory or the District of Columbia, in going to any place for the purpose of prostitution or debauchery, or for any other immoral purpose, or with the intent or purpose on the part of such person to induce, entice, or compel her to give herself up to the practice of prostitution, or to give herself up to the practice of debauchery, or any other immoral practice, whereby any such woman or girl shall be transported in interstate or foreign commerce, or in any Territory or the District of Columbia, shall be deemed guilty of a felony, and upon conviction thereof shall be punished by a fine not exceeding five thousand dollars, or by imprisonment of not more than five years, or by both such fine and imprisonment, in the discretion of the court.

SEC. 3. That any person who shall knowingly persuade, induce, entice, or coerce, or cause to be persuaded, induced, enticed, or coerced, or aid or assist in persuading, inducing, enticing or coercing any woman or girl to go from one place to another in interstate or foreign commerce, or in any Territory or the District of Columbia, for the purpose of prostitution or debauchery, or for any other immoral purpose, or with the intent and purpose on the part of such person that such woman or girl shall engage in the practice of prostitution or debauchery, or any other immoral practice, whether with or without her consent, and who shall thereby knowingly cause or aid or assist in causing such woman or girl to go and be carried or transported as a passenger upon the line or route of any common carrier or carriers in interstate or foreign commerce, or any Territory or the District of Columbia, shall be deemed guilty of a felony and on conviction thereof shall be punished by a fine of not more than five thousand dollars, or by imprisonment for a term not exceeding five years, or by both fine and imprisonment, in the discretion of the court. . . .

SEC. 6. That for the purpose of regulating and preventing the transportation in foreign commerce of alien women and girls for purposes of prostitution and debauchery, and in pursuance of and for the purpose of carrying out the terms of the agreement of project of arrangement for the suppression of the white-slave traffic, . . . adhered to by the United States on June sixth, nineteen hundred and eight, as shown by the proclamation of the President of the United States, dated June fifteenth, nineteen hundred and eight, the Commissioner-General of Immigration is hereby designated as the authority of the United States to receive and centralize information concerning the procuration of alien women and girls with a view to their debauchery, and to exercise supervision over such alien women and girls, receive their declarations, establish their identity, and ascertain from them who induced them to leave their native countries, respectively; and it shall be the duty of said Commissioner-General of Immigration to receive and keep on file in his office the statements and declarations which may be made by such alien women and girls. . . .

Every person who shall keep, maintain, control, support or harbor in any house or place for the purpose of prostitution, or for any other immoral purpose, any alien woman or girl within three years after she shall have entered the United States from any country, party to the said arrangement for the suppression of the white-slave traffic, shall file with the Commissioner-General of Immigration a statement in writing setting forth the name of such alien woman or girl, the place at which she is kept, and all facts as to the date of her entry into the United States, . . . shall be deemed guilty of a misdemeanor, and on conviction shall be punished by a fine of not more than two thousand dollars, or by imprisonment for a term not exceeding two years, or by both such fine and imprisonment, in the discretion of the court.

In any prosecution brought under this section, if it appear that any such statement required is not on file in the office of the Commissioner-General of Immigration, the person whose duty it shall be to file such statement shall be presumed to have failed to file said statement, as herein required, unless such person or persons shall prove otherwise. No person shall be excused from furnishing the statement. . . .

SEC. 8. That this Act shall be known and referred to as the "White-slave traffic Act."

Glossary

alien: coming from a different country, race, or group

debauchery: excessive indulgence in sensual pleasures, especially sexual activities

Short-Answer Questions

1. According to the "White-Slave Traffic Act," what are the potential penalties for transporting women or girls across state lines or internationally?

2. What responsibilities are assigned to the Commissioner-General of Immigration under the act regarding alien women and girls?

3. What does Congress imply by referring to the Mann Act as the "White-Slave Traffic Act"? What ramifications might that have?

Mackenzie v. Hare

Author
Joseph McKenna

Date
1915

Document Type
Legal

Significance
Ruled that a woman's citizenship could be taken away based on who she married

Overview

Mackenzie v. Hare was a Supreme Court case decided in 1915. The case revolved around the constitutionality of the Expatriation Act of 1907, a provision in the United States Code that stated that American women who married foreigners would take the nationality of their husbands. This legislation did not apply to American men who married women of other nationalities.

The Plaintiff, Ethel Mackenzie, was a native-born American woman who had married a British citizen. When she applied to register to vote in California, her request was denied on the grounds that because she had married a British subject, she had taken the nationality of her husband and therefore ceased to be a citizen of the United States. Mrs. Mackenzie argue that the Expatriation Act of 1907 went beyond the authority of Congress and violated her constitutional rights.

In a unanimous decision, the Supreme Court upheld the constitutionality of the legislation. The Court reasoned that Congress did possess the authority to pass laws related to citizenship and the nation's relationships with foreign countries. It rejected the plaintiff's argument that citizenship, once acquired, could only be taken away as a punishment for a crime or through voluntary expatriation. It acknowledged that citizenship held great value but emphasized the importance of considering broader national interests and international policy concerns. The Court concluded that the legislation in question was a valid exercise of government power and necessary to prevent potential complications arising from the marriage of American women to foreigners.

Mackenzie v. Hare established the principle that marriage to a foreigner could result in the temporary loss of American citizenship for women, subject to the termination of the marital relationship. The case upheld the authority of Congress to regulate matters of citizenship and highlighted the balance between individual rights and the government's interest in managing international relations. It also reinforced the patriarchal status quo as a codification into law.

Document Text

The facts are not in dispute and are stated . . . as follows: "The plaintiff was born and ever since has resided in the State of California. On August 14, 1909, being then a resident and citizen of this state and of the United States, she was lawfully married to Gordon Mackenzie, a native and subject of the kingdom of Great Britain. . . . On January 22, 1913, she applied to the defendants to be registered as a voter. . . . Registration was refused to her on the ground that, by reason of her marriage to Gordon Mackenzie, a subject of Great Britain, she thereupon took the nationality of her husband and ceased to be a citizen of the United States."

On March 2, 1907, that is, prior to the marriage of plaintiff in error, Congress enacted a statute the third section of which provides:

"That any American woman who marries a foreigner shall take the nationality of her husband. At the termination of the marital relation, she may resume her American citizenship, if abroad, by registering as an American citizen within one year with a consul of the United States, or by returning to reside in the United States, or, if residing in the United States at the termination of the marital relation, by continuing to reside therein."

Plaintiff contends that "such legislation, if intended to apply to her, is beyond the authority of Congress."

. . . An earnest argument is presented to demonstrate its invalidity. Its basis is that the citizenship of plaintiff was an incident to her birth in the United States, and, under the Constitution and laws of the United States, it became a right, privilege, and immunity which could not be taken away from her except as a punishment for crime or by her voluntary expatriation. . . .

Their foundation principles, we may assume, are known. The identity of husband and wife is an ancient principle of our jurisprudence. It was neither accidental nor arbitrary, and worked in many instances for her protection. There has been, it is true, much relaxation of it, but in its retention, as in its origin, it is determined by their intimate relation and unity of interests, and this relation and unity may make it of public concern in many instances to merge their identity, and give dominance to the husband. It has purpose if not necessity in purely domestic policy; it has greater purpose, and, it may be, necessity, in international policy. And this was the dictate of the act in controversy. Having this purpose, has it not the sanction of power?

Plaintiff contends, as we have seen, that it has not, and bases her contention upon the absence of an express gift of power. But there may be powers implied, necessary or incidental to the expressed powers. As a government, the United States is invested with all the attributes of sovereignty. As it has the character of nationality, it has the powers of nationality, especially those which concern its relations and intercourse with other countries. We should hesitate long before limiting or embarrassing such powers. But monition is not necessary in the present case. There need be no dissent from the cases cited by plaintiff; there need be no assertion of very extensive power over the right of citizenship or of the imperative imposition of conditions upon it. It may be conceded that a change of citizenship cannot be arbitrarily imposed—that is, imposed without the concurrence of the citizen. The law in controversy does not have that feature. It deals with a condition voluntarily entered into, with notice of the consequences. We concur with counsel that citizenship is of tangible worth, and we sympathize with plaintiff in her desire to retain it and in her earnest assertion of it. But there is involved more than personal considerations. As we have seen, the legislation was urged by conditions of national moment. And this is an answer to the apprehension of counsel that our construction of the legislation will make every act, though lawful, as marriage, of course, is, a renunciation of citizenship. The marriage of an American woman with a foreigner has consequences of like kind, may involve national complications of like kind, as her physical expatriation may involve. Therefore, as long as the relation lasts, it is made tantamount to expatriation. This is no arbitrary exercise of government. It is one which, regarding the international aspects, judicial opinion has taken for granted would not only be valid, but demanded. It is the conception of the legislation under review that such an act may bring the government into embarrassments, and, it may be, into controversies. It is as voluntary and distinctive as expatriation, and its consequence must be considered as elected.

Glossary

expatriate: a person who resides outside their native country

jurisprudence: the official power to make legal decisions and judgments

monition: a warning of impending danger

Short-Answer Questions

1. What is the basis for Ethel Mackenzie's argument against the legislation?

2. Why does the passage argue that the legislation regarding citizenship and marriage is necessary from an international perspective?

3. Why does the legislation consider the marriage of an American woman to a foreigner as tantamount to expatriation?

Christine Jorgensen: "The Story of My Life"

Author
Christine Jorgensen

Date
1953

Document Type
Essays, Reports, Manifestos

Significance
Disrupted conventional notions of gender, igniting widespread public discussion about the intricacies of identity

Overview

"The Story of My Life" is a five-part, serialized and autobiographical account of the life of Christine Jorgensen, a transgender woman who became a prominent figure in the mid-twentieth century. It initially appeared in the February 15, 1953, issue of *The American Weekly*. Her story played a crucial role in shaping public discourse around gender identity and transgender issues.

In 1951, Jorgensen made headlines around the world after she traveled to Denmark to undergo gender confirmation surgery. At the time, medical advancements in sex reassignment procedures were limited, and Jorgensen's journey sparked widespread fascination and controversy. She became one of the first individuals to publicly discuss gender reassignment and share her personal experiences with the media.

In "The Story of My Life" (and later, her autobiography, published in 1967), Jorgensen's openness about her transition challenged prevailing notions of gender and sparked public conversations about the complexities of identity. In an era when transgender rights were virtually nonexistent, her story shed light on the struggles faced by transgender individuals and brought their existence into the public consciousness. Jorgensen's visibility helped debunk myths and misconceptions surrounding transgender people and provided a human face to the transgender community.

Document Text

It was an average cold, gray morning in Copenhagen and there was nothing unusual to suggest that this day, December 1, 1952, was to be one of the most memorable days of my life as I lay in my bed at the famous Rigshospitalet.

I was momentarily lost in thought. In a matter of weeks I would be home in New York, if my plans worked well, and for the first time my parents would see their new 26-year-old daughter, Christine—the girl who would forever replace the only son they ever had.

Knowing George Jorgensen, Jr., the boy I had been, would never return because he no longer existed, I had come to Denmark in 1950 when life as George was no longer tolerable. . . .

In my mind I saw a picture of a frail little boy praying before he went to sleep: "Dear God," he said, "Send me a dolly for Christmas, just like those my sister Dorothy has." . . .

I never grew to be as husky as other little boys in the community and, as early as I can remember, I wondered why I had to wear clothes so different from my sister Dorothy's pretty dresses.

I hated boys' suits and I hated little boys for their rough-and-tumble games, which I never joined, and for the questioning look I always seemed to see in their eyes. . . .

I recall one incident which left a vivid impression upon me, so vivid that even now it remains clear in my mind. I was about eight or nine years of age at the time. I had found, or in some way acquired, a piece of needlepoint. I loved that little piece of handwork.

I kept it in my desk at school and was quite upset one day to find it missing. I suddenly was confronted by the teacher, and, much to my surprise, my mother. In the teacher's hand was my needlepoint, held up for ridicule.

Christine Jorgensen
(Wikimedia Commons)

I hated that teacher. She cheapened something I loved, and she hurt my mother. That teacher should have realized that this little boy, who was not going to follow the normal pattern of development, needed help, not ridicule. . . .

At this teen-age stage of my life I had found one boy, Tom, who did not make me feel awkward or embarrassed. . . . We corresponded frequently and I had a great affection for him.

It was an affection that worried me and, therefore, increased my problem. . . .

Then there came a momentous day when a letter arrived from Tom. He wrote that he had joined the service since seeing me last and after his initial training would be sent to the South Pacific.

It was then that I knew I loved Tom, not as a buddy, but as a woman loves a man. I was filled with a consuming fear at the thought of sending him off to unknown dangers. . . .

The only love I had known—my love for Tom which the world would have considered sinful, and which yet remained a fine and shining thing in my memory. I could not understand why the world should hate me and this love which had meant so much to me. . . .

I consulted a New York doctor. Would it be possible, I asked him, for me to take female sex hormones in large quantities and feminize myself to an extent where I could look and act like a woman—and really be a woman?

That, I was told, was an impossible dream. Impossible! That word was a challenge to me. How did anyone dare say it in the Atomic Age? . . .

"Do you think I ought to be treated by a psychiatrist?" I asked. . . .

"It is possible, and eventually I may direct you to do so," Dr. Hamburger replied, "but I feel, from what you have told me, that he can't do a great deal for you because, in my opinion, your trouble is deep-rooted in all the cells of your body.

"Outwardly you have the sex characteristics of a man. You were declared a boy at birth and you have grown up, so very unhappily, in the guise of a young man. But inwardly it is quite possible that you are a woman." . . .

"I don't want to charge you anything," the doctor said, "but I will tell you quite frankly that, at the same time that we are testing and treating you, you could serve as a guinea pig in some other hormone experiments which require observing a person for months, or perhaps years. They are based on analyses over a long period of time." . . .

One day, while in consultation with Dr. Hamburger, I asked, "What do we do now? Do I go on indefinitely taking hormones?"

"That would be possible," he said, "and I don't think it would do any harm. However, we have proven that the male element of your body is no longer of any use to you and perhaps a surgical operation would be better. . . .

"Had I said, 'No, I will not recommend an operation,' I would have been attempting to push you back into the character you hated. I would have been dooming you to despair. . . ."

My greatest contribution, perhaps, can be an appeal to doctors in all countries to study the problem of the soul-sick men and women who find themselves, through no fault of their own, in the disheartening no-man's-land of sex. . . .

When I set out on my own quest for relief, it didn't enter my mind that I ever would be called upon to be anything but an inconspicuous individual fitting into a new social role.

I was forced into the public eye, . . . and now I can only accept the responsibility to others that my unsought fame has placed upon me. I hope I may not be found wanting.

Glossary

needlepoint: embroidery worked over canvas, typically in a diagonal stitch covering the entire surface of the fabric

Rigshospitalet: a highly specialized hospital in Denmark

sex hormones: hormones, such as estrogen or testosterone, that affect sexual development or reproduction

Short-Answer Questions

1. How did Jorgensen's feelings about her gender identity manifest during childhood?

2. How did Jorgensen's realization of her feelings for Tom influence her understanding of her own identity?

3. How did the doctor in New York influence Jorgensen even though he did not treat her?

Denise Harmon: "Stonewall Means Fight Back!"

Author
Denise Harmon

Date
1973

Document Type
Essays, Reports, Manifestos

Significance
Described the Stonewall Inn rebellion in 1969, recognized as the catalyst for the gay rights movement in the United States, as the first time members of the gay and trans community physically resisted police harassment

Overview

Denise Harmon's article "Stonewall Means Fight Back!" first appeared in the periodical *Women of Youth against War and Fascism* in the summer of 1973 and described the police attack and subsequent rebellion four years earlier at a bar that served a largely lesbian, gay, bisexual, and transgender (LGBT) clientele.

The LGBT community was not new, but it had existed mainly on the fringes of society and kept largely secret and private. Inevitably, however, a movement for LGBT rights joined the civil rights movement, the Chicano movement, second-wave feminism, the anti-war movement, and other social justice movements of the mid-twentieth century. The era was a tumultuous one, in which people gathered across the country to protest and advocate change. At this time, homosexuality was not legal, and the police targeted gay men, lesbians, and transgender individuals for persecution. In the past, resistance had been seen as futile. The three-day rebellion that broke out at the Stonewall Inn, a known gathering place for LGBTs in New York's Greenwich Village, marked the first time that LGBT people stood up for themselves in large numbers and resisted. This action prompted the first Gay Pride March and an annual Gay Pride Week and launched the modern gay rights movement, better known today as the LGBTQIA+ movement.

The Stonewall Inn (Wikimedia Commons)

Document Text

On June 29, 1969, the police attacked the Stonewall Inn, a popular gay bar in New York City. The raid was not unusual, but the response was, because for the first time gays fought back in a rebellion that lasted three days. The raid was not unusual because all through history gay people have been beaten, harassed, drugged, and even murdered for being gay. Only a few years ago James Clay, a Black transvestite from Chicago, was shot down in cold blood by the racist cops simply because he was Black and gay.

The New York cops claimed that the Stonewall was supposed to have a state liquor license, but in actuality since the Stonewall was a private lounge, it was not required to have one. The police marched into the bar and announced the raid, and then started to release the customers one by one. Instead of running away, the gay customers stayed outside to await the outcome of the raid, and soon 400 gays gathered.

Many people, including gays, think that men started the Stonewall rebellion, but this is not exactly true. As the cops were arresting three gay men, those standing by were yelling threats and curses. Then the cops made the mistake of attempting to arrest a gay woman. She fought back and called for her gay brothers' and sisters' help. The cops were met with bricks, bottles, cans, coins, fists—real gay power. The next night gay people from all over New York marched down Christopher Street in the first Gay Pride March in history.

In fact, for several nights running, large crowds of gay people challenged the right of the police to invade their social gathering places. The street battles that occurred as a result of continuing police harassment and brutality (with the police actually drawing their guns on one occasion) made it clear that gay people now had the consciousness to fight back when pushed too hard. The Stonewall rebellion was more than justified and long overdue.

The next year Gay Pride Week was called to commemorate the Stonewall rebellion with numerous marches, demonstrations, and rallies. And each year in cities all over the country similar celebrations are held.

Gay pride is gay unity, strength, and love for each other. It affirms our pride in ourselves and in our lifestyle. For us to come to the realization that our love is right and good is a beautiful and courageous act. Gay pride is also not feeling guilty about being gay, but feeling beautiful, strong in love, and unafraid. We refuse to be frightened any more. We must join with all our oppressed sisters and brothers, gay and straight, to build a new society, one where all can determine their own lives free from all forms of oppression.

Glossary

Christopher Street: the location of the Stonewall Inn and regarded at a center of the gay rights movement

James Clay: a Black man living in Chicago in 1970 when he was chased and shot by police, and whose death led to formation of the Transvestites Legal Committee in 1971, which advocated for the political rights of the transgender community

Stonewall Inn: a bar in Greenwich Village, New York, known for its gay, lesbian, and transgender patronage

transvestite: a term (now considered archaic) for a person who wears clothes not reflecting their apparent gender

Short-Answer Questions

1. Why was the response to the police raid of the Stonewall Inn unusual?

2. Why do you think that gay people stood up for their rights during this raid and at this time, and not at another, earlier time in history?

3. What does Harmon consider the goals of gay pride, and how did this proliferate after the Stonewall rebellion?

Sylvia Rivera: "Y'All Better Quiet Down"

Author
Sylvia Rivera

Date
1973

Document Type
Speeches/Addresses

Significance
Called for equal rights and fair treatment for trans men and women and for people of color within the LGBTQ+ community

Overview

Sylvia Rivera (1951–2002) was a gay rights and transgender rights activist in the late twentieth century. Born Ray Rivera in New York City to Puerto Rican and Venezuelan parents, she was orphaned by the age of three and identified as a drag queen by 1962. She fled her abusive grandmother, who had raised her, and found welcome in the city's drag community. By the later 1960s she had become well-known as an activist, speaking and marching against the Vietnam War and for civil rights and women's rights causes.

In 1970, along with fellow drag queen Marsha P. Johnson (1945–1992), Rivera founded STAR, the Street Transvestite Action Revolutionaries, as a refuge for gay, lesbian, and trans youths. These young people were systematically excluded from services extended to cis-gendered and heterosexual young men and women. Rivera and Johnson often met with pushback from some people within the LGBTQ+ community, who found them too radical for their own comfort. In the speech excerpted below, Rivera pushes back against those people.

Sylvia Rivera (Wikimedia Commons)

Document Text

I may be . . . You all better quiet down. I've been trying to get up here all day for your gay brothers and your gay sisters in jail that write me every m****rf***ing week and ask for your help, and you all don't do a goddamn thing for them. Have you ever been beaten up and raped in jail? Now think about it. They've been beaten up and raped after they've had to spend much of their money in jail to get their self home and to try to get their sex changes. The women have tried to fight for their sex changes or to become women of the Women's Liberation and they write STAR, not to the women's groups, they do not write to men, they write STAR because we're trying to do something for them. I have been to jail. I have been raped, and beaten. Many times. By men, heterosexual men that do not belong in the homosexual shelter. But, do you do anything for me? No. You tell me to go and hide my tail between my legs. I will not put up with this shit. I have been beaten. I have had my nose broken. I have been thrown in jail. I have lost my job. I have lost my apartment for gay liberation and you all treat me this way? What the f***'s wrong with you all? Think about that! I do not believe in a revolution, but you all do. I believe in the Gay Power. I believe in us getting our rights, or else I would not be out there fighting for our rights. That's all I wanted to say to you people. If you all want to know about the people in jail—and do not forget Bambi L'Amour, Andorra Marks, Kenny Messner, and other gay people in jail—come and see the people at STAR House on Twelfth Street on 640 East Twelfth Street between B and C apartment 14. The people are trying to do something for all of us, and not men and women that belong to a white, middle-class white club. And that's what you all belong to! Revolution now! Gimme a "G"! Gimme an "A"! Gimme a "Y"! Gimme a "P"! Gimme an "O"! Gimme a "W"! Gimme an "E"! Gimme an "R"! huh—Gay Power. Louder! Gay Power!

Glossary

Andorra Marks: an important figure in the early trans rights movement

Bambi L'Amour: an activist in the LGBTQ+ movement in the 1960s and one of the founders of STAR

Gay Power: a call for political rights and protection for LGBTQ+ individuals, and a movement said to have been sparked by the Stonewall Riot in 1969

Kenny Messner: an important figure in the early trans rights movement

STAR: Street Transvestite Action Revolutionaries, co-founded by Rivera and Marsha P. Johnson in 1970 to fight for trans rights

Short-Answer Questions

1. Who does Rivera address in this speech?

2. Why does Rivera object to mainstream gay activism?

3. What is the primary message that Rivera is communicating in the speech?

Adrienne Rich: "Compulsory Heterosexuality and Lesbian Experience"

Author
Adrienne Rich

Date
1980

Document Type
Essay, Reports, Manifestos

Significance
Made the case that lesbianism and feminism were compatible and should join forces to fight the true oppressor, the political institution of heterosexuality

Overview

Adrienne Rich (1929–2012) was an award-winning writer known especially for her poetry examining the lesbian experience, promoting women's liberation, and urging feminism toward intersectionality.

"Compulsory Heterosexuality and Lesbian Experience," published in 1980, is one of many essays written in the 1980s that identified a particular flaw within the feminist movement: its lack of inclusion of women considered outside the realm of normalcy. It called for inclusion of lesbian women and the value of their experiences. Rich emphasized the need for deeper understanding between feminists and lesbians, claiming that the ideology that framed heterosexuality and heteronormative behavior as ideal excluded and negated other experiences. She also drew attention to the idea that heterosexuality was a tool of society's structural inequality and served to reinforce male superiority and dominance. The essay reviews existing feminist theory and highlights the case that British feminist theorist Kathleen Gough makes that male domination throughout history has served to curtail female creativity and autonomy. Feminism and feminist theory, Rich concludes, can benefit by including lesbian women. Such inclusion can also serve to reorder the imbalance found in heterosexuality and examine it as a political institution serving only men.

Adrienne Rich (right) alongside Audre Lorde (left) and Meridel Lesueur (center) (Flickr)

Document Text

The bias of compulsory heterosexuality, through which lesbian experience is perceived on a scale ranging from deviant to abhorrent, or simply rendered invisible, could be illustrated from many texts....

The assumption made by Rossi, that women are "innately sexually oriented" toward men, or by Lessing, that the lesbian choice is simply an acting-out of bitterness toward men, are by no means theirs alone; they are widely current in literature and in the social sciences.

I am concerned here with two other matters as well: first, how and why women's choice of women as passionate comrades, life partners, co-workers, lovers, tribe has been crushed, invalidated, forced into hiding and disguise; and second, the virtual or total neglect of lesbian existence in a wide range of writings, including feminist scholarship. Obviously there is a connection here....

It is not enough for feminist thought that specifically lesbian texts exist. Any theory or cultural/political creation that treats lesbian existence as a marginal or less "natural" phenomenon, . . . is profoundly weakened. . . . Feminist theory can no longer afford merely to voice a toleration of "lesbianism" as an "alternative life-style," or make token allusion to lesbians. A feminist critique of compulsory heterosexual orientation for women is long overdue....

Heterosexuality is presumed as a "sexual preference" of most women, either implicitly or explicitly. In none of these books, which concern themselves with mothering, sex roles, relationships, and societal prescriptions for women, is compulsory heterosexuality ever examined as an institution powerfully affecting all these; or the idea of "preference" or "innate orientation" even indirectly questioned....

I am suggesting that heterosexuality, like motherhood, needs to be recognized and studied as a *political institution*—even, or especially, by those individuals who feel they are, in their personal experience, the precursors of a new social relation between the sexes....

In her essay "The Origin of the Family," Kathleen Gough lists eight characteristics of male power in archaic and contemporary societies that I would like to use as a framework.... Below, Gough's words appear in italics; the elaboration of each of her categories, in brackets, is my own.

Characteristics of male power include the power of men:

1. *to deny women* [our own] *sexuality*

[by means of ... chastity belts; punishment, including death, for female adultery; punishment, including death, for lesbian sexuality ...];

2. *or to force it* [male sexuality] *upon them*

[by means of rape ... and wife beating; father-daughter, brother-sister incest; the socialization of women to feel that male sexual "drive" amounts to a right, idealization of heterosexual romance in art, literature, media, advertising, and so forth; child marriage; arranged marriage; prostitution ...];

3. *to command or exploit their labor to control their produce*

[by means of the institutions of marriage and motherhood as unpaid production; the horizontal segregation of women in paid employment; the decoy of the upwardly mobile token woman; male control of abortion, contraception, and childbirth; enforced sterilization; pimping, female infanticide ...];

4. *to control or rob them of their children*

[by means of father-right and "legal kidnapping"; enforced sterilization; systematized infanticide; seizure of children from lesbian mothers by the courts, the malpractice of male obstetrics ...];

5. *to confine them physically and prevent their movement*

[by means of rape as terrorism, keeping women off the streets; purdah, foot-binding; atrophying of women's athletic capabilities; haute couture, "feminine" dress codes; the veil; sexual harassment on the streets, horizontal segregation of women in employment; prescriptions for "full-time" mothering; enforced economic dependence of wives];

6. *to use them as objects in male transactions*

[use of women as "gifts," bride-price; pimping; arranged marriage; use of women as entertainers to facilitate male deals, for example, wife-hostess, cocktail waitress required to dress for male sexual titillation, call girls, "bunnies," geisha, *kisaeng* prostitutes, secretaries];

7. *to cramp their creativeness*

[witch persecutions as campaigns against midwives and female healers and as pogrom against independent, "unassimilated" women; definition of male pursuits as more valuable than female within any culture, so that cultural values become embodiment of male subjectivity, restriction of female self-fulfillment to marriage and motherhood, sexual exploitation of women by male artists and teachers; the social and economic disruption of women's creative aspirations; erasure of female tradition]; and

8. *to withhold from them large areas of the society's knowledge and cultural attainments*

[by means of noneducation of females (60 percent of the world's illiterates are women); . . . sex-role stereotyping that deflects women from science, technology, and other "masculine" pursuits; male social/professional bonding that excludes women; discrimination against women in the professions].

These are some of the methods by which male power is manifested and maintained. Looking at the schema, what surely impresses itself is the fact that we are confronting not a simple maintenance of inequality and property possession, but a pervasive cluster of forces, ranging from physical brutality to control of consciousness. . . .

In her brilliant study *Sexual Harassment of Working Women: A Case of Sex Discrimination*, Catharine A. MacKinnon delineates the intersection of compulsory heterosexuality and economics. Under capitalism, women are horizontally segregated by gender and occupy a structurally inferior position in the workplace; this is hardly news, but MacKinnon raises the question why, even if capitalism "requires some collection of individuals to occupy low-status, low-paying positions . . . such persons must be biologically female," and goes on to point out that "the fact that male employers often do not hire qualified women, *even when they could pay them less than men* suggests that more than the profit motive is implicated" (emphasis added). She cites a wealth of material documenting the fact that women are not only segregated in low-paying service jobs (as secretaries, domestics, nurses, typists, telephone operators, childcare workers, waitresses) but that "sexualization of the woman" is part of the job. . . .

The fact is that the workplace, among other social institutions, is a place where women have learned to accept male violation of our psychic and physical boundaries as the price of survival. . . .

Incidents of sexual harassment suggest that male sexual desire itself may be aroused by female vulnerability. . . . Men feel they can take advantage, so they want to, so they do. . . .

The question inevitably will arise: Are we then to condemn all heterosexual relationships, including those that are least oppressive? I believe this question, though often heartfelt, is the wrong question here. We have been stalled in a maze of false dichotomies that prevents our apprehending the institution as a whole: "good" versus "bad" marriages; "marriage for love" versus arranged marriage; "liberated" sex versus prostitution; heterosexual intercourse versus rape. . . . The absence of choice remains the great unacknowledged reality, and in the absence of choice, women will remain dependent on the chance or luck of particular relationships and will have no collective power to determine the meaning and place of sexuality in their lives. As we address the institution itself, moreover, we begin to perceive a history of female resistance that has never fully understood itself because it has been so fragmented, miscalled, erased. It will require a courageous grasp of the politics and economics, as well as the cultural propaganda, of heterosexuality to carry us beyond individual cases or diversified group situations into the complex kind of overview needed to undo the power men everywhere wield over women, power that has become a model for every other form of exploitation and illegitimate control.

Glossary

compulsory heterosexuality: the idea that society functions to marginalize or remove the concept of gay and lesbian sexuality and only recognizes heterosexuality as normal and correct

Gough: Kathleen Gough (1925–1990), British anthropologist and feminist

MacKinnon: Catharine A. MacKinnon (1946–), American legal scholar and feminist

pogrom: organized massacre

Rossi: Alice Rossi (1922–2009), an American sociologist and feminist

Short-Answer Questions

1. Adrienne Rich calls for the inclusion of the lesbian experience in the contemporary feminist movement. What other elements does she specify need consideration for a more complete, comprehensive feminist theory?

2. Of the eight examples that Kathleen Gough cites as male dominance and power, which are the most relevant to the women's liberation movement of the 1980s? Do they remain pertinent, or have they become largely irrelevant? Please explain.

3. Why do you think the women's liberation movement neglected to include the experiences of lesbians? How would their inclusion improve the movement's success? How might it be detrimental?

June Jordan:
"A New Politics of Sexuality"

Author
June Jordan

Date
1991

Document Type
Speeches/Addresses; Essays, Reports, Manifestos

Significance
A rallying cry for the inclusion of bisexuality in human rights and a challenge to identity politics that practice exclusion

Overview

June Jordan (1936–2002) was one of the most prolific Black writers of the later twentieth century. Born in Harlem to parents from Jamaica, she attended Barnard College, married a white graduate student, had a son, and joined the civil rights movement. The couple divorced in 1965, and Jordan was faced with the challenge of raising her son as a single parent. In 1967 she began to teach at the City College of New York. She later joined the faculties of Connecticut College, Sarah Lawrence College, and Yale University before moving on to the State University of New York at Sony Brook. There she directed the Poetry Center and held a post as professor of English until 1989.

In 1989 Jordan joined the faculty as professor of English, women's studies, and African American studies at the University of California, Berkeley, where she founded the Poetry for the People program. She held those posts at the university until her death from breast cancer in June 2002.

"A New Politics of Sexuality" was originally an address to Stanford University's Bisexual, Gay, and Lesbian Student Association. In it, Jordan expresses her dissatisfaction with the idea of identity politics—not its political aims, but the idea of having to adhere to a group identity that was not chosen by the individual involved.

Document Text

I believe the Politics of Sexuality is the most ancient and probably the most profound arena for human conflict. Increasingly, it seems clear to me that deeper and more pervasive than any other oppression, than any other bitterly contested human domain, is the oppression of sexuality, the exploitation of the human domain of sexuality for power.

When I say sexuality, I mean gender. I mean male subjugation of human beings because they are female. When I say sexuality I mean heterosexual institutionalization of rights and privileges denied to homosexual men and women. When I say sexuality I mean gay or lesbian contempt for bisexual modes of human relationship.

The Politics of Sexuality therefore subsumes all of the different ways in which some of us seek to dictate to others of us what we should do, what we should desire, what we should dream about, and how we should behave ourselves, generally. From China to Iran, from Nigeria to Czechoslovakia, from Chile to California, the politics of sexuality—enforced by traditions of state-sanctioned violence plus religion and the law—reduces to male domination of women; heterosexist tyranny, and, among those of us who are in any case deemed despicable or deviant by the powerful, we find intolerance for those who choose a different, a more complicated—for example, interracial or bisexual—mode of rebellion and freedom.

We must move out from the Shadows of our collective subjugation—as people of color/as women/as gay/as lesbian/as bisexual human beings. . . .

Recently, I have come upon gratuitous and appalling pseudoliberal pronouncements on sexuality. Too often, these utterances fall out of the mouths of men and women who first disclaim any sentiment remotely related to homophobia, but who then proceed to issue outrageous opinions like the following:

* That it is blasphemous to compare the oppression of gay, lesbian, or bisexual people to the oppression, say, of Black people, or of the Palestinians.

* That the bottom line about gay or lesbian or bisexual identity is that you can conceal it whenever necessary and, so, therefore, why don't you do just that? Why don't you keep your deviant sexuality in the closet and let the rest of us—we who suffer oppression for reasons of our ineradicable and always visible components of our personhood such as race or gender—get on with our more necessary, our more beleaguered struggle to survive?

Well, number one, I believe I have worked as hard as I could, and then harder than that, on behalf of equality and justice—for African Americans, for the Palestinian people, and for people of color everywhere.

And no, I do not believe it is blasphemous to compare oppressions of sexuality to oppressions of race and ethnicity: Freedom is indivisible, or it is nothing at all besides sloganeering and temporary, short-sighted, and short-lived advancement for a few. Freedom is indivisible, and either we are working for freedom or you are working for the sake of your self-interests and I am working for mine.

If you can finally go to the bathroom wherever you find one, if you can finally order a cup of coffee and drink it wherever coffee is available, but you cannot follow your heart—you cannot respect the response of your own honest body in the world—then how much of what kind of freedom does any one of us possess? . . .

What tyranny could exceed a tyranny that dictates to the human heart and that attempts to dictate the public career of an honest human body? . . .

This is a New Politics of Sexuality. And even as I despair of identity politics—because identity is given and principles of justice/equality/freedom cut across given gender and given racial definitions of being, and because I will call you my brother, I will call you my sister, on the basis of what you *do* for justice, what you *do* for equality, what you do for freedom and *not* on the basis of who you are, even so I look with admiration and respect upon the new, bisexual politics of sexuality. . . .

If you are free, you are not predictable and you are not controllable. To my mind, that is the keenly positive, politicizing significance of bisexual affirmation:

To insist upon complexity, to insist upon the validity of all of the components of social/ sexual complexity, to insist upon the equal validity of all of the components of social/ sexual complexity. . . .

Glossary

"for the Palestinian people": a reference to the Palestinian movement called the First Intifada, in which Palestinians protested Israeli occupation through strikes, riots, and civil disobedience, and more than one thousand Palestinians died at the hands of Israeli security forces, prompting international protests against the treatment of the Palestinians

ineradicable: incapable of being erased or forgotten

subjugation: placing someone or something under outside control

Short-Answer Questions

1. How does Jordan define the politics of sexuality?

2. What differences does Jordan draw between the old politics of sexuality and the new politics she calls for?

3. What is Jordan's stated objection to identity politics? How does she contrast it with what she calls the "new, bisexual politics of sexuality"?

Lawrence v. Texas

Author
Anthony M. Kennedy

Date
2003

Document Type
Legal

Significance
Ruled that laws banning sodomy were unconstitutional, effectively creating a constitutional right to privacy for same-sex couples in the United States

Overview

In 1986, in *Bowers v. Hardwick*, the U.S. Supreme Court upheld as constitutional a Georgia law criminalizing sodomy between consenting adults. The defendant in the case was a gay man who had been convicted under the statute. He argued that he had a constitutional right to privacy that extended to private, consensual sexual conduct. Reframing the legal question as whether the Constitution created "a fundamental right to engage in homosexual sodomy," the Court rejected the defendant's arguments and answered that the Constitution provided no such right.

Seventeen years later, in *Lawrence v. Texas*, the Supreme Court faced a direct challenge to the holding of *Bowers*. In *Lawrence*, two men convicted of illegal sexual intercourse under a Texas statute criminalizing oral and anal sex by consenting same-sex couples argued that the Texas law was unconstitutional for the very reasons rejected by the Court in *Bowers*. In its decision in *Lawrence*, the Court took the unusual step of overruling itself and striking down the Texas statute. Writing for the majority, Justice Anthony M. Kennedy declared *Bowers* to have been wrongly decided and held that the defendants were free as adults to engage in private sexual conduct in the exercise of their right to liberty as guaranteed by the due process clause of the Fourteenth Amendment.

It is rare for the Supreme Court to reverse established legal precedent, as it did in *Lawrence*. The Constitutional arguments that decided the case were based on the equal protection clause of the Fourteenth Amendment and the implicit right to privacy. The implications of these arguments, and the *Lawrence* decision overall, were profound. The decision created a possibility for lesbian, gay, bisexual, and transgender (LGBT) people to openly serve in the military, marry, and parent children. Historians and legal scholars consider the case a landmark in the evolution of civil rights law because the decision established that the governments could not intrude into the personal sexual lives of consenting adults. The decision showed the relatively rapid pace of social change for LGBT people in the United States.

Document Text

Liberty protects the person from unwarranted government intrusions into a dwelling or other private places. In our tradition the State is not omnipresent in the home. And there are other spheres of our lives and existence, outside the home, where the State should not be a dominant presence. Freedom extends beyond spatial bounds. Liberty presumes an autonomy of self that includes freedom of thought, belief, expression, and certain intimate conduct. The instant case involves liberty of the person both in its spatial and more transcendent dimensions.

I

The question before the Court is the validity of a Texas statute making it a crime for two persons of the same sex to engage in certain intimate sexual conduct....

The petitioners were adults at the time of the alleged offense. Their conduct was in private and consensual.

II

We conclude the case should be resolved by determining whether the petitioners were free as adults to engage in the private conduct in the exercise of their liberty under the Due Process Clause of the Fourteenth Amendment to the Constitution. For this inquiry we deem it necessary to reconsider the Court's holding in *Bowers*....

The laws involved in *Bowers* and here are, to be sure, statutes that purport to do no more than prohibit a particular sexual act. Their penalties and purposes, though, have more far-reaching consequences, touching upon the most private human conduct, sexual behavior, and in the most private of places, the home. The statutes do seek to con-

Justice Kennedy wrote the Court's opinion in **Lawrence v. Texas.**
(Supreme Court of the United States)

trol a personal relationship that, whether or not entitled to formal recognition in the law, is within the liberty of persons to choose without being punished as criminals.

This, as a general rule, should counsel against attempts by the State, or a court, to define the meaning of the relationship or to set its boundaries absent injury to a person or abuse of an institution the law protects. It suffices for us to acknowledge that adults may choose to enter upon this relationship in the confines of their homes and their own private lives and still retain their dignity as free persons. When sexuality finds overt expression in intimate conduct with another person, the conduct can be but one element in a personal bond that is more enduring. The liberty protected by the Constitution allows homosexual persons the right to make this choice. . . .

Equality of treatment and the due process right to demand respect for conduct protected by the substantive guarantee of liberty are linked in important respects, and a decision on the latter point advances both interests. If protected conduct is made criminal and the law which does so remains unexamined for its substantive validity, its stigma might remain even if it were not enforceable as drawn for equal protection reasons. When homosexual conduct is made criminal by the law of the State, that declaration in and of itself is an invitation to subject homosexual persons to discrimination both in the public and in the private spheres. The central holding of *Bowers* has been brought into question by this case, and it should be addressed. Its continuance as precedent demeans the lives of homosexual persons. . . .

The present case does not involve minors. It does not involve persons who might be injured or coerced or who are situated in relationships where consent might not easily be refused. It does not involve public conduct or prostitution. It does not involve whether the government must give formal recognition to any relationship that homosexual persons seek to enter. The case does involve two adults who, with full and mutual consent from each other, engaged in sexual practices common to a homosexual lifestyle. The petitioners are entitled to respect for their private lives. The State cannot demean their existence or control their destiny by making their private sexual conduct a crime. Their right to liberty under the Due Process Clause gives them the full right to engage in their conduct without intervention of the government. . . . The Texas statute furthers no legitimate state interest which can justify its intrusion into the personal and private life of the individual.

Had those who drew and ratified the Due Process Clauses of the Fifth Amendment or the Fourteenth Amendment known the components of liberty in its manifold possibilities, they might have been more specific. They did not presume to have this insight. They knew times can blind us to certain truths and later generations can see that laws once thought necessary and proper in fact serve only to oppress. As the Constitution endures, persons in every generation can invoke its principles in their own search for greater freedom.

The judgment of the Court of Appeals for the Texas Fourteenth District is reversed, and the case is remanded for further proceedings not inconsistent with this opinion.

It is so ordered.

Glossary

Bowers: *Bowers v. Hardwick* (1986), a case in which the Supreme Court held that there was no constitutional protection for sodomy, and that states could outlaw it and other private sexual practices.

Due Process Clause: a clause found in both the Fifth and Fourteenth Amendments; in the former it guarantees no one shall be "deprived of life, liberty or property without due process of law," and in the latter it guarantees that governments cannot "make or enforce any law which shall abridge the privileges or immunities of citizens of the United States"

Fifth Amendment: protects criminal defendants from having to testify if they may incriminate themselves through their testimony

Short-Answer Questions

1. Describe the basic argument Justice Kennedy presents in the majority opinion, excerpted here. Why is this argument considered a landmark by scholars of human rights and LGBT civil liberties?

2. Explain how Justice Kennedy links the existence of anti-sodomy laws with the creation and perpetuation of social stigma faced by LGBT individuals in the United States.

3. Analyze the paragraph in the excerpt beginning with the words "Had those who drew . . ." Summarize the argument Kennedy is making about history and the intent of the Constitution's authors. After summarizing this argument, explain some of the implications of his reasoning on other political, social, and legislative issues.

Obergefell v. Hodges

Author
Anthony Kennedy

Date
2015

Document Type
Legal

Significance
Established the constitutional right to marry for same-sex couples

Overview

In *Obergefell v. Hodges* (2015), the U.S. Supreme Court, in a 5–4 decision authored by Anthony Kennedy, held that same-sex couples in the United States had the same right to marry as opposite-sex couples. It also held that states had to recognize legal marriages performed in other states. *Obergefell* expressly overturned the decision in *Baker v. Nelson* (1971), a Minnesota Supreme Court case that the U.S. Supreme Court declined to consider via a one-sentence dismissal in 1972, saying that the issue of same-sex marriage did not rise to "a substantial federal question" and was not properly to be heard before the Court. The Court's decision in *Obergefell v. Hodges* was predicated on the established right to marriage. The Court concluded that marriage is a fundamental and essential part of an individual's autonomy and that it is a vital institution, needed to foster lasting, emotional relationships and protect families with children. Moreover, the Court applied the language of the equal protection clause, found in the Fifth and Fourteenth Amendments, to conclude that denying same-sex couples the right to marry violated their rights to equal protection under the law. *Obergefell* was a landmark piece of civil rights legislation.

The Supreme Court's ruling marked a pivotal moment in the nation's history. It affirmed the efforts of LGBTQ+ activists who had made the campaign for marriage a central part of their agenda. This had been a strategic decision, since it was felt that advocating for the right to marry would appeal to the American public's widely shared assumptions about privacy and relationships. The Court's decision vindicated this strategy. The Court's opinion had immediate implications. It effectively legalized same-sex marriage across the United States, thus granting same-sex couples the legal protections previously denied to them. More profoundly, however, the decision signaled a wider transformation in societal attitudes about same-sex relationships, encouraging a growing acceptance for LGBTQ+ individuals and an emerging emphasis on equality and inclusion.

The White House on the evening of the ruling (Flickr)

Document Text

The Constitution promises liberty to all within its reach, a liberty that includes certain specific rights that allow persons, within a lawful realm, to define and express their identity. The petitioners in these cases seek to find that liberty by marrying someone of the same sex and having their marriages deemed lawful on the same terms and conditions as marriages between persons of the opposite sex. . . .

From their beginning to their most recent page, the annals of human history reveal the transcendent importance of marriage. The lifelong union of a man and a woman always has promised nobility and dignity to all persons, without regard to their station in life. Marriage is sacred to those who live by their religions and offers unique fulfillment to those who find meaning in the secular realm. Its dynamic allows two people to find a life that could not be found alone, for a marriage becomes greater than just the two persons. Rising from the most basic human needs, marriage is essential to our most profound hopes and aspirations.

The centrality of marriage to the human condition makes it unsurprising that the institution has existed for millennia and across civilizations. Since the dawn of history, marriage has transformed strangers into relatives, binding families and societies together. Confucius taught that marriage lies at the foundation of government. . . . There are untold references to the beauty of marriage in religious and philosophical texts spanning time, cultures, and faiths, as well as in art and literature in all their forms. It is fair and necessary to say these references were based on the understanding that marriage is a union between two persons of the opposite sex.

That history is the beginning of these cases. The respondents say it should be the end as well. To them, it would demean a timeless institution if the concept and lawful status of marriage were extended to two persons of the same sex. Marriage, in their view, is by its nature a gender-differentiated union of man and woman. . . .

The petitioners acknowledge this history but contend that these cases cannot end there. Were their intent to demean the revered idea and reality of marriage, the petitioners' claims would be of a different order. But that is neither their purpose nor their submission. To the contrary, it is the enduring importance of marriage that underlies the petitioners' contentions. This, they say, is their whole point. Far from seeking to devalue marriage, the petitioners seek it for themselves because of their respect and need for its privileges and responsibilities. And their immutable nature dictates that same-sex marriage is their only real path to this profound commitment. . . .

The ancient origins of marriage confirm its centrality, but it has not stood in isolation from developments in law and society. The history of marriage is one of both continuity and change. That institution even as confined to opposite-sex relations has evolved over time. . . .

The nature of injustice is that we may not always see it in our own times. The generations that wrote and ratified the Bill of Rights and the Fourteenth Amendment did not presume to know the extent of freedom in all of its dimensions, and so they entrusted to future generations a charter protecting the right of all persons to enjoy liberty as we learn its meaning. When new insight reveals discord between the Constitution's central protections and a received legal stricture, a claim to liberty must be addressed. . . .

As this Court held in *Lawrence*, same-sex couples have the same right as opposite-sex couples to enjoy intimate association. *Lawrence* invalidated laws that made same-sex intimacy a criminal act. . . . But while *Lawrence* confirmed a dimension of freedom that allows individuals to engage in intimate association without criminal liability, it does not follow that freedom stops there. Outlaw to outcast may be a step forward, but it does not achieve the full promise of liberty.

A third basis for protecting the right to marry is that it safeguards children and families and thus draws meaning from related rights of childrearing, procreation, and education. . . .

As all parties agree, many same-sex couples provide loving and nurturing homes to their children, whether biological or adopted. And hundreds of thousands of children are presently being raised by such couples. . . . Most States have allowed gays and lesbians to adopt, either as individuals or as couples, and many adopted and foster children have same-sex parents. . . . This provides powerful confirmation from the law itself that gays and lesbians can create loving, supportive families.

Excluding same-sex couples from marriage thus conflicts with a central premise of the right to marry. Without the recognition, stability, and predictability marriage offers, their children suffer the stigma of knowing their families are somehow lesser. They also suffer the significant material costs of being raised by unmarried parents, relegated through no fault of their own to a more difficult and uncertain family life. The marriage laws at issue here thus harm and humiliate the children of same-sex couples. . . .

It is now clear that the challenged laws burden the liberty of same-sex couples, and it must be further acknowledged that they abridge central precepts of equality. Here the marriage laws enforced by the respondents are in essence unequal: same-sex couples are denied all the benefits afforded to opposite-sex couples and are barred from exercising a fundamental right. Especially against a long history of disapproval of their relationships, this denial to same-sex couples of the right to marry works a grave and continuing harm. The imposition of this disability on gays and lesbians serves to disrespect and subordinate them. . . .

These considerations lead to the conclusion that the right to marry is a fundamental right inherent in the liberty of the person, and under the Due Process and Equal Protection Clauses of the Fourteenth Amendment couples of the same-sex may not be deprived of that right and that liberty. The Court now holds that same-sex couples may exercise the fundamental right to marry. No longer may this liberty be denied to them.

Glossary

Due Process and Equal Protection Clauses: the legal rights and guarantees promised in the Fifth Amendment, extended in the Fourteenth Amendment, in which Section 1 states the following: "No state shall make or enforce any law which shall abridge the privileges or immunities of citizens of the United States; nor shall any state deprive any person of life, liberty, or property, without due process of law; nor deny to any person within its jurisdiction the equal protection of the laws"

Fourteenth Amendment: ratified in 1868, granted citizenship to all persons "born or naturalized in the United States," including formerly enslaved people, and provided all citizens with "equal protection under the laws," extending the guarantees of the Fifth Amendment's due process clause

Lawrence: *Lawrence v. Texas*, a landmark 2003 Supreme Court case in which the Court reversed established precedent and invalidated sodomy laws across the United States and made same-sex sexual activity legal in every U.S. state and territory

Short-Answer Questions

1. Describe the arguments Kennedy makes in his excerpted opinion regarding the history and evolution of the institution of marriage. In your view, what rhetorical purpose was he trying to achieve by summarizing this history?

2. Analyze how Kennedy links the issue of marriage with parenting. Summarize his arguments and then examine his purpose for linking these two issues. How does he use this connection to create an argument for same-sex marriage?

3. The concept of precedent is an important one in legal scholarship. Precedent refers to the concept that a court's earlier decisions are considered authoritative when deciding subsequent cases with similar facts or similar legal issues. How does Kennedy use legal and constitutional precedents to support his ruling that same-sex individuals cannot be denied the right to marry.

Chapter 12
Modern, Postmodern, and Postcolonial Feminisms

Modern, postmodern, and postcolonial feminisms are terms that are used to describe different forms of feminist theory that emerged, mostly in the post-World War II era, that were influenced by second-wave feminism. These were forms of thinking that tried to reclaim universal female rights from worldwide male oppression. Because of the diversity of forms that oppression took, different flavors of feminism emerged. Over the past sixty-plus years, those feminisms, informed by modern, postmodern, and postcolonial thinking, have become ways in which women who suffer from different forms of oppression can come together under a common feminist banner.

Simone de Beauvoir and the Second Sex

All three of these different forms of feminism can trace their roots back to Simone de Beauvoir's groundbreaking 1949 work, *Le deuxième sexe* (1949; English translation as *The Second Sex,* 1953). De Beauvoir (1908–1986) argued that there was a difference between biological sex, which was rooted in the body, and gender, which was defined socially and historically. She pointed out that the oppression of women found worldwide was primarily because, throughout history, men and masculinity had been the baseline against which all differences had been compared and, as a result, women were considered secondary: the "second sex." Men, de Beauvoir argued, had enshrined women as mysterious, but in the process they also confined them and limited their potential. Women needed to break free of the confines of male definitions of gender and sex. Only then would women be truly free.

This was a radical idea, and it spread rapidly, diffused by feminist theorists and scholars. By 1977 the French philosopher Luce Irigaray (1930–) was arguing that, intellectually, strict feminism really meant that there should be no differences between men and women. But although first-wave feminists, who fought for the right to vote, called for the unity of all women to demand civil rights, there were nonetheless significant differences in class, wealth, race, and sexual identity that tore women apart even as the feminist movement tried to bring them together. As a result, different forms of feminism emerged worldwide in the 1960s and 1970s.

Intersectionality and "Othering"

But women, despite the call for transnational and trans-class unity, were also members of their own distinct classes in societies. One term that has come into use to describe these different forms of feminism is *intersectionality*, but intersectionality is usually used in a more restricted sense. Modern, postmodern, and particularly postcolonial feminism create ways in which women of color, women living in poverty, and women living in non-Western postcolonial societies can find commonalities to discuss their common oppression and devise ways of resisting it.

De Beauvoir used the Hegelian term *other* to describe what men had done to disempower women. That word was also used to describe the basis of other forms of oppression, such as racism. In 1963 Celina Simango, wife of the vice-president of FRELIMO, the Marxist-Leninist Liberation Front of the African nation of Mozambique, addressed the International Women's Congress in Moscow. Simango pointed out that women were supporting the struggle for rights in Mozambique, but they were being deprived of those same rights. Yale professor of African American Studies Hazel Carby suggested that one of the primary ways to resisting the "othering" of women of color living in a post-imperial world is through personal and family history. By making history personal, the Other ceases to be different and strange. It becomes familiar—overturning the imperialist attempts to alienate colonialized peoples from their history.

Throughout the 1980s this postcolonial feminism continued to develop in different parts of the world. Syracuse University professor Chandra Talpade Mohanty (1955–) pointed out ways in which transnational feminism could help create a feminist solidarity that did not rely on imperialist and colonialist tropes. Chinese feminist artist Xiao Lu (1962–), who became renowned shortly before the Tiananmen Square rallies in 1989 when she destroyed her own artwork with a shotgun at the opening of the China/Avant-Garde Exhibition, demonstrated ways in which China's ruling Communist Party has violated the freedom for women promised by Mao Zedong in 1949. Ghanian playwright and novelist Ama Ata Aidoo (1940–2023) likewise honored women who broke with tradition and defied stereotypes in her work. In 2010 Binghampton University professor María Lugones (1944–2020), in "Toward a Decolonial Feminism," suggested that gender itself, which de Beauvoir had said was a cultural construct, was also a colonial construct, a relic of imperialism that continued its oppression of women long after the imperialists had departed.

Audre Lorde and Gloria E. Anzaldúa

Perhaps the clearest statement of the ways in which culture, class, and color divided the feminist movement came from African American poet and activist Audre Lorde (1934–1992). Although primarily remembered as a poet, Lorde was a fierce feminist and an outspoken critic of the racism and classism endemic in the American movement. In "The Master's Tools Will Never Dismantle the Master's House," Lorde pointed out that until women of color were welcomed into the feminist movement and their viewpoints given equal credence to those of white feminists, the movement would remain oppressive—undermining the very goals toward which it worked.

Lorde spoke not only as a Black woman but as a lesbian, a member of the LGBTQ+ community that was similarly deprived of rights yet never fully accepted into the mainstream feminist movement. Chicana scholar Gloria E. Anzaldúa (1942–2004), best known for her semi-autobiographical work *Borderlands/La Frontera* (1987), likewise spoke up for oppressed Chicana women and queer people in the Hispanic community.

These scholars and writers have shown that, far from being simple acts of rebellion aimed toward a single goal, modern, postmodern, and postcolonial feminisms are complex, multifaceted systems of thought that require recognition and respect of a multiplicity of identities.

Further Reading

Articles

Barei-Guyot, Isis. "Layers of Honesty: Postcolonial Feminism and Ethical Research Relationships Post-Pandemic." *Ethics In /Of Geographical Research* (November 2, 2022). Available at https://doi.org/10.1111/area.12852.

Ling, L.H.M. "Postcolonial-Feminism: Transformative Possibilities in Thought and Action, Heart and Soul." *Postcolonial Studies* 19, no. 4 (2016): 478–480.

Marchand, Marianne H. "The Future of Gender and Development after 9/11: Insights from Postcolonial Feminism and Transnationalism." *Third World Quarterly* 30, no. 5, (2009): 921–935.

Sa'ar, Amalia. "Postcolonial Feminism, the Politics of Identification, and the Liberal Bargain." *Gender and Society* 19, no. 5 (2005): 680–700.

Safia Mirza, Heidi. "Plotting a History: Black and Postcolonial Feminisms in 'New Times.'" *Race Ethnicity and Education* 12, no. 1 (2009), 1-10.

Simone de Beauvoir: *The Second Sex*

Author
Simone de Beauvoir

Date
1949

Document Type
Essays, Reports, Manifestos

Significance
Challenged the idea that women were inferior to women because of their biological differences

Overview

In 1945, women in France were granted the right to vote. The inclusion of women in the political and social future of France had long been taken up by women activists across France, dating back to the founding of First Republic, in which Olympe de Gouges in *The Declaration of the Rights of Woman* denounced the customary treatment of women as second class and argued that women should be included in France's future. In 1949, Simone de Beauvoir followed in the footsteps of de Gouges with *The Second Sex*. The title is a criticism of women being categorized as the secondary or inferior sex. De Beauvoir was writing during the Fourth Republic of France, a period defined as the French restructuring and rebuilding of the republic after the tumultuous years of World War II, which brought about the collapse of the Third Republic. De Beauvoir's work is helpful for understanding the conditions of women not only in France but around the world. Women after World War II were demanding greater inclusion in political and social affairs, challenging the historical arguments that women were inherently inferior to men and therefore could never be equal, paving the way for the future of the feminist movement.

Document Text

Woman? Very simple, say those who like simple answers: She is a womb, an ovary; she is a female: this word is enough to define her. From a man's mouth, the epithet "female" sounds like an insult; but he, not ashamed of his animality, is proud to hear: "He's a male!" The term "female" is pejorative not because it roots woman in nature but because it confines her in her sex, and if this sex, even in an innocent animal, seems despicable and an enemy to man, it is obviously because of the disquieting hostility woman triggers in him. Nevertheless, he wants to find a justification in biology for this feeling. The word "female" evokes a saraband of images: an enormous round egg snatching and castrating the agile sperm; monstrous and stuffed, the queen termite reigning over the servile males; the praying mantis and the spider, gorged on love, crushing their partners and gobbling them up; the dog in heat running through back alleys, leaving perverse smells in her wake; the monkey showing herself off brazenly, sneaking away with flirtatious hypocrisy. And the most splendid wildcats, the tigress, lioness, and panther, lie down slavishly under the male's imperial embrace, inert, impatient, shrewd, stupid, insensitive, lewd, fierce, and humiliated. Man projects all females at once onto woman. And the fact is that she is a female. But if one wants to stop thinking in commonplaces, two questions arise. What does the female represent in the animal kingdom? And what unique kind of female is realized in woman?

Simone de Beauvoir
(Flickr)

Glossary

animality: animal nature or character

disquieting: inducing feelings of anxiety or worry

servile: having or showing an excessive willingness to serve or please others

Short-Answer Questions

1. How does de Beauvoir explain how men have constructed the definition of the term "woman"? Explain the significance of her argument.

2. De Beauvoir highlights several qualities of women that differ from those of men. Why is highlighting those qualities important to understanding the significant role women play in society?

3. De Beauvoir writes, "From a man's mouth, the epithet 'female' sounds like an insult; but he, not ashamed of his animality, is proud to hear: 'He's a male!'" How does this quote highlight de Beauvoir's argument surrounding the sexism found in gender construction?

Luce Irigaray: "Women on the Market"

Author
Luce Irigaray

Date
1977

Document Type
Essays, Reports, Manifestos

Significance
Argued that common theoretical approaches to women's sexuality and social status are inherently structured using sexualized, masculine language and knowledge systems

Overview

Born in 1930, Luce Irigaray is a Belgian-born French scholar whose works have bridged the gap between psychoanalysis and feminist theory. Active in feminist movements in France and Italy and a pivotal figure in the rise of gender studies in the 1980s, Irigaray is a prolific writer. In 1974, she published her first work, *Speculum of the Other Woman,* which deconstructed texts in the Western philosophical canon using the theoretical lens of phallocentrism. As understood by feminist scholars, phallocentrism is the perspective that asserts that the masculine, as expressed through the phallus, or male sexual organ, has become central to the Western understanding of meaning, language, economy, and social relations. Phallocentrism has been widely used in literary criticism, psychoanalysis, psychology, linguistics, medicine, and philosophy. Irigaray used the concept in her early works to deconstruct texts by philosophers and by her predecessors in the psychoanalytic tradition, showing that, for earlier psychoanalysts, the phallus served as both a supreme symbol of masculine power and of female weakness.

Irigaray published additional works during the 1980s and 1990s, including *This Sex Which Is Not One*. This collection of eleven essays—including the chapter excerpted here, "Women on the Market"—expanded on her earlier commentaries on psychoanalysis. Each of the essays in this work can be read individually, but taken together, the arguments presented make the case that Western culture's use of language and signs structure how female identity is represented, which in turn influences the ways women see themselves and see their world. In her essays, Irigaray explores a host of linked topics, including the boundaries of masculinist language systems and discourses and the ways in which this language has come to define female sexuality. In addition, she draws on the analytical approaches of the structuralist anthropologist Claude Lévi-Strauss, contending that the essentially phallic nature of the market economy equates women and sexuality with barter and exchange. The radical nature of this text placed Irigaray at the forefront of the feminist movement in the 1980s. Her early works became foundational texts in the emerging field of gender studies.

Irigaray's deconstructivist writings have contributed to an understanding of the sexualized nature of language and systems of knowledge. Her works make clear that signs, symbols, and words are not neutral; they are, in themselves, highly sexualized contributors to patriarchal social systems.

Document Text
Chapter 8: Women on the Market

The society we know, our own culture, is based upon the exchange of women. Without the exchange of women, we are told, we would fall back into the anarchy (?) of the natural world, the randomness (?) of the animal kingdom. The passage into the social order, into the symbolic order, into order as such, is assured by the fact that men, or groups of men, circulate women among themselves, according to a rule known as the incest taboo.

Whatever familial form this prohibition may take in a given state of society, its signification has a much broader impact. It assures the foundation of the economic, social, and cultural order that has been ours for centuries. . . .

Are men all equally desirable? Do women have no tendency toward polygamy? The good anthropologist does not raise such questions. *A fortiori*: why are men not objects of exchange among women? It is because women's bodies—through their use, consumption, and circulation—provide for the condition making social life and culture possible, although they remain an unknown "infrastructure" of the elaboration of that social life and culture. The exploitation of the matter that has been sexualized female is so integral a part of our sociocultural horizon that there is no way to interpret it except within this horizon.

In still other words: all the systems of exchange that organize patriarchal societies and all the modalities of productive work that are recognized, valued, and rewarded in these societies are men's business. The production of women, signs, and commodities is always referred back to men (when a man buys a girl, he "pays" the father or the brother, not the mother . . .), and they always pass from one man to another, from one group of men to another. The work force is thus always assumed to be masculine, and "products" are objects to be used, objects of among men alone.

Which means that the possibility of our social life, of our culture, depends upon a ho(m)mo-sexual monopoly? The law that orders our society is the exclusive valorization of men's needs/desires, of exchanges among men. What the anthropologist calls the passage from nature to culture thus amounts to the institution of the reign of hom(m)o-sexuality. . . .

In this new matrix of History, in which man begets man as his own likeness, wives, daughters, and sisters have value only in that they serve as the possibility of, and potential benefit in, relations among men. . . .

Their situation of specific exploitation in exchange operations—sexual exchange, and economic, social, and cultural exchanges in general—might lead them to offer a new critique of the political economy. . . .

For, without the exploitation of women, what would become of the social order? What modifications would it undergo if women left behind their condition as commodities—subject to being produced, consumed, valorized, circulated, and so on, by men alone—and took part in elaborating and carrying out exchanges? Not by reproducing, by copying, the "phallocratic" models that have the force of law today, but by socializing in a different way the relation to nature, matter, the body, language, and desire.

Glossary

a fortiori: signals an argument that it is based on an even stronger argument

ho(m)mo-sexual: a pun suggesting relations among patrilineal clans are based in homosocial desire

matrix of History: a reference to the German philosopher Georg Wilhelm Friedrich Hegel's theory of history and historical development

Short-Answer Questions

1. Describe the argument Irigaray presents in this excerpt from Chapter 8 of her book. In your response, outline what connections she draws between property, economics, and women's status.

2. Explain how you feel about Irigaray's basic contention that the social order is underpinned by the economic exploitation of women. In your response, discuss your personal reaction to this idea and reference specific words, phrases, or ideas in the excerpt.

3. Analyze the final paragraph of this excerpt. What is Irigaray urging readers to do in this paragraph? Be specific in your interpretations of this challenging text.

Hazel V. Carby: "White Woman Listen! Black Feminism and the Boundaries of Sisterhood"

Author
Hazel V. Carby

Date
1982

Document Type
Essays, Reports, Manifestos

Significance
Analyzed the ways white American feminism marginalizes and discounts the experiences of women of color and women from underdeveloped countries

Overview

Hazel V. Carby's 1982 essay "White Woman Listen! Black Feminism and the Boundaries of Sisterhood" is a scathing indictment of feminism in the 1980s, calling out the elements of racism and subjugation that white feminism directs toward "the forgotten woman": women of color and women from underdeveloped countries. Carby argues that "white feminism" is not inclusive and lacks the insight to be representative of minority women. Her critique stems from the distinctive treatment that Black, minority, and Asian women experience as a result of their complex intersectional identities. It is not enough for white women to examine women's lives in general in the light of patriarchy. They must research, investigate, and listen to the specific experiences of Black and minority women to gain a fuller understanding of the ways their lives are different from those of white women.

Carby, professor emerita of African American studies and of American studies at Yale University, utilizes an anticolonial approach in her essay and mentions the different ways that family and intricate support networks allow Black and minority women to navigate the world. She also highlights the position of Black men in the hierarchy of patriarchy, where they still face bigotry, which affects their ability to support and contribute to their families' standard of living.

Carby's essay highlighted the experiences of women of color and women from underdeveloped countries. (Flickr)

Document Text

The black women's critique of *history* has not only involved us in coming to terms with "absences"; we have also been outraged by the ways in which it has made us visible, when it has chosen to see us. *History* has constructed our sexuality and our femininity as deviating from those qualities with which white women, as the prize objects of the Western world, have been endowed. We have also been defined in less than human terms. We cannot hope to constitute ourselves in all our absences, or to rectify the ill-conceived presences that invade herstory from *history*, but we do wish to bear witness to our own herstories. The connections between these and the herstories of white women will be made and remade in struggle. Black women have come from Africa, Asia and the Caribbean and we cannot do justice to all their herstories in a single chapter. Neither can we represent the voices of all black women in Britain, our herstories are too numerous and too varied. What we will do is to offer ways in which the "triple" oppression of gender, race and class can be understood, in their specificity, and also as they determine the lives of black women.

Much contemporary debate has posed the question of the relation between race and gender, in terms which attempt to parallel race and gender divisions. It can be argued that as processes, racism and sexism are similar. Ideologically for example, they both construct common sense through reference to "natural" and "biological" differences. It has also been argued that the categories of race and gender are both socially constructed and that, therefore, they have little internal coherence as concepts. Furthermore, it is possible to parallel racialized and gendered divisions in the sense that the possibilities of amelioration through legislation appear to be equally ineffectual in both cases. Michèle Barrett, however, has pointed out that it is not possible to argue for parallels because as soon as historical analysis is made, it becomes obvious that the institutions which have to be analysed are different, as are the forms of analysis needed. We would agree that the construction of such parallels is fruitless and often proves to be little more than a mere academic exercise; but there are other reasons for our dismissal of these kinds of debate. The experience of black women does not enter the parameters of parallelism. The fact that black women are subject to the *simultaneous* oppression of patriarchy, class and "race" is the prime reason for not employing parallels that render their position and experience not only marginal but also invisible.

We can point to no single source for our oppression. When white feminists emphasize patriarchy alone, we want to redefine the term and make it a more complex concept. Racism ensures that black men do not have the same relations to patriarchal/capitalist hierarchies as white men.

It is only in the writings by black feminists that we can find attempts to theorize the interconnection of class, gender and race as it occurs in our lives and it has only been in the autonomous organizations of black women that we have been able to express and act upon the experiences consequent upon these determinants. . . . Black feminists have been, and are still, demanding that the existence of racism must be acknowledged as a structuring feature of our relationships with white women. Both white feminist theory and practice have to recognize that white women stand in a power relation as oppressors of black women. This compromises any feminist theory and practice founded on the notion of simple equality.

Three concepts which are central to feminist theory become problematic in their application to black women's lives: "the family," "patriarchy" and "reproduction." When used they are placed in a context of the herstory of white (frequently middle-class) women and become contradictory when applied to the lives and experiences of black women. In a recent comprehensive survey of contemporary feminist theory, *Women's Oppression Today*, Michèle Barrett sees the contemporary family (effectively the family under capitalism) as the source of oppression of women.

We would not wish to deny that the family can be a source of oppression for us but we also wish to examine how the black family has functioned as a prime source of resistance to oppression. We need to recognize that during slavery, periods of colonialism and under the present authoritarian state, the black family has been a site of political and cultural resistance to racism. Furthermore, we cannot easily separate the two forms of oppression because racist theory and practice is frequently gender-specific. Ideologies of black female sexuality do not stem primarily from the black family. The way the gender of black women is constructed differs from constructions of white femininity because it is also subject to racism.

Black women are constantly challenging these ideologies in their day-to-day struggles.

Glossary

authoritarian: concentrating power in a leader or system not responsible to the people

colonialism: a system in which a developed country controls and profits from an underdeveloped country's resources, people, and location, almost always at a detriment to the native people and usually involving violence

herstory: history about women or from a feminist point of view

patriarchy: social organization in which men have power and control

slavery: a system of oppression in which one person owns or controls another person completely; referring here to the institution of slavery in the United States through the mid-nineteenth century

Short-Answer Questions

1. Who is Carby's audience, and why is it significant that she address them at this time in history?

2. What does Carby list as the concepts fundamental to feminism? Why does she consider them imprecise when analyzing Black women's experiences?

3. How does Carby compare white women's experiences to Black women's experiences? Why does she assert that white women benefit from racism and colonialism?

Chandra Talpade Mohanty: "Under Western Eyes"

Author
Chandra Talpade Mohanty

Date
1984

Document Type
Essays, Reports, Manifestos

Significance
Argued that Western feminist scholars have ignored the specifics of women's experiences around the world and essentialized non-Western women

Overview

Chandra Talpade Mohanty is a postcolonial and transnational feminist theorist. Postcolonial feminism is a form of feminism that examines the ways in which racism and the effects of colonialism affect non-white, non-Western women in the postcolonial world. Transnational feminism is a related perspective that is rooted more clearly in an activist agenda. Transnational feminism began as a critique of the international women's movement of the 1970s and 1980s. Transnational feminist thinkers view any global or international approach to gender equality as suspect, arguing that these points of view are inherently rooted in Eurocentric, colonialist perspectives. Mohanty's writings in this area have been extensive, and she is a key figure in the development of an explicitly anticolonial feminist perspective.

Mohanty is currently Distinguished Professor of Women's and Gender Studies, Sociology, and the Cultural Foundations of Education at Syracuse University in Syracuse, New York. Born in Mumbai, India, in 1955 and educated in the United States, Mohanty became known among feminist thinkers after the publication of her 1984 essay "Under Western Eyes: Feminist Scholarship and Colonial Discourses." This pivotal essay was a pointed critique of Western feminist political assumptions. In it, Mohanty argued that Western feminists tended to turn women in the developing world into a flat, homogenous category and often disregarded important differences in the experiences of women globally. Moreover, she found that Western feminists often labeled all non-Western women as poor, uneducated, victimized, and passive. From these observations, she contended that the specifics of women's experiences deserve consideration, even if they shared a universal experience with gender-based oppression.

Mohanty's significance as a scholar and essayist lies in her deconstruction of the ethnocentric notions common among Western feminists. In addition, she alerts scholars and activists to the ways in which their own rhetoric can split women into two opposed groups: Western women, who are liberated and enjoy equality, and non-Western women, who need salvation. This framing perpetuates a colonial approach to feminism and prevents the development of a truly global women's movement.

Document Text

What I wish to analyze is specifically the production of the "third world woman" as a singular monolithic subject in some recent (Western) feminist texts. The definition of colonization I wish to invoke here is a predominantly discursive one, focusing on a certain mode of appropriation and codification of "scholarship" and "knowledge" about women in the third world by particular analytic categories employed in specific writings on the subject which take as their referent feminist interests as they have been articulated in the U.S. and Western Europe. . . .

The relationship between "Woman"—a cultural and ideological composite Other constructed through diverse representational discourses (scientific, literary, juridical, linguistic, cinematic, etc.)—and "women"—real, material subjects of their collective histories—is one of the central questions the practice of feminist scholarship seeks to address. This connection between women as historical subjects and the representation of Woman produced by hegemonic discourses is not a relation of direct identity, or a relation of correspondence or simple implication. It is an arbitrary relation set up by particular cultures. I would like to suggest that the feminist writings I analyze here discursively colonize the material and historical heterogeneities of the lives of women in the third world, thereby producing/re-presenting a composite, singular "third world woman"—an image which appears arbitrarily constructed, but nevertheless carries with it the authorizing signature of Western humanist discourse.

I argue that assumptions of privilege and ethnocentric universality, on the one hand, and inadequate self-consciousness about the effect of Western scholarship on the "third world" in the context of a world system dominated by the West, on the other, characterize a sizable extent of Western feminist work on women in the third world. An analysis of "sexual difference" in the form of a cross-culturally singular, monolithic notion of patriarchy or male dominance leads to the construction of a similarly reductive and homogeneous notion of what I call the "third world difference"—that stable, ahistorical something that apparently oppresses most if not all the women in these countries. . . .

I argue that . . . a homogeneous notion of the oppression of women as a group is assumed, which, in turn, produces the image of an "average third world woman." This average third world woman leads an essentially truncated life based on her feminine gender (read: sexually constrained) and her being "third world" (read: ignorant, poor, uneducated, tradition-bound, domestic, family-oriented, victimized, etc.). This, I suggest, is in contrast to the (implicit) self-representation of Western women as educated, as modern, as having control over their own bodies and sexualities and the freedom to make their own decisions. . . .

What happens when this assumption of "women as an oppressed group" is situated in the context of Western feminist writing about third world women? It is here that I locate the colonialist move. By contrasting the representation of women in the third world with what I referred to earlier as Western feminisms' self-presentation in the same context, we see how Western feminists alone become the true "subjects" of this counterhistory. Third world women, on the other hand, never rise above the debilitating generality of their "object" status. . . .

A comparison between Western feminist self-presentation and Western feminist representation of women in the third world yields significant results. Universal images of "the third world woman" (the veiled woman, chaste virgin, etc.), images constructed from adding the "third world difference" to "sexual difference," are predicated upon (and hence obviously bring into sharper focus) assumptions about Western women as secular, liberated, and having control over their own lives. . . . It is time to move beyond the Marx who found it possible to say: They cannot represent themselves; they must be represented.

Glossary

discourse, discursive: in academia, particularly in the humanities and social sciences, relating to a formal way of thinking about a topic as expressed through language; a social boundary or a set of rules defining what can be said about a topic

humanist: relating to humanism, a Western philosophical stance that assumes the central importance of the individual and argues for the universal agency of all human beings

Marx: Karl Marx, a German-born philosopher, economist, historian, sociologist, political theorist, journalist, critic of political economy, and socialist revolutionary, whose extensive writings are often cited in the humanities and in the fields of postcolonial and gender studies

third world: an unfashionable term now, but widely used beginning in the 1960s to represent countries in Africa, Asia, and Latin America that were considered underdeveloped by Western economic standards

Short-Answer Questions

1. Describe the characteristics of the "third world woman" archetype that Mohanty argues Western feminists have created.

2. According to Mohanty, how did Western feminists create the image of women in the developing world as a homogenous monolith?

3. Why, in your view, is it problematic that some Western feminists group all third-world women together? How might this warp and distort movements and organizations attempting to support women around the world?

Xiao Lu: "China: Feudal Attitudes, Party Control, and Half the Sky"

Author
Xiao Lu

Date
1984

Document Type
Essays, Reports, Manifestos

Significance
Analyzed the status of women in the People's Republic of China, where equality between the sexes was legally mandated in theory but rarely achieved in practice

Overview

For most of its history, China was a strictly patriarchal society. Confucianism, the worldview and ethical stance propagated by Confucius in the sixth and fifth centuries BCE, was the guiding outlook of Chinese culture for more than two millennia. According to traditional Confucian ethics, women were expected to be chaste, demure, pleasant, and domestic. They were expected to be subservient to the men in their lives. Confucius believed that society should be centered on patriarchal relationships and familial obligations; consequently, women were supposed to support their husbands, fathers, and brothers without question. Women's behavior was determined by the overlapping kinship roles they occupied as daughters, sisters, wives, daughters-in-law, mothers, and mothers-in-law. Regardless of the role, Confucian scholars expected that women would agree with the wishes and support the needs of the men around them.

Despite the historical oppression of women, in modern China the lives of women have changed significantly. During the late Qing dynasty (1636–1912), reformist political leaders and philosophers contended that China's economic stagnation and political weakness resulted from the country's strict adherence to traditional social structures. Reforms were enacted in the 1800s that improved the lives of women, and these were expanded during the subsequent Republican period (1912–1949) and during the long and bloody Chinese Civil War (1927–1949). When the Chinese Communist Party took complete control of China in 1949, it made the achievement of women's liberation a major part of its political agenda. In part, this was in recognition of the militant role that peasant women had played in the Chinese Civil War. Chairman Mao Zedong, the Communist revolutionary who was the founder of the People's Republic of China (PRC), famously said, in support of his efforts to promote gender equality, that "women hold up half the sky."

Women's rights in China have improved dramatically in the past century. Chinese women contribute to the paid labor force in numbers exceeding most other countries. And most of the world's self-made female billionaires are from China. But, as this document demonstrates, the PRC's stated goal of achieving gender equality remains stubbornly elusive. Women are still accorded a lower social, political, and economic status compared to men. For instance, no woman has ever been among the nine members of the Standing Committee of the Communist Party's Politburo, China's most important political body. Xiao Lu's essay shows that formal and legal equality has not eradicated a legacy of patriarchal oppression.

Lu references China's patriarchal history. (Wikimedia Commons)

Document Text

In comparison with the state of women before 1949, women's situation in the People's Republic of China (PRC) today is much improved. However, despite constitutional guarantees and official pronouncements of the Chinese Communist Party, equality between the sexes has yet to be achieved. The situation is worse in the countryside than in rural areas, but even in large cities women do not have the same access to opportunities as men do. Traditional attitudes towards women are still widespread, and the consciousness of people at every level of society, including cadres and Party members, remains low. While most people recognize that no government can undo 3000 years of history in 30 years, they are uncertain about the government's commitment and determination to make women's rights a priority....

One of the most serious problems the PRC faces in achieving its goal of modernization is the generally low level of development of its humanpower. . . . Owing to the lack of economic resources and qualified instructors, the number of spaces [in colleges and universities] has been severely limited. Currently about 25–30 percent of college students are women. While during the early years no explicit consideration was given to the gender of the applicant, beginning in 1982, officials decided to raise women's admission score by two points. In other words, while a male applicant can get into the university with, say, 360 points, a female applicant will not be admitted unless she has scored 362 points or even higher. Some universities are instituting a quota system designed to limit the number of female students on their campuses. . . .

Young women are complaining that many of the most desirable jobs are not open to them. The more prestigious the unit, the more unlikely that it will accept a woman as an employee. Unit heads give the same reasons for discriminating against women as those given in the case of university admissions: the need for maternity leave, time pressure for childcare and housework, physical and mental "limitations," etc. . . . In the countryside, despite numerous campaigns for "equal work, equal pay," peasant women still receive fewer workpoints than their male counterparts generally and even when they do the same task . . . the prevalent view among the rural masses is still that women's main responsibility is housework and men's responsibility is income-producing work. . . .

In the PRC one's sexual and public lives are intertwined to such an extent that an undesirable personal style (usually referring to sexual behavior) is often detrimental to one's career and lifelong development. The loss of virginity before marriage or an extramarital affair is cause enough for social ostracism, job dismissal, or denial of promotion. Although it applies to both men and women, the effect is usually much more serious for women.

Despite what is stated in the marriage law, parental and kin interference in marriage is not uncommon, especially among peasant families. . . . Feudal attitudes towards women and general ignorance of the legal system have led to the beating and severe mistreatment of peasant women. . . . The recent "one-child" policy has resulted in widespread resistance by both men and women, and in a number of tragedies. Since women are considered responsible for the gender of the child in rural areas, giving birth to a baby girl has led to ridicule and resulted in suicides and female infanticides. . . .

The root of the problem lies in the persistence of feudal attitudes and the total control of political life by the Communist Party—which does not allow an independent women's movement to exist. The Constitution of the PRC, the Marriage Law, and the Party platform all proclaim equality between the sexes, yet feudal attitudes die hard and, given the social organization of China, these attitudes seep through every sphere of life, consciously and unconsciously affecting the making of administrative policies and their implementation. . . .

If the apparatus of Party control can be convinced to truly engage the feudal attitudes, then, perhaps, it will be possible for women not only to—in Mao Zedong's words—"hold up half the sky" but do so with respect, compassion, and on their own terms.

Glossary

Mao Zedong: founder of the People's Republic of China in 1949 and chairman of the Chinese Communist Party who famously said that "women hold up half the sky"

Marriage Law: also called the New Marriage Law, a civil marriage law passed in the People's Republic of China on May 1, 1950, marking a radical departure from the strictly patriarchal Confucian marriage customs that had governed Chinese marriages for more than 2,000 years

one-child policy: a population planning mandate in China implemented between 1979 and 2015, instituted to curb the country's population growth by restricting many families to a single child

unit: also called a *danwei*, an organizational grouping of employees in China

Short-Answer Questions

1. Describe some of the ways women in China, despite official pronouncements, remain marginalized in the labor force and education. In your response, cite data from the text to support your conclusions.

2. Describe the unofficial ways in which contemporary Chinese culture remains deeply sexist and patriarchal, according to the excerpt. In your response, discuss the information on marriages and sexual behavior discussed in the text.

3. Analyze this excerpt considering your own experience and cultural upbringing. How does the information presented in this passage compare with your own experience and with your understanding of the status of women and girls in the United States? What are some intriguing similarities and differences?

Ama Ata Aidoo:
"Ghana: To Be a Woman"

Author
Ama Ata Aidoo

Date
1984

Document Type
Essays, Reports, Manifestos

Significance
Described the challenges of navigating cultural norms and social expectations as an African female writer and academic living in a postcolonial society

Overview

Ama Ata Aidoo was born in 1942 in southern Ghana to a royal family of the Fante ethnic community, a subgroup of Akan people living primarily in coastal areas of contemporary Ghana. A precocious and ambitious child, she was encouraged to pursue Western education by her family and began writing when she was just fifteen. After attending the University of Ghana, where she studied English literature, she published her first play, *The Dilemma of the Ghost,* in 1964. The work was published to widespread acclaim, marking Aidoo's entrance onto the global literary stage and making her the first published female African playwright. Aidoo briefly served as the secretary for education in Ghana and was also a prolific dramatist, essayist, and novelist, as well as an academic and lecturer. At the time of her death in 2023, Aidoo was widely recognized as one of Africa's most important literary voices.

Aidoo's work was probing and nuanced, and nearly all of her literary oeuvre focused on the challenges facing her strong, independent female protagonists. The challenges facing these characters limit their actions and their independence, placing boundaries on what is possible for them. Aidoo's works exhibit an anthropological engagement with the effects of history and the impositions of culture and society. She applied a feminist lens to the lives of African women, examining the ways in which patriarchy and the legacies of colonialism worked in concert to shape the female experience. For her, local norms, customs, and traditions shaped the textures of women's lives in granular, highly specific ways. Aidoo's narratives complicated the stereotypical portrayals of women in male-authored African works of literature, displaying female characters as individuals, universally strong, intelligent, and outspoken but bounded by history and circumstance.

Aidoo's overall literary agenda sought to reclaim African women's voices from the margins. Recurrent themes in her works include colonialism and its legacies, the history of slavery, the conflict between tradition and modernity, and the relationship between Ghana and its diasporic communities around the world. In her essay "Ghana: To Be a Woman," Aidoo discusses the challenges faced by many Ghanaian women but also describes her specific experiences with oppression and patriarchy as a writer and academic in a society where women are expected to abide by traditional gender binaries.

Document Text

I had sensed vaguely as a child living among adult females that everything which had to do exclusively with being a woman was regarded as dirty. At definite traditional landmarks in a woman's life cycle, she was regarded literally as untouchable. The scope and frequency of the restrictions depended on such factors as the family's mode of ancestral worship and the propinquity of the woman's domicile to private and public shrines. These landmarks included the first menstruation and (for some) all other menstruations; all of the post-partum forty days for the first-born and subsequent births; a whole year of widowhood (compare forty days at most for a widower), and dying pregnant—in which latter case, it was the corpse of the woman which was now exposed to ostracism and humiliation.

A girl's first menstrual flow was celebrated after a whole week of confinement. Put "celebrated" in quotation marks. Because we know now that the "celebration" was really a broadcasting of the fact that she was ready for procreation. And once you, the young man, had been bold enough to go forward and take her off her mother's back, you could also take it for granted that you had acquired

a sexual aid;
a wet-nurse and nursemaid for your children;
a cook-steward and general housekeeper;
a listening post;
an economic and general consultant;
a field-hand and,
if you are that way inclined,
a punch-ball.

No, the position of a woman in Ghana is no less ridiculous than anywhere else. The few details that differ are interesting only in terms of local color and family needs.

... As a writer, I not only can *cope* with aloneness; I have to actively *seek* it in order to produce. Yet as an academic, can I maintain a vibrant intellect, condemned as I am to ostracism because I refuse to consider marriage the only way to live? Male colleagues resent your professional standing and punish your presumption in mean little ways. They blame your *femininity* for what one would have thought was evidence of a regular *human* frailty: ill health, laziness, and other excuses of poor productivity. Yet rather than avail themselves of your expertise, they consult other male colleagues, however mediocre. If they do not find you physically repulsive, they take your continued single state as an insult to their manhood. ...

Certainly it is a little easier on the nerves of your high-minded colleagues if, with the unmarried state, you are childless. For then they just put you down for being a bitter old maid. Definitely, it is not fair to anybody that together with the outrage of your unmarried state, you should also insist, shamelessly, on being a single parent.

In any case, as a woman, your persistence in staying in the academic field is a total waste of time, since articulateness and other manifestations of intelligence are all masculine. ...

An inquiry of this nature runs the risk of getting charged with pettiness. Yet petty or not, it is legitimate. The ancients have said that if you assume indifference at a meat-sharing, you end up with the bones.

And we all know that with not only our indifference but also our acquiescence (and even connivance), women have ended up with very much less than bones. Primarily resting on women's fears of physical (and economic) insecurity, but tightly encased in the myth of male superiority and moral blackmail, marriage has proved singularly effective as an instrument of suppression. It has put half (or often more than half) of humanity through mutations that are thoroughly humiliating and at best ridiculous. . . .

At the very foundation of the family, marriage has maintained a chameleon-like capacity to change its nature in time and space and to serve the ignominious aims of every society: slave-owning, feudal, or modern bourgeois. Throughout history and among all peoples, marriage has made it possible for women to be owned like property, abused and brutalized like serfs, privately corrected and, like children, publicly scolded, overworked, underpaid, and much more thoroughly exploited than the lowest male worker on any payroll. . . .

And you know the solution does not lie with you, the individual woman, married or unmarried, no matter how keenly aware you are of the problems in your environment. . . .

It is obvious that for a long-term answer, if one is at all possible, only collective action would be meaningful. We must organize. . . .

Glossary

acquiescence: passive acceptance

connivance: active consent

propinquity: nearness in place; proximity

Short-Answer Questions

1. Describe the tone of these excerpts from Aidoo's essay, analyzing the rhetorical effect she was likely attempting to achieve with this tone.

2. Summarize Aidoo's thesis regarding marriage. In your response, evaluate how she presents male attitudes toward marriage as well as the social and historical function of marriage as an institution.

3. Aidoo has been noted for her textured understanding of women's experiences with oppression. Her works address both general structural forms of patriarchy and the specific and individualized ways women are oppressed by gender norms. Analyze how, in these excerpts, Aidoo explores general patriarchal norms and their effects on women, as well as how male attitudes have affected her life specifically.

Audre Lorde: "The Master's Tools Will Never Dismantle the Master's House"

Author
Audre Lorde

Date
1984

Document Type
Essays, Reports, Manifestos; Speeches/Addresses

Significance
An admonition to women of color that they must recognize oppression and discrimination in all of its forms and must embrace their differences as a way to contest systemic injustice

Overview

Audre Lorde (1934–1992) described herself as a "Black, lesbian, mother, warrior, poet." She was a prolific essayist and poet and a professor at Lehman College, John Jay College of Criminal Justice, and Hunter College. As a panelist at a New York University Institute for the Humanities conference in 1979 focusing on feminism, Lorde addressed the audience on the hypocrisy of feminism and its marginalization of certain sectors of women due to their class, race, sexual orientation, or economic circumstances. She found that the same systems of oppression and patriarchy that feminism espoused to combat ran rampant within feminism itself, and she pointed out evidence of racism and inequality at the conference. She felt the tokenism of being one of only two Black scholars asked to speak. She chastised the group for maintaining the status quo by "playing by their oppressor's rules." Lorde's speech, published in 1984 in her collection *Sister Outsider: Essays and Speeches*, warns her audience that they cannot be successful in achieving social justice and equity while adhering to old concepts established by elite, white males.

Document Text

I agreed to take part in a New York University Institute for the Humanities conference a year ago, with the understanding that I would be commenting upon papers dealing with the role of difference within the lives of American women: difference of race, sexuality, class, and age. The absence of these considerations weakens any feminist discussion of the personal and the political.

It is a particular academic arrogance to assume any discussion of feminist theory without examining our many differences, and without a significant input from poor women, Black and Third World women, and lesbians. And yet, I stand here as a Black lesbian feminist, having been invited to comment within the only panel at this conference where the input of Black feminists and lesbians is represented. What this says about the vision of this conference is sad, in a country where racism, sexism, and homophobia are inseparable. To read this program is to assume that lesbian and Black women have nothing to say about existentialism, the erotic, women's culture and silence, developing feminist theory, or heterosexuality and power. And what does it mean in personal and political terms when even the two Black women who did present here were literally found at the last hour? What does it mean when the tools of a racist patriarchy are used to examine the fruits of that same patriarchy? It means that only the most narrow parameters of change are possible and allowable.

The absence of any consideration of lesbian consciousness or the consciousness of Third World women leaves a serious gap within this conference and within the papers presented here. For example, in a paper on material relationships between women, I was conscious of an either/or model of nurturing which totally dismissed my knowledge as a Black lesbian. In this paper there was no examination of mutuality between women, no systems of shared support, no interdependence as exists between lesbians and women-identified women. Yet it is only in the patriarchal model of nurturance

Audre Lorde
(Elsa Dorfman)

that women "who attempt to emancipate themselves pay perhaps too high a price for the results," as this paper states.

For women, the need and desire to nurture each other is not pathological but redemptive, and it is within that knowledge that our real power I rediscovered. It is this real connection which is so feared by a patriarchal world. Only within a patriarchal structure is maternity the only social power open to women.

Interdependency between women is the way to a freedom which allows the *I* to *be*, not in order to be used, but in order to be creative. This is a difference between the passive *be* and the active *being*.

Advocating the mere tolerance of difference between women is the grossest reformism. It is a total denial of the creative function of difference in our lives. Difference must be not merely tolerated, but seen as a fund of necessary polarities between which our creativity can spark like a dialectic. Only then does the necessity for interdependency become unthreatening. Only within that interdependency of difference strengths, acknowledged and equal, can the power to seek new ways of being in the world generate, as well as the courage and sustenance to act where there are no charters.

Within the interdependence of mutual (nondominant) differences lies that security which enables us to descend into the chaos of knowledge and return with true visions of our future, along with the concomitant power to effect those changes which can bring that future into being. Difference is that raw and powerful connection from which our personal power is forged.

As women, we have been taught either to ignore our differences, or to view them as causes for separation and suspicion rather than as forces for change. Without community there is no liberation, only the most vulnerable and temporary armistice between an individual and her oppression. But community must not mean a shedding of our differences, nor the pathetic pretense that these differences do not exist.

Those of us who stand outside the circle of this society's definition of acceptable women; those of us who have been forged in the crucibles of difference—those of us who are poor, who are lesbians, who are Black, who are older—know that *survival is not an academic skill*. It is learning how to stand alone, unpopular and sometimes reviled, and how to make common cause with those others identified as outside the structures in order to define and seek a world in which we can all flourish. It is learning how to take our differences and make them strengths. *For the master's tools will never dismantle the master's house.* They may allow us temporarily to beat him at his own game, but they will never enable us to bring about genuine change. And this fact is only threatening to those women who still define the master's house as their only source of support.

Poor women and women of Color know there is a difference between the daily manifestations of marital slavery and prostitution because it is our daughters who line 42nd Street. If white American feminist theory need not deal with the differences between us, and the resulting difference in our oppressions, then how do you deal with the fact that the women who clean your houses and tend your children while you attend conferences on feminist theory are, for the most part, poor women and women of Color? What is the theory behind racist feminism?

In a world of possibility for us all, our personal visions help lay the groundwork for political action. The failure of academic feminists to recognize difference as a crucial strength is a failure to reach beyond the first patriarchal lesson. In our world, divide and conquer must become define and empower.

Why weren't other women of Color found to participate in this conference? Why were two phone calls to me considered a consultation? Am I the only possible source of names of Black feminists? And although the Black panelist's paper ends on an important and powerful connection of love between women, what about interracial cooperation between feminists who don't love each other?

In academic feminist circles, the answer to these questions is often, "We do not know who to ask." But that is the same evasion of responsibility, the same cop-out, that keeps Black women's art our of women's exhibitions, Black women's work out of most feminist publications except for the occasional "Special Third World Women's Issue," and Black women's texts off your reading lists. But as Adrienne Rich pointed out in a recent talk, which feminists have educated themselves about such an enormous amount over the past ten years, how come you haven't also educated yourselves about Black women and the differences between us—white and Black—when it is key to our survival as a movement?

Women of today are still being called upon to stretch across the gap of male ignorance and to educate men as to our existence and our needs. This is an old and primary tool of all oppressors to keep the oppressed occupied with the master's concerns. Now we hear that it is the task of women of Color to educate white women—in the face of tremendous resistance—as to our existence, our differences, our relative roles in our joint survival. This is a diversion of energies and a tragic repetition of racist patriarchal thought.

Simone de Beauvoir once said: "It is in the knowledge of the genuine conditions of our lives that we must draw our strength to live and our reasons for acting."

Racism and homophobia are real conditions of all our lives in this place and time. *I urge each one of us here to reach down into that deep place of knowledge inside herself and touch that terror and loathing of any difference that lives there. See whose face it wears.* Then the personal as the political can begin to illuminate all our choices.

Glossary

academic: theoretical

Adrienne Rich: American feminist poet and essayist

racist feminism: a feminism that represents mainly middle-class, heterosexual white women and their interests while overlooking or ignoring the concerns of women of color, lesbians, poor women, and women in developing countries

Simone de Beauvoir: French existentialist philosopher, feminist writer, and author of the book *The Second Sex* (1949)

Third World: referring to developing nations

Short-Answer Questions

1. Why does Lorde believe that maternity is "the only social power open to women" within a patriarchal structure? What social powers does she identify outside of a patriarchal structure?

2. What are some possible explanations for the conference's omission of a significant portion of women in its scope?

3. What is the "old and primary tool of all oppressors" that Lorde refers to toward the end of the essay? How does she see white women wielding the tool? How does Lorde propose women overcome this tendency?

Gloria Anzaldúa:
Borderlands/La Frontera: The New Mestiza

Author
Gloria Anzaldúa

Date
1987

Document Type
Essays, Reports, Manifestos

Significance
Offered a probing and semi-autobiographical analysis of the Chicana experience through an intersectional lens, exploring issues such as gender, identity, race, and colonialism

Overview

Gloria Anzaldúa (1942–2004) was an American scholar and an important voice in the development of a distinctive Chicana feminism. In addition, she contributed to the academic disciplines of cultural theory and queer theory, an activist academic perspective that insists scholars deconstruct traditional assumptions about gender and sexual identities and that challenges traditional academic approaches to gender. Anzaldúa, who was born on the Mexico-Texas border, used her lived experiences to ground her academic work. The liminality of the South Texas borderlands prompted her to examine cultural marginalization from the lens of her own life story. Her primary academic focus was on chronicling the marginalized, fluid, and mixed cultures in borderlands communities.

A prolific author of essays and poetry, as well as an educator and academic, Anzaldúa's best-remembered work is *Borderlands/La Frontera: The New Mestiza*. In this 1987 work, she discusses her life growing up on the Mexico-Texas border and summarizes a variety of specific Chicana experiences, including life in a heteronormative culture, the lingering vestiges of colonial domination, and patriarchal social norms. In addition, she explores the unique forms of oppression encountered by Chicana lesbians and the loneliness and challenges they face in a culture where gendered expectations strictly govern the behaviors of women. The most significant contribution of Anzaldúa's work is the development of the idea of the "new mestiza," a fluid identity that will break down the male/female and straight/gay binaries that govern social relations.

For Anzaldúa, the concept of the borderland is more than just a geographic and physical space. She uses the term to explore the ways in which linguistic and cultural borders are created to govern and police identities. The people on the borderlands of Mexico and the United

States exist in a hybrid space, neither fully Mexican or American, and are forced to become conversant in the rules of both spaces. She suggests that there are unseen borders between Latinas/os and non-Latinas/os, men and women, heterosexuals and homosexuals, and other marginalized groups. *Borderlands/La Frontera: The New Mestiza* is now recognized as a foundational text in the development of Latinx philosophy and an important work in the evolution of a distinctive Chicana feminism.

Document Text
Chapter 7: *La conciencia de la mestiza/* Towards a New Consciousness

José Vascocelos, Mexican philosopher, envisaged *una raza mestiza*. . . . He called it a cosmic race, *la raza cósmica*, a fifth race embracing the four major races of the world. Opposite to the theory of the pure Aryan, and to the policy of racial purity that white America practices, his theory is one of inclusivity. At the confluence of two or more genetic streams, with chromosomes constantly "crossing over," this mixture of races, rather than resulting in an inferior being, provides hybrid progeny, a mutable, more malleable species with a rich gene pool. From this racial, ideological, cultural and biological cross pollination, an "alien" consciousness is presently in the making—a new *mestiza* consciousness. . . . It is a consciousness of the Borderlands. . . .

The ambivalence from the clash of voices results in mental and emotional states of perplexity. Internal strife results in insecurity and indecisiveness. The mestiza's dual or multiple personality is plagued by psychic restlessness.

In a constant state of mental nepantilism, an Aztec word meaning torn between ways, *la mestiza* is a product of the transfer of the cultural and spiritual values of one group to another. Being tricultural, monolingual, bilingual, or multilingual, speaking a patois, and in a state of perpetual transition, the *mestiza* faces the dilemma of the mixed breed: which collectivity does the daughter of a dark-skinned mother listen to? . . .

Cradled in one culture, sandwiched between two cultures, straddling all three cultures and their value systems, *la mestiza* undergoes a struggle of flesh, a struggle of borders, an inner war. Like all people, we perceive the version of reality that our culture communicates. Like others having or living in more than one culture, we get multiple, often opposing messages. The coming together of two self-consistent but habitually incompatible frames of reference causes *un choque*, a cultural collision.

Within us and within *la cultura chicana*, commonly held beliefs of the white culture attack commonly held beliefs of the Mexican culture, and both attack commonly held beliefs of the indigenous culture. . . .

Gloria Anzaldúa
(Flickr)

These numerous possibilities leave *la mestiza* floundering in uncharted seas. In perceiving conflicting information and points of view, she is subjected to a swamping of her psychological borders. She has discovered that she can't hold concepts or ideas in rigid boundaries. The borders and walls that are supposed to keep the undesirable ideas out are entrenched habits and patterns of behavior; these habits and patterns are the enemy within. Rigidity means death. Only by remaining flexible is she able to stretch the psyche horizontally and vertically. *La mestiza* constantly has to shift out of habitual formations, from convergent thinking, analytical reasoning that tends to use rationality to move toward a single goal (a Western mode), to divergent thinking, characterized by movement away from set patterns and goals and toward a more whole perspective, one that includes rather than excludes.

The new *mestiza* copes by developing a tolerance for contradictions, a tolerance for ambiguity. She learns to be an Indian in Mexican culture, to be Mexican from an Anglo point of view. She learns to juggle cultures. She has a plural personality. . . .

The work of *mestiza* consciousness is to break down the subject-object duality that keeps her a prisoner and to show in the flesh and through the images in her work how duality is transcended. The answer to the problem between the white race and the colored, between males and females, lies in healing the split that originates in the very foundation of our lives, our culture, our languages, our thoughts. A massive uprooting of dualistic thinking in the individual and collective consciousness is the beginning of a long struggle, but one that could, in our best hopes, bring us to the end of rape, of violence, of war.

Glossary

choque: shock

José Vascocelos: a significant Mexican writer, philosopher, and politician whose philosophy of the "cosmic race" influenced Mexican political thought, and who advanced the then-unorthodox position that the mixing of races was a natural and desirable direction for humankind

mestiza: an emergent, fluid identity that Anzaldúa urges Chicana women to develop to reinvent themselves and attain a higher level of consciousness

Nepantilism: torn between two things, from the Nahuatl word *nepantla*, which means "in the middle of it" or "middle"

"pure Aryan": a reference to an obsolete and discredited historical race concept that emerged in the late nineteenth century to describe people of proto-Indo-European heritage

raza mestiza: an emerging race

Short-Answer Questions

1. Describe the challenges Anzaldúa identifies as associated with "having a consciousness of the Borderlands."

2. Analyze the concluding paragraphs to the excerpt above. How does Anzaldúa suggest that Chicanas reconcile the conflicting identities at the heart of the Borderlands consciousness?

3. Intersectionality refers to the ways different aspects of a person's gender, sexual, cultural, and racial identity can expose them to overlapping forms of marginalization and disadvantage. Based on the excerpt above, how does Anzaldúa's work explore the idea of intersectionality? In your response, cite specific words, phrases, and concepts she uses that connect with this idea.

María Lugones: "Toward a Decolonial Feminism"

Author
María Lugones

Date
2010

Document Type
Essays, Reports, Manifestos

Significance
Argued that gender, as a social classification, was imposed on colonized peoples and used as a tool along with class, ethnicity, religion, and other intersectional factors to divide and subjugate them

Overview

Born in 1944, María Lugones was an Argentine feminist philosopher, activist, and academic. She was a professor of comparative literature and women's studies at Carleton College in Northfield, Minnesota, and at Binghamton University in New York State. Lugones, who died in 2020, is remembered as a forceful advocate for Latina philosophy and for developing multiple models of resistance against intersectional forms of oppression in Latin America and across the globe. Her primary theoretical contribution to feminist thought and decolonial studies is her theory of "a plurality of selves." This concept, which posits that one's self is really a multiplicity of composite, plural, contradictory identities, allows for the existence of multiple social "worlds" and for multiple selves that interact with those "worlds." Lugones's work on the self and on self-knowledge are significant because of their connections with ideas of intersectionality and overlapping, interrelating forms of oppression and discrimination.

Lugones was also widely recognized for her theoretical work on gender and colonialism. In two late-career essays, "Heterosexualism and the Colonial/Modern Gender System" and "Toward a Decolonial Feminism," Lugones applied concepts from postcolonial studies to a sustained study of gender in colonized spaces. She used the theory of the coloniality of power—a theory stating that, in colonial societies, social relations were configured to be relations of domination. These social relations, according to this theory, are a living, extant legacy of colonial rule. Forms of social discrimination and oppression that were developed by colonizers were integrated into the social orders of contemporary societies, long after those colonizers departed. Lugones applied this theory to the study of gender, arguing that gender, as a social category, was largely an imposition of colonial powers and that it was articulated and used as a system for dividing, classifying, and ruling subjugated peoples. Gender, for Lugones, operated as a tool of oppression and domination.

Lugones's work relied heavily on her deep engagement with and understanding of Native American societies. For instance, she uses the indigenous Chilean Mapuche culture to show how subjugated peoples understood gender. The Mapuche see gender as interchangeable, malleable, and combinable. The Spanish, who colonized Chile, had a strictly binary understanding of gender, and the contemporary Chilean government still operates under this Western knowledge paradigm. The gender binary imposed by the Spanish is continually enforced and policed, which has required the repression of Mapuche gender norms. Lugones's work on gender in colonial spaces is important. It forces scholars to reckon with the subtle ways in which colonial rules created boundaries of knowledge and cultural norms that continue to shape contemporary societies.

Document Text

Modernity organizes the world ontologically in terms of atomic, homogeneous, separable categories. Contemporary women of color and third-world women's critique of feminist universalism centers the claim that the intersection of race, class, sexuality, and gender exceeds the categories of modernity. If *woman* and *black* are terms for homogeneous, atomic, separable categories, then their intersection shows us the absence of black women rather than their presence. . . . I want to emphasize categorial, dichotomous, hierarchical logic as central to modern, colonial, capitalist thinking about race, gender, and sexuality. . . .

I understand the dichotomous hierarchy between the human and the non-human as the central dichotomy of colonial modernity. Beginning with the colonization of the Americas and the Caribbean, a hierarchical, dichotomous distinction between human and non-human was imposed on the colonized in the service of Western man. It was accompanied by other dichotomous hierarchical distinctions, among them that between men and women. This distinction became a mark of the human and a mark of civilization. Only the civilized are men or women. Indigenous peoples of the Americas and enslaved Africans were classified as not human in species—as animals, uncontrollably sexual and wild. The European, bourgeois, colonial, modern man became a subject/agent, fit for rule, for public life and ruling, a being of civilization, heterosexual, Christian, a being of mind and reason. The European bourgeois woman was not understood as his complement, but as someone who reproduced race and capital through her sexual purity, passivity, and being home-bound in the service of the white, European, bourgeois man. The imposition of these dichotomous hierarchies became woven into the historicity of relations, including intimate relations. . . .

Under the imposed gender framework, the bourgeois white Europeans were civilized; they were fully human. The hierarchical dichotomy as a mark of the human also became a normative tool to damn the colonized. The behaviors of the colonized and their personalities/souls were judged as bestial and thus non-gendered, promiscuous, grotesquely sexual, and sinful. Though at this time the understanding of sex was not dimorphic, animals were differentiated as males and females, the male being the perfection, the female the inversion and deformation of the male. Hermaphrodites, sodomites, viragos, and the colonized were all understood to be aberrations of male perfection. . . .

I am certainly not advocating not reading, or not "seeing" the imposition of the human/non-human, man/woman, or male/female dichotomies in the construction of everyday life, as if that were possible. To do so would be to hide the coloniality of gender, and it would erase the very possibility of sensing—reading—the tense inhabitation of the colonial difference and the responses from it. As I mark the colonial translation from *chachawarmi* to man/woman, I am aware of the use of man and woman in everyday life in Bolivian communities, including in interracial discourse. The success of the complex gender norming introduced with colonization that goes into the constitution of the coloniality of gender has turned this colonial translation into an everyday affair, but resistance to the coloniality of gender is also lived linguistically in the tension of the colonial wound. The political erasure, the lived tension of languaging—of moving between ways of living in language—between *chachawarmi* and man/woman constitutes loyalty to the coloniality of gender as it erases the history of resistance at the colonial difference. . . .

One does not resist the coloniality of gender alone. One resists it from within a way of understanding the world and living in it that is shared and that can understand one's actions, thus providing recognition. Communities rather than individuals enable the doing; one does with someone else, not in individualist isolation. The passing from mouth to mouth, from hand to hand of lived practices, values, beliefs, ontologies, space-times, and cosmologies constitutes one. The production of the everyday within which one exists produces one's self as it provides particular, meaningful clothing, food, economies and ecologies, gestures, rhythms, habitats, and senses of space and time. But it is important that these ways are not just different. They include affirmation of life over profit, communalism over individualism, "estar" over enterprise, beings in relation rather than dichotomously split over and over in hierarchically and violently ordered fragments. These ways of being, valuing, and believing have persisted in the resistant response to the coloniality.

Glossary

***chachawarmi*:** literally, "man-woman," a term used by the Aymaras, an indigenous people in the Andes of Bolivia who believe in gender fluidity and in men and women being represented equally

coloniality: the assumptions or structures considered normal by Western colonial powers

estar: being; the Spanish for the verb "to be"

historicity: actuality

ontologically: of or relating to the philosophical study of being, the study of what it means to exist

viragos: a domineering, violent, or assertive woman

Short-Answer Questions

1. Summarize Lugones's thesis presented in the excerpts from her essay "Toward a Decolonial Feminism." In your response, focus on explaining what Lugones argues was the central project of colonial powers in the Americas and the Caribbean.

2. Analyze the implications of Lugones's thesis. How does Lugones argue that the gender categories imposed by colonial powers are still enforced in postcolonial spaces?

3. How convincing do you find Lugones's argument? What might be some critiques of her thesis? In your response, use references from the excerpt, knowledge drawn from other courses, and your personal experiences.

Chapter 13

Intersectionality in the United States

Intersectionality is a term coined in 1989 by legal scholar Kimberlé Crenshaw (1959–) to describe the ways in which discrimination cuts across traditional boundaries such as race, sex or gender, and wealth or poverty. It is often associated with critical race theory, another term coined by Crenshaw, which examines the ways in which race is defined and discrimination is produced in America. Intersectionality can be used to describe relations that are legacies of imperialism and colonialism, but in the United States it is most often used to describe the layers of discrimination produced as a result of race and as a result of gender. Intersectionality is particularly important when considering the history of women of color, who have been the victims of discrimination both because of their race and because of their gender.

The Roots of Intersectionality

Intersectionality has its roots in the struggle for the abolition of slavery before the Civil War. Advocates for women's rights and advocates for the abolishment of slavery were allies, working toward a common goal. Women worked throughout the Civil War, some of them for the army as nurses or cooks. However, many more worked at home, bringing in crops, tending farm animals, or working in factories. The contribution of women toward the war effort in the North was substantial, and women's rights advocates expected that their contribution would be recognized by the government. But when the Fourteenth Amendment was ratified, it awarded rights only to men. Women—and especially women of color—were excluded. As a result, feminists such as Elizabeth Cady Stanton and Susan B. Anthony created a movement for women's suffrage. It was not until 1920 that the Nineteenth Amendment established a woman's right to vote.

Almost immediately after the ratification of the Nineteenth Amendment, women of color began protesting that they were excluded from many of the advantages that were supposed to accrue to all women. The Langton Dakota author and musician Zitkala-Ša (1876–1938) described in an essay titled "The Cutting of My Long Hair" (1921) how as a child she had been forced into a school run by white educators who tried to destroy her Native identity by erasing all its physical signs. Despite legal efforts to win recognition for women with disabilities, discrimination still persists against them, as Judith Heumann (1947–2023) pointed out in her 2018 TED talk, "Our Fight for Disability Rights and Why We're Not Done Yet."

Black Women Writers Speak Out

Although slavery had been ended as a result of the Thirteenth Amendment, Black citizens more often than not found that civil rights still remained outside their grasp. During the Harlem Renaissance of the 1920s, Black women writers spoke out against the discrimination they received from Black men. Jessie Fauset (1882–1961), one of the most significant editors of the time, who worked as literary editor of *The Crisis*, the NAACP's newspaper, pointed out in "Some Notes on Color" (1922) how her own freedom as a writer was limited because of her race. Marita O. Bonner (1899–1971), one of the first Black students admitted to Radcliffe College and a talented musician, wrote in "On Being Young—A Woman—And Colored" (1925) about how race and gender limited her opportunities for success. Zora Neale Hurston (1891–1960), best known as a novelist and anthropologist, wrote in the essay "How It Feels to Be Colored Me" (1928) about how she was made to feel isolated and alone when she was forced to leave her majority-Black community in Florida. Even the liberal administration of Franklin D. Roosevelt (1933–1945), which tried to reduce racial inequalities, fell short, as Mary McLeod Bethune (1875–1955) noted in "What Does American Democracy Mean to Me?" (1939).

While the struggle that culminated in the Civil Rights Act of 1965 helped reduce some of the inequalities that Black Americans faced in exercising the right to vote and the right to an equal education, at the same time it left other forms of discrimination unaddressed. In particular, it did not deal with sexism and homophobia among the Black civil rights leadership. Nor did it deal with the racism found among the (mostly white) leadership of the second-wave women's rights movement—rising to prominence as the civil rights movement was achieving its main objectives. By 1977 the situation had become dire enough that the Combahee River Collective, a group made up of prominent feminist women of color, issued "The Combahee River Collective Statement." This statement was designed to allow the broadest and most inclusive interpretation of identity. In *Feminist Theory: From Margin to Center* (1984), the feminist writer bell hooks (pseudonym of Gloria Jean Watkins, 1952–2021) explicitly pointed out that racism within second-wave feminism continued to undermine the ultimate goals of the feminist movement.

The question of sexism within the Black community came into the public eye when Clarence Thomas was nominated to the Supreme Court by President George H.W. Bush. During the Senate hearings for Thomas's nomination, attorney Anita Hill (1956–), who had worked with Thomas in a government position, spoke about Thomas's sexist treatment of her. In her "Opening Statement at the Senate Confirmation Hearing of Clarence Thomas" (1991), Hill accused Thomas of inappropriate behavior and sexual harassment. During the hearings, a group of Hill's supporters took out an advertisement in the *New York Times*, "African American Women in Defense of Ourselves" (1991). This piece clearly showed that Hill was not alone and that sexism and harassment were problems within the Black community as well as the larger society as a whole.

#BlackLivesMatter and #MeToo

The rise in violence against Black people in the early twenty-first century, following the 2013 murder of teenager Trayvon Martin, led to a series of social media-based protests circulating under the hashtag #BlackLivesMatter. Alicia Garza (1981–) pointed out in "A Herstory of the #BlackLivesMatter Movement" (2014) that the ways in which #BlackLivesMatter was appropriated or changed by different organizations working against violence toward different groups effectively diffused its original intent: to focus on the ways in which extrajudicial violence severely impacted the lives of Black Americans The following year, "Say Her Name," launched under the hashtag #SayHerName, focused attention on the ways violence impacted Black women in particular. Crenshaw herself explicitly linked violence against Black women to what she called "intersectional failure"—the point at which many different lines of discrimination intersect—at her keynote speech at the Women of the World conference in 2016.

The following year another hashtag movement, #MeToo, emerged as a way for women who had suffered from sexual abuse or harassment to talk about and share their experiences with one another. The term had originally been introduced in 2006 on the social media platform MySpace by sexual assault survivor Tarana Burke

(1973–). It spread quickly following the filing of sexual assault allegations against producer Harvey Weinstein. Television personality and entrepreneur Oprah Winfrey (1954–) alluded to it in her Cecil B. DeMille Award acceptance speech in 2018. Burke herself made a public call for unity against sexual violence in her "Full Power of Women" speech the same year. "[I]f you are ready to do the work that's necessary to end sexual violence," she said, "I can only leave you with these two words: Me Too."

Further Reading

Books

Lynn, Marvin, and Adrienne D. Dixson, eds. *Handbook of Critical Race Theory in Education.* 2nd edition. New York: Routledge, 2021.

Articles

Covarrubias, Alejandro. "Quantitative Intersectionality: A Critical Race Analysis of the Chicana/o Educational Pipeline." *Journal of Latinos and Education* 10, no. 2 (2011): 86–105.

Crenshaw, Kimberlé. "Demarginalizing the Intersection of Race and Sex: A Black Feminist Critique of Antidiscrimination Doctrine, Feminist Theory and Antiracist Politics." *University of Chicago Legal Forum* 1 no. 8 (1989). Available at http://chicagounbound.uchicago.edu/uclf/vol1989/iss1/8.

Gillborn, David. "Intersectionality, Critical Race Theory, and the Primacy of Racism: Race, Class, Gender, and Disability in Education." *Qualitative Inquiry* 21, no. 3 (2015): 277–287.

Kupupika, Trust. "Shaping Our Freedom Dreams: Reclaiming Intersectionality through Black Feminist Legal Theory." *Virginia Law Review Online* 107 (2021): 27–47.

Zitkala-Ša: "The Cutting of My Long Hair"

Author
Zitkala-Ša (Gertrude Simmons Bonnin)

Date
1921

Document Type
Essays, Reports, Manifestos

Significance
Offered a first-person perspective on the abusive treatment of Native Americans by white Americans under the excuse of civilizing them

Overview

Zitkala-Ša (1876–1938), meaning "Red Bird," was a Yankton Dakota writer, educator, musician, and activist. She is also known Gertrude Simmons Bonnin, a name given to her by the Quaker missionaries who took her from her mother and her homeland in South Dakota in 1884. The missionaries were on the Yankton reservation to recruit students for their residential school, White's Indiana Manual Labor Institute in Wabash, Indiana. Zitkala-Ša spent three years at the institute receiving a basic education and being indoctrinated into Western culture—a culture that did not accept her as a full participant.

At the school, Zitkala-Ša was brutally stripped of all signs of her Dakota heritage, but she also learned to read, write, and play the violin, all of which she loved to do. When she returned to the Yankton reservation in 1887, she found that she no longer fully fit in there. She returned to the institute and graduated in 1895. She moved on to study music at Earlham College in Richmond, Indiana, and at the New England Conservatory of Music before joining the faculty of the Carlisle Indian Industrial School in Carlisle, Pennsylvania. Conflict with Carlisle's founder Richard Henry Pratt led to her dismissal from the school in 1901, and she took up a position with the Bureau of Indian Affairs on the Yankton reservation.

"The Cutting of My Long Hair" was originally composed as part of Zitkala-Ša's autobiography. It was reprinted in her collection *American Indian Stories* (1921), and the excerpt reprinted here is taken from the later work.

Document Text

The first day in the land of apples was a bitter-cold one; for the snow still covered the ground, and the trees were bare. A large bell rang for breakfast, its loud metallic voice crashing through the belfry overhead and into our sensitive ears. The annoying clatter of shoes on bare floors gave us no peace. The constant clash of harsh noises, with an undercurrent of many voices murmuring an unknown tongue, made a bedlam within which I was securely tied. And though my spirit tore itself in struggling for its lost freedom, all was useless.

A paleface woman, with white hair, came up after us. We were placed in a line of girls who were marching into the dining room. These were Indian girls, in stiff shoes and closely clinging dresses. The small girls wore sleeved aprons and shingled hair. As I walked noiselessly in my soft moccasins, I felt like sinking to the floor, for my blanket had been stripped from my shoulders. I looked hard at the Indian girls, who seemed not to care that they were even more immodestly dressed than I, in their tightly fitting clothes. While we marched in, the boys entered at an opposite door. I watched for the three young braves who came in our party. I spied them in the rear ranks, looking as uncomfortable as I felt. . . .

Late in the morning, my friend Judéwin gave me a terrible warning. Judéwin knew a few words of English, and she had overheard the paleface woman talk about cutting our long, heavy hair. Our mothers had taught us that only unskilled warriors who were captured had their hair shingled by the enemy. Among our people, short hair was worn by mourners, and shingled hair by cowards!

We discussed our fate some moments, and when Judéwin said, "We have to submit, because they are strong," I rebelled.

"No, I will not submit! I will struggle first!" I answered.

Zitkala-Ša
(National Museum of American History)

I watched my chance, and when no one noticed I disappeared. I crept up the stairs as quietly as I could in my squeaking shoes,—my moccasins had been exchanged for shoes. Along the hall I passed, without knowing whither I was going. Turning aside to an open door, I found a large room with three white beds in it. The windows were covered with dark green curtains, which made the room very dim. Thankful that no one was there, I directed my steps toward the corner farthest from the door. On my hands and knees I crawled under the bed, and cuddled myself in the dark corner.

From my hiding place I peered out, shuddering with fear whenever I heard footsteps near by. Though in the hall loud voices were calling my name, and I knew that even Judéwin was searching for me, I did not open my mouth to answer. Then the steps were quickened and the voices became excited. The sounds came nearer and nearer. Women and girls entered the room. I held my breath, and watched them open closet doors and peep behind large trunks. Some one threw up the curtains, and the room was filled with sudden light. What caused them to stoop and look under the bed I do not know. I remember being dragged out, though I resisted by kicking and scratching wildly. In spite of myself, I was carried downstairs and tied fast in a chair.

I cried aloud, shaking my head all the while until I felt the cold blades of the scissors against my neck, and heard them gnaw off one of my thick braids. Then I lost my spirit. Since the day I was taken from my mother I had suffered extreme indignities. People had stared at me. I had been tossed about in the air like a wooden puppet. And now my long hair was shingled like a coward's! In my anguish I moaned for my mother, but no one came to comfort me. Not a soul reasoned quietly with me, as my own mother used to do; for now I was only one of many little animals driven by a herder.

Glossary

bedlam: noise and confusion; the word comes from the nickname of a London hospital in which mentally ill people were confined

shingled hair: a short bob, in which the hair is cut above the neckline

Short-Answer Questions

1. What does Zitkala-Ša say is the reason she fears having her hair cut? Why might the teachers at the school insist on cutting it?

2. How does Zitkala-Ša describe the moment when her spirit is broken by the Quaker teachers at the school?

3. What form does Zitkala-Ša's resistance to indoctrination take?

Jessie Redmon Fauset: "Some Notes on Color"

Author
Jessie Redmon Fauset

Date
1922

Document Type
Essays, Reports, Manifestos

Significance
Called attention to the "color question" and the disparities between middle-class whites and African Americans on the same socioeconomic scale

Overview

Jessie Redmon Fauset (1882–1961) was born into poverty, but after studies at Cornell University and the University of Pennsylvania, her career as a teacher and as an editor elevated her to middle-class status. Her work at *The Crisis* made her integral to the Harlem Renaissance as she helped foster the works of such prolific African American writers as Langston Hughes and Georgia Douglas Johnson.

In addition to being an editor of *The Crisis*, Fauset wrote a number of literary works and contributed to other magazines and periodicals, including *The World Tomorrow*, a magazine that embraced the idea of Christian Socialism, which combined Christian thought with leftist political ideologies. In "Some Notes on Color," Fauset calls attention to the struggles of middle-class African Americans who were having difficulty integrating into white middle-class society.

Written in 1922 during the Harlem Renaissance, Fauset called attention to her experiences fitting into white middle-class America. She noted that as much as she tried to fit in, the stigma remained that she was different and lesser because she was Black. Additionally, she stated, if whites were told to be judged by "their statues and not their actions," then the same rules should apply to all people, regardless of race. As an example, she encountered the hypocrisy of this argument when she was on the subway and an available seat opened up. As chivalry dictated, women were prioritized over men for the vacant seat. But because she was Black, a white gentleman did not see her as worthy of chivalrous standards and therefore denied her the seat. Fauset wondered why race was the overriding factor in equality when both Black people and white people were afforded the same virtues and values designated by the United States and held accountable to the same laws.

Jessie Redmon Fauset
(Library of Congress)

Document Text

A distinguished novelist said to me not long ago: "I think you colored people make a great mistake in dragging the race problem into your books and novels. It isn't art."

"But good heavens," I told him, "it's life, it's colored life. Being colored is being a problem."

That attitude and the sort of attitude instanced by a journalist the other day who thought colored people ought to be willing to permit the term "n*****" because it carries with it so much picturesqueness defines pretty well, I think, our position in the eyes of the white world. . . .

Of course we do think about the white world, we have to. But not at all in the sense in which that white world thinks it. For the curious thing about white people is that they expect us to judge them by their statute-books and not by their actions. But we colored people have learned better, so much so that when we prepare for a journey, when we enter on a new undertaking, when we decide on where to go to school, if we want to shop, to move, to go to the theatre, to eat (outside of our own houses) we think quite consciously, "If we can pull it through without some white person interfering."

I have hesitated more than once about writing this article because my life has been spent in the localities which are considered favorable to colored people and in the class which least meets the grossest forms of prejudice. . . .

Being colored in America at any rate means: Facing the ordinary difficulties of life, getting education, work, in fine getting a living plus fighting every day against some inhibition of natural liberties.

Let me see if I can give you some idea. I am a colored woman, neither white nor Black, neither pretty nor ugly, neither specially graceful nor at all deformed. I am fairly well educated, of fair manners and deportment. In brief, the average American done over in brown. In the morning I go to work by means of the subway, which is crowded. Presently somebody gets up. The man standing in front of the vacant place looks around meaning to point it out to a woman. I am the nearest one, "But oh," says his glance, "you're colored. I'm not expected to give it to you." And down he plumps. According to my reflexes that morning, I think to myself "hypocrite" or "pig." And make a conscious effort to shake the unpleasantness of it off, for I don't want my day spoiled. . . .

But I hate to be pitied even so sincerely. I hate to have this position thrust upon me.

All of us are passionately interested in the education of our children, our younger brothers and sisters. And just as deliberately, as earnestly as white people discuss tuition, relative ability of professors, expenses, etc., so we in addition discuss the question of prejudice....

I think the thing that irks us most is the teasing uncertainty of it all. Did the man at the box-office give us the seat behind the post on purpose? Is the shop-girl impudent or merely nervous? Had the position really been filled before we applied for it? What actuates the teacher who tells Alice—oh, so kindly—that the college preparatory course is really very difficult. Even remarkably clever pupils have been known to fail. Now if she were Alice—

Other things cut deeper, undermine the very roots of our belief in mankind. In school we sing "America," we learn the Declaration of Independence, we read and even memorize some of the passages in the Constitution. Chivalry, kindness, consideration are the ideals held up before us....

So much is this difference impressed on us, "this for you but that quite other thing for me," that finally we come to take all expressions of a white man's justice with a cynical disbelief, our standard of measure being a provident "How does he stand on the color question?"

Glossary

"America": referring to the song "America the Beautiful"

color question: differences in race or skin color, and relations between groups of people distinguished in these ways, as matters for debate or consideration

Constitution: the document that embodies the fundamental laws and principles by which the United States is governed

Declaration of Independence: the public act by which the Second Continental Congress, on July 4, 1776, declared the Colonies to be free and independent of England

Short-Answer Questions

1. What does Fauset mean when she says, "I hate to be pitied even so sincerely. I hate to have this position thrust upon me"? Explain how this fits into her overall argument.

2. Fauset notes there is a "double standard" surrounding social norms. What evidence does she give to support her claim?

3. How does Fauset look to solve the color question?

Marita O. Bonner: "On Being Young—A Woman—And Colored"

Author
Marita O. Bonner

Date
1925

Document Type
Essays, Reports, Manifestos

Significance
Addressed the residential segregation and social constraints faced by Black women living in the "Black Ghetto"

Overview

Growing up in a middle-class Boston community, Marita Bonner experienced racial segregation firsthand. While attending school, she was denied certain opportunities, such as housing and access to clubs, because of her race and gender. She channeled her experiences into her writing, which depicted the limited opportunities for upward mobility that affected African Americans and women in particular. Bonner contributed in various ways to the Harlem Renaissance, but her writings primarily addressed the struggles of Black people who lived outside of Harlem to form a strong racial and gender identity. While being outspoken herself through her writing, she advised Black women to remain silent to gain the understanding, knowledge, and truth necessary to fight racial and gender oppression. In her work, she addressed the barriers that African American women faced when they attempted to follow the Harlem Renaissance's call for self-improvement through education and issues surrounding discrimination.

In this essay, Bonner addresses the distinct identity of Black womanhood and the difficulties that come with belonging to two oppressed groups: African Americans and women. African American women were discriminated against not only by white society but also by African American men. The essay calls attention to racial and gender barriers that Bonner experienced despite having the opportunities that are afforded to the middle class. While the liberalism of the 1920s offered middle-class white women more opportunities of expression, African American women were limited by racial, social, and gender norms. Bonner's work also shows the limitations of the influence of the Harlem Renaissance; although she was influential in shaping its course, for African Americans, especially women, who lived outside Harlem, opportunities were limited.

Document Text

You start out after you have gone from kindergarten to sheepskin covered with sundry Latin phrases.

At least you know what you want life to give you. A career as fixed and as calmly brilliant as the North Star. The one real thing that money buys. Time. Time to do things. A house that can be as delectably out of order and as easily put in order as the doll-house of "playing-house" days. And of course, a husband you can look up to without looking down on yourself. . . .

That's Youth.

But you know that things learned need testing— acid testing—to see if they are really after all, an interwoven part of you. All your life you have heard of the debt you owe "Your People" because you have managed to have the things they have not largely had. . . .

If you have never lived among your own, you feel prodigal. Some warm untouched current flows through them—through you—and drags you out into the deep waters of a new sea of human foibles and mannerisms; of a peculiar psychology and prejudices. And one day you find yourself entangled—enmeshed—pinioned in the seaweed of a Black Ghetto.

Not a Ghetto, placid like the Strasse that flows, outwardly unperturbed and calm in a stream of religious belief, but a peculiar group. . . .

You hear that up at New York this is to be seen; that, to be heard.

You decide the next train will take you there.

You decide the next second that that train will not take you, nor the next—nor the next for some time to come.

For you know that—being a woman—you cannot twice a month or twice a year, for that matter, break away to see or hear anything in a city that is supposed to see and hear too much.

That's being a woman. A woman of any color.

You decide that something is wrong with a world that stifles and chokes; that cuts off and stunts; hedging in, pressing down on eyes, ears and throat. Somehow all wrong.

You wonder how it happens there that—say five hundred miles from the Bay State—Anglo Saxon intelligence is so warped and stunted. How judgment and discernment are bred out of the race. And what has become of discrimination? Discrimination of the right sort. Discrimination that the best minds have told you weighs shadows and nuances and spiritual differences before it catalogues. The kind they have taught you all of your life was best: that looks clearly past generalization and past appearance to dissect, to dig down to the real heart of matters. . . .

But—"In Heaven's name, do not grow bitter. Be bigger than they are",—exhort white friends who have never had to draw breath in a Jim- Crow train. Who have never had petty putrid insult dragged over them—drawing blood—like pebbled sand on your body where the skin is tenderest. On your body where the skin is thinnest and tenderest. You long to explode and hurt everything white; friendly; unfriendly. But you know that you cannot live with a chip on your shoulder even if you can manage a smile around your eyes—without getting steely and brittle and losing the softness that makes you a woman.

For chips make you bend your body to balance them. And once you bend, you lose your poise, your balance, and the chip gets into you. The real you. You get hard.

. . . And many things in you can ossify. . . .

You must sit quietly without a chip. Not sodden—and weighted as if your feet were cast in the iron of your soul. Not wasting strength in enervating gestures as if two hundred years of bonds and whips had really tricked you into nervous uncertainty.

But quiet; quiet. Like Buddha—who brown like I am—sat entirely at ease, entirely sure of himself; motionless and knowing, a thousand years before the white man knew there was so very much difference between feet and hands.

Motionless on the outside. But inside?

Silent.

Still . . . "Perhaps Buddha is a woman." . . .

And then you can, when Time is ripe, swoop to your feet—at your full height—at a single gesture.

Ready to go where?

Why . . . Wherever God motions.

Glossary

Anglo-Saxon: ethnic group that hails from northern and western Europe; a term commonly used as a measure of whiteness

Black Ghetto: neighborhood with a higher concentration of Black residents than others, and often isolated and segregated regardless of social or economic class

ossify: to become rigid or fixed in attitude or position; to cease developing

Short-Answer Questions

1. Bonner evokes the image of Buddha in describing how women should act in the face of oppression and even notes that perhaps "Buddha is a woman." Why?

2. What is Bonner's message in evoking the image of "youth"?

3. Although the Harlem Renaissance was influential in shaping the lives of many prominent African Americans, including Bonner's, its limitations are noted by the author. Describe those limitations and how their existence runs counter to the ideals put forth by the movement.

Zora Neale Hurston: "How It Feels to Be Colored Me"

Author
Zora Neale Hurston

Date
1928

Document Type
Essays, Reports, Manifestos

Significance
Argued that race is not an essential feature that a person is born with but emerges in specific social contexts

Overview

Zora Neale Hurston (1891–1960) wrote in a time when racism had proven relentless and oppression undaunting. However, having been raised in Eatonville, Florida, an all-Black town, she was guarded against many of the cruelties of racial strife. Hurston uses "How It Feels to Be Colored Me" as a vehicle to vividly describe her realization of what it meant to be Black in America.

Recalling her childhood, she expresses the insignificance of the color of one's skin and how unaware she was of the racial division that existed outside her world. Even after realizing that she is of color, Hurston does not place a significant emphasis on the racial inequalities that exist in America. This can be observed in many of her other works as well.

Having recognized the consequences of being Black, she makes a clear distinction between herself as a person of color and "the sobbing school of Negrohood." Here she exhibits an ambition that carries her past the obstacles faced by African Americans in the course of their lifetimes. With her outspoken, high-spirited, and ambitious personality, Hurston obtains an education and explores the complexities of African American society through her research and writing.

Much of her work is interpreted as autobiographical. Throughout her writings, many characters exude a strong sense of courage, determination, and willfulness to achieve their goals. These characters are often interpreted as having attributes characteristic of Hurston. She expresses pride and appreciation for her people and recognizes African heritage as a significant factor in determining a cultural identity.

Portrait of Zora Neale Hurston
(Carl Van Vechten)

Document Text

I remember the very day that I became colored. Up to my thirteenth year I lived in the little Negro town of Eatonville, Florida. It is exclusively a colored town. The only white people I knew passed through the town going to or coming from Orlando. The native whites rode dusty horses, the Northern tourists chugged down the sandy village road in automobiles. The town knew the Southerners and never stopped cane chewing when they passed. But the Northerners were something else again. They were peered at cautiously from behind curtains by the timid. The more venturesome would come out on the porch to watch them go past and got just as much pleasure out of the tourists as the tourists got out of the village. . . .

But changes came in the family when I was thirteen, and I was sent to school in Jacksonville. . . . I was now a little colored girl. I found it out in certain ways. . . .

But I am not tragically colored. There is no great sorrow dammed up in my soul, nor lurking behind my eyes. I do not mind at all. I do not belong to the sobbing school of Negrohood who hold that nature somehow has given them a lowdown dirty deal and whose feelings are all but about it. . . . No, I do not weep at the world—I am too busy sharpening my oyster knife.

Someone is always at my elbow reminding me that I am the granddaughter of slaves. It fails to register depression with me. Slavery is sixty years in the past. The operation was successful and the patient is doing well, thank you. The terrible struggle that made me an American out of a potential slave said "On the line!" The Reconstruction said "Get set!" and the generation before said "Go!" I am off to a flying start and I must not halt in the stretch to look behind and weep. Slavery is the price I paid for civilization, and the choice was not with me. It is a bully adventure and worth all that I have paid through my ancestors for it. No one on earth ever had a greater chance for glory. The world to be won and nothing to be lost. It is thrilling to think—to know that for any act of mine, I shall get twice as much praise or twice as much blame. It is quite exciting to hold the center of the national stage, with the spectators not knowing whether to laugh or to weep. . . .

I do not always feel colored. Even now I often achieve the unconscious Zora of Eatonville before the Hegira. I feel most colored when I am thrown against a sharp white background. . . .

I have no separate feeling about being an American citizen and colored. I am merely a fragment of the Great Soul that surges within the boundaries. My country, right or wrong.

Sometimes, I feel discriminated against, but it does not make me angry. It merely astonishes me. How can any deny themselves the pleasure of my company? It's beyond me.

But in the main, I feel like a brown bag of miscellany propped against a wall. Against a wall in company with other bags, white, red and yellow. Pour out the contents, and there is discovered a jumble of small things priceless and worthless. A first-water diamond, an empty spool, bits of broken glass, lengths of string, a key to a door long since crumbled away, a rusty knife-blade, old shoes saved for a road that never was and never will be, a nail bent under the weight of things too heavy for any nail, a dried flower or two still a little fragrant. In your hand is the brown bag. On the ground before you is the jumble it held—so much like the jumble in the bags, could they be emptied, that all might be dumped in a single heap and the bags refilled without altering the content of any greatly. A bit of colored glass more or less would not matter. Perhaps that is how the Great Stuffer of Bags filled them in the first place—who knows?

Glossary

bully: very good; excellent

Hegira: referring to the Prophet Muhammad's migration, in 622 CE, from Mecca to Yathrib (Medina) upon invitation to escape persecution

miscellany: a group or collection of different items; a mixture

Short-Answer Questions

1. Consider Hurston's use of imagination in her descriptions of growing up in Eatonville. How does she use specific details to ground these flights of imagination? How does she use the imaginative moments to make her points?

2. How do you respond to the conception of race with which Hurston ends her essay? Does it agree with how you understand race?

3. Hurston notes that she is "merely a fragment of the Great Soul that surges within the boundaries." Explain what she means by this phrase.

Mary McLeod Bethune: "What Does American Democracy Mean to Me?"

Author
Mary McLeod Bethune

Date
1939

Document Type
Speeches/Addresses

Significance
Called for a nationwide reappraisal of segregation and discrimination and for recognition of the historical contributions of African Americans to American democracy

Overview

On the evening of November 23, 1939, Mary McLeod Bethune was part of a panel discussion on *America's Town Meeting of the Air*, a weekly public affairs broadcast on NBC Radio—one of the nation's first "talk radio" programs—revolving around the title question "What Does American Democracy Mean to Me?" Bethune was eminently qualified to join the panel that evening. She was the founder of a school that evolved into the modern-day Bethune-Cookman University. She was a past president of the National Association of Colored Women and the founder of the National Council of Negro Women. She was also a key figure in the Black Cabinet, formally called the Federal Council on Negro Affairs, an advisory group that kept the administration of President Franklin Roosevelt apprised of the concerns of the Black community. She delivered her remarks during what would prove to be the tail end of the Great Depression, a time when African American workers faced enormous challenges. Looming on the horizon was American entry into World War II, which had started less than three months earlier with the German invasion of Poland. As Americans vigorously discussed issues involving the direction the country should take, both economically and militarily, the topic of the panel that evening was particularly timely.

Document Text

Democracy is for me, and for 12 million Black Americans, a goal towards which our nation is marching. It is a dream and an ideal in whose ultimate realization we have a deep and abiding faith. For me, it is based on Christianity, in which we confidently entrust our destiny as a people. Under God's guidance in this great democracy, we are rising out of the darkness of slavery into the light of freedom. Here my race has been afforded [the] opportunity to advance from a people 80 percent illiterate to a people 80 percent literate; from abject poverty to the ownership and operation of a million farms and 750,000 homes; from total disfranchisement to participation in government; from the status of chattels to recognized contributors to the American culture.

As we have been extended a measure of democracy, we have brought to the nation rich gifts. We have helped to build America with our labor, strengthened it with our faith and enriched it with our song. We have given you Paul Laurence Dunbar, Booker T. Washington, Marian Anderson and George Washington Carver. But even these are only the first fruits of a rich harvest, which will be reaped when new and wider fields are opened to us.

The democratic doors of equal opportunity have not been opened wide to Negroes. In the Deep South, Negro youth is offered only one-fifteenth of the educational opportunity of the average American child. The great masses of Negro workers are depressed and unprotected in the lowest levels of agriculture and domestic service, while the Black workers in industry are barred from certain unions and generally assigned to the more laborious and poorly paid work. Their housing and living conditions are sordid and unhealthy. They live too often in terror of the lynch mob; are deprived too often of the Constitutional right of suffrage; and are humiliated too often by the denial of civil liberties. We do not believe that justice and common decency will allow these conditions to continue.

1949 portrait of Mary McLeod Bethune
(Library of Congress

Our faith in visions of fundamental change as mutual respect and understanding between our races come in the path of spiritual awakening. Certainly there have been times when we may have delayed this mutual understanding by being slow to assume a fuller share of our national responsibility because of the denial of full equality. And yet, we have always been loyal when the ideals of American democracy have been attacked. We have given our blood in its defense—from Crispus Attucks on Boston Commons to the battlefields of France. We have fought for the democratic principles of equality under the law, equality of opportunity, equality at the ballot box, for the guarantees of life, liberty and the pursuit of happiness. We have fought to preserve one nation, conceived in liberty and dedicated to the proposition that all men are created equal. Yes, we have fought for America with all her imperfections, not so much for what she is, but for what we know she can be.

Perhaps the greatest battle is before us, the fight for a new America: fearless, free, united, morally re-armed, in which 12 million Negroes, shoulder to shoulder with their fellow Americans, will strive that this nation under God will have a new birth of freedom, and that government of the people, for the people and by the people shall not perish from the earth. This dream, this idea, this aspiration, this is what American democracy means to me.

Glossary

battlefields of France: an allusion to World War I

Booker T. Washington: founder of the Tuskegee Institute in Alabama

Crispus Attucks: a man of African and Native American descent who was killed in the Boston Massacre prior to the Revolutionary War

George Washington Carver: a prominent Black scientist and educator

Marian Anderson: a singer who gave an open-air concert on the steps of the Lincoln Memorial in Washington, D.C., on Easter Sunday 1939

Paul Laurence Dunbar: the first Black poet to achieve national recognition

Short-Answer Questions

1. How does Bethune support the claim, made in her first paragraph, that "we are rising out of the darkness of slavery into the light of freedom"? What evidence and persuasive writing techniques does she employ to support this argument, and how successful is she?

2. Summarize Bethune's rhetorical purpose in the paragraph beginning with the words "Our faith in visions of fundamental change as mutual respect and understanding between our races come in the path of spiritual awakening." Analyze how this paragraph supports her overall theme, and evaluate its effectiveness.

3. Bethune was sometimes criticized by other African Americans for her accommodating tone toward white Americans. Using excerpts from her address, analyze how she balances this accommodating tone with reminders of the sacrifices Black Americans have made for their country. In your response, consider why she adopted this tone and how it might have affected audiences.

Combahee River Collective Statement

Author
Combahee River Collective

Date
1977

Document Type
Essays, Reports, Manifestos

Significance
Provided a clear statement of the goals of Black feminism and a history of the challenges the movement faced

Overview

The Combahee River Collective was an organization made up of Black feminist lesbian socialists who were active in the area of Boston, Massachusetts, from roughly 1974 to 1980. The collective had its origins as a regional chapter of the National Black Feminist Organization, which had held its inaugural meeting in New York City in 1973. The collective's membership changed over the years in which it met, but it included some notable Black feminists such as Cheryl Clarke, Demita Frazier, Gloria Akasha Hull, Audre Lorde, Chirlane McCray, Margo Okazawa-Rey, Barbara Smith, Beverly Smith, and Helen L. Stewart. These women saw their work as an outgrowth of the labor and sacrifice of countless generations of women who had struggled before them, such as Sojourner Truth, Harriet Tubman, and Ida B. Wells.

The collective's statement was composed because the membership recognized that every group that struggled for civil and social rights had a history of excluding certain parts of their own bodies. Historically, women's rights advocates had been racist, while the Black civil rights movement had often been led by sexists and homophobes. The collective was designed to allow the broadest and most inclusive interpretation of identity. In fact, the "Combahee River Collective Statement" is often credited with creating the term "identity politics" as a way of describing its intentions.

Chirlane McCray was a member of the Combahee River Collective. (Benjamin Kanter)

Document Text

We are a collective of Black feminists who have been meeting together since 1974. During that time we have been involved in the process of defining and clarifying our politics, while at the same time doing political work within our own group and in coalition with other progressive organizations and movements. The most general statement of our politics at the present time would be that we are actively committed to struggling against racial, sexual, heterosexual, and class oppression, and see as our particular task the development of integrated analysis and practice based upon the fact that the major systems of oppression are interlocking. The synthesis of these oppressions creates the conditions of our lives. As Black women we see Black feminism as the logical political movement to combat the manifold and simultaneous oppressions that all women of color face. . . .

Black feminists often talk about their feelings of craziness before becoming conscious of the concepts of sexual politics, patriarchal rule, and most importantly, feminism, the political analysis and practice that we women use to struggle against our oppression. The fact that racial politics and indeed racism are pervasive factors in our lives did not allow us, and still does not allow most Black women, to look more deeply into our own experiences and, from that sharing and growing consciousness, to build a politics that will change our lives and inevitably end our oppression. Our development must also be tied to the contemporary economic and political position of Black people. . . .

We believe that sexual politics under patriarchy is as pervasive in Black women's lives as are the politics of class and race. We also often find it difficult to separate race from class from sex oppression because in our lives they are most often experienced simultaneously. We know that there is such a thing as racial-sexual oppression which is neither solely racial nor solely sexual, e.g., the history of rape of Black women by white men as a weapon of political repression.

Although we are feminists and Lesbians, we feel solidarity with progressive Black men and do not advocate the fractionalization that white women who are separatists demand. Our situation as Black people necessitates that we have solidarity around the fact of race, which white women of course do not need to have with white men, unless it is their negative solidarity as racial oppressors. We struggle together with Black men against racism, while we also struggle with Black men about sexism. . . .

During our years together as a Black feminist collective we have experienced success and defeat, joy and pain, victory and failure. We have found that it is very difficult to organize around Black feminist issues, difficult even to announce in certain contexts that we are Black feminists. We have tried to think about the reasons for our difficulties, particularly since the white women's movement continues to be strong and to grow in many directions . . . . The major source of difficulty in our political work is that we are not just trying to fight oppression on one front or even two, but instead to address a whole range of oppressions. We do not have racial, sexual, heterosexual, or class privilege to rely upon, nor do we have even the minimal access to resources and power that groups who possess any one of these types of privilege have. . . .

The reaction of Black men to feminism has been notoriously negative. They are, of course, even more threatened than Black women by the possibility that Black feminists might organize around our own needs. They realize that they might not only lose valuable and hardworking allies in their struggles but that they might also be forced to change their habitually sexist ways of interacting with and oppressing Black women. Accusations that Black feminism divides the Black struggle are powerful deterrents to the growth of an autonomous Black women's movement.

Still, hundreds of women have been active at different times during the three-year existence of our group. And every Black woman who came, came out of a strongly-felt need for some level of possibility that did not previously exist in her life. . . .

Glossary

fractionalization: dividing something up into smaller parts; divisions within groups of oppressed people that let a dominant faction suppress the interests of another

separatists: a faction that wants to separate itself from a larger group; here, a reference to white feminists who want to separate their lives and goals from those of men

"sexual politics, patriarchal rule, and . . . feminism": respectively, the power differences between men and women; the placement of all power in the hands of men; and support for women's rights

Short-Answer Questions

1. What does the Combahee River Collective define as its primary aim or purpose?

2. The Combahee River Collective says that it tries to struggle against a range of oppressions. What does it say these oppressions are?

3. What is the Combahee River Collective's stated position on race? Are problems of race the collective's primary focus? What supports that conclusion?

bell hooks:
Feminist Theory: From Margin to Center

Author
bell hooks

Date
1984

Document Type
Essays, Reports, Manifestos

Significance
Severely critiqued contemporary feminism in the 1980s, noting its lack of diversity and need for an inclusive approach

Overview

bell hooks (1952–2021) was the Distinguished Professor in Residence at Berea College. Born Gloria Jean Watkins, she adopted the name bell hooks to honor her grandmother and used lowercase letters in her name as a way to highlight her message rather than herself. In addition to her role as educator, hooks was a prolific poet, essayist, social commentator, and feminist. Her work analyzed feminism's need for inclusivity to thrive and serve its true purpose: to change social structures.

Feminist Theory: From Margin to Center offers a severe critique of contemporary feminism in the 1980s. hooks notes the lack of diversity in its fundamental theoretical analysis and its need for an inclusive approach. Such an approach would include the stories and experiences of all women, not simply the predominantly white, middle-class women leading the women's liberation movement of the era. Each chapter of the book addresses a different aspect of feminist theory and highlights its failures in inclusivity. hooks demonstrates how feminism would benefit by uniting all women, by including men as allies, and by changing social and political structures from within, and she emphasized the need for education and understanding. Rather than weakening the movement, such inclusion was necessary for its ultimate realization. hooks also made the case that feminism as a theory needed more explanation. To make it viable, the ideology needed to be seen as a way for all people to become free rather than a way for women to become superior to men. It was a reminder at the time that the second wave of feminism was not bringing all people along for a better life, and it would fail if its leaders did not heed her warning.

Document Text

A central tenet of modern feminist thought has been the assertion that "all women are oppressed." This assertion implies that women share a common lot, that factors like class, race, religion, sexual preference, etc., do not create a diversity of experience that determines the extent to which sexism will be an oppressive force in the lives of individual women. Sexism as a system of domination is institutionalized but it has never determined in an absolute way the fate of all women in this society. Being oppressed means the *absence of choices*. It is the primary point of contact between the oppressed and the oppressor. Many women in this society do have choices (as inadequate as they are), therefore exploitation and discrimination are words that more accurately describe the lot of women collectively in the United States. Many women do not join organized resistance against sexism precisely because sexism has not meant an absolute lack of choices. They may know they are discriminated against on the basis of sex, but they do not equate this with oppression. Under capitalism, patriarchy is structured so that sexism restricts women's behavior in some realms even as freedom from limitations is allowed in other spheres. The absence of extreme restrictions leads many women to ignore the areas in which they are exploited or discriminated against; it may even lead them to imagine that no women are oppressed. . . .

Although the impulse towards unity and empathy that informed the notion of common oppression was directed at building solidarity, slogans like "organize around your own oppression" provided the excuse many privileged women needed to ignore the differences between their social status and the status of masses of women. It was a mark of race and class privilege, as well as the expression of freedom from the many constraints sexism places on working-class women, that middle-class white women were able to make their interests the primary focus of feminist movement and employ a rhetoric of commonality that made their condition synonymous with "oppression." Who was there

bell hooks
(Wikimedia Commons)

to demand a change in vocabulary? What other group of women in the United States had the same access to universities, publishing houses, mass media, money? Had middle-class black women begun a movement in which they had labeled themselves "oppressed," no one would have taken them seriously. Had they established public forums and given speeches about their "oppression," they would have been criticized and attacked from all sides. This was not the case with white bourgeois feminists for they could appeal to a large audience of women, like themselves, who were eager to change their lot in life. Their isolation from women of other class and race groups provided no immediate comparative base by which to test their assumptions of common oppression. . . .

As a group, black women are in an unusual position in this society, for not only are we collectively at the bottom of the occupational ladder, but our overall social status is lower than that of any other group. Occupying such a position, we bear the brunt of sexist, racist, and classist oppression. At the same time, we are the group that has not been socialized to assume the role of exploiter/oppressor in that we are allowed no institutionalized "other" that we can exploit or oppress. (Children do not represent an institutionalized other even though they may be oppressed by parents.) White women and black men have it both ways. They can act as oppressor or be oppressed. Black men may be victimized by racism, but sexism allows them to act as exploiters and oppressors of women. White women may be victimized by sexism, but racism enables them to act as exploiters and oppressors of black people. Both groups have led liberation movements that favor their interests and support the continued oppression of other groups. Black male sexism has undermined struggles to eradicate racism just as white female racism undermines feminist struggle. As long as these two groups or any group defines liberation as gaining social equality with ruling-class white men, they have a vested interest in the continued exploitation and oppression of others.

Black women with no institutionalized "other" that we may discriminate against, exploit, or oppress often have a lived experience that directly challenges the prevailing classist, sexist, racist social structure and its concomitant ideology. This lived experience may shape our consciousness in such a way that our world view differs from those who have a degree of privilege (however relative within the existing system). It is essential for continued feminist struggle that black women recognize the special vantage point our marginality gives us and make use of this perspective to criticize the dominant racist, classist, sexist hegemony as well as to envision and create a counter-hegemony....

Feminism defined as a movement to end sexist oppression enables women and men, girls and boys to participate equally in revolutionary struggle. So far, contemporary feminist movement has been primarily generated by the efforts of women; men have rarely participated. This lack of participation is not solely a consequence of antifeminism. By making women's liberation synonymous with women gaining social equality with men, liberal feminists effectively created a situation in which they, not men, designated feminist movement "women's work." Even as they were attacking sex role divisions of labor, the institutionalized sexism which assigns unpaid, devalued, "dirty" work to women, they were assigning to women yet another sex role task: making feminist revolution. Women's liberationists called upon all women to join feminist movement, but they did not continually stress that men should assume responsibility for actively struggling to end sexist oppression. Men, they argued, were all-powerful, misogynist, oppressor—the enemy. Women were the oppressed—the victims. Such rhetoric reinforced sexist ideology by positing in an inverted form the notion of a basic conflict between the sexes, the implication being that the empowerment of women would necessarily be at the expense of men.

As with other issues, the insistence on a "woman-only" feminist movement and a virulent anti-male stance reflected the race and class background of participants. Bourgeois white women, especially radical feminists, were envious and angry at privileged white men for denying them an equal share in class privilege. In part, feminism provided them with a public forum for the expression of their anger as well as a political platform they could use to call attention to issues of social equality, demand change, and promote specific reforms. They were not eager to call attention to the fact that men do not share a common social status; that patriarchy does not negate the existence of class and race privilege or exploitation; that all men do not benefit equally from sexism. They did not want to acknowledge that bourgeois white women, though often victimized by sexism, have more power and privilege, are less likely to be exploited or oppressed, than poor, uneducated, nonwhite males. At the time, many white women's liberationists did not care about the fate of oppressed groups of men. In keeping with the exercise of race and/or class privilege, they deemed the life experiences of these men unworthy of their attention, dismissed them, and simultaneously deflected attention away from their support of continued exploitation and oppression. Assertions like "all men are the enemy" and "all men hate women" lumped all groups of men in one category, thereby suggesting that they share equally in all forms of male privilege.

Glossary

bourgeois: related to the middle class; materialistic

hegemony: domination

patriarchy: systematic organization of a society based on male superiority, in which males hold the predominance of power, rights, and privileges

solidarity: unity of sentiment, purpose, or action

Short-Answer Questions

1. Identify three ways that the inclusion of women of color would improve the feminist movement.

2. Does the idea that not all women experience the same type of oppression resonate with you? How does bell hooks make this evident in her work?

3. According to bell hooks, how does the failure to include men in feminist theory and action limit feminism? How would their inclusion benefit all of society?

Anita Hill: Opening Statement at the Senate Confirmation Hearing of Clarence Thomas

Author
Anita Hill

Date
1991

Document Type
Speeches/Addresses

Significance
Made plain the fact that sexual harassment transcends race and can be not just physical but verbal

Overview

Anita Hill's Opening Statement at the Senate Confirmation Hearing of Clarence Thomas in 1991 was a bold and revealing account of sexual harassment in the workplace that also brought up issues related to gender discrimination and racism. During the course of the grueling proceedings conducted by the Senate Judiciary Committee regarding the nomination of Clarence Thomas to the U.S. Supreme Court, startling accusations of sexual harassment were raised by Hill against Thomas. A law professor at the University of Oklahoma who had been one of Thomas's coworkers, Hill only reluctantly came forward with detailed allegations. Her statement and subsequent testimony, which were broadcast on national television, provided a public glimpse into the confirmation process as well as the complex web of issues surrounding sexual harassment, gender discrimination, and racial stereotyping. Despite the controversy over his nomination, Thomas was confirmed by a close vote on the Senate floor, and he was sworn in as the 106th U.S. Supreme Court justice on October 23, 1991. He became only the second African American to hold the position, replacing the first African American Supreme Court justice, Thurgood Marshall.

Hill's opening statement was historically and culturally significant in a number of ways. It exposed the profound damage that could be inflicted by verbal rather than physical sexual harassment. Moreover, Hill's account demonstrated that the "he said, she said" dilemma posed by many sexual harassment claims could be a difficult hurdle to overcome. Hill's statement also gave expression to the gender and racial discrimination she had endured and how they had been important factors in her decision to come forward. The statement was also significant because it pitted two African Americans against each other in the public eye and provoked widespread disagreement in the Black community.

Hill testifying in front of the Senate Judiciary Committee (Library of Congress)

Document Text

Mr. Chairman, Senator Thurmond, Members of the Committee, my name is Anita F. Hill, and I am a Professor of Law at the University of Oklahoma. I was born on a farm in Okmulge, Oklahoma in 1956, the 13th child, and had my early education there. My father is Albert Hill, a farmer of that area. My mother's name is Erma Hill; she is also a farmer and housewife. My childhood was the childhood of both work and poverty; but it was one of solid family affection as represented by my parents who are with me as I appear here today. I was reared in a religious atmosphere in the Baptist faith and I have been a member of the Antioch Baptist Church in Tulsa since 1983. It remains a warm part of my life at the present time. . . .

Upon graduation from law school I became a practicing lawyer with the Washington, D.C. firm of Wald, Harkrader & Ross. In 1981, I was introduced to now Judge Thomas by a mutual friend. Judge Thomas told me that he anticipated a political appointment shortly and asked if I might be interested in working in that office. He was in fact appointed as Assistant Secretary of Education, in which capacity he was the Director of the Office for Civil Rights. After he was in that post, he asked if I would become his assistant and I did then accept that position. In my early period there I had two major projects. The first was an article I wrote for Judge Thomas' signature on "Education of Minority Students." The second was the organization of a seminar on high risk students, which was abandoned because Judge Thomas transferred to the EEOC before that project was completed.

During this period at the Department of Education, my working relationship with Judge

Thomas was positive. I had a good deal of responsibility as well as independence. I thought that he respected my work and that he trusted my judgment. After approximately three months of working together, he asked me to go out with him socially. I declined and explained to him that I thought that it would only jeopardize what, at the time, I considered to be a very good working relationship. I had a normal social life with other men outside of the office and, I believed then, as now, that having a social relationship with a person who was supervising my work would be ill-advised. I was very uncomfortable with the idea and told him so.

I thought that by saying "no" and explaining my reasons, my employer would abandon his social suggestions. However, to my regret, in the following few weeks he continued to ask me out on several occasions. He pressed me to justify my reasons for saying "no" to him. These incidents took place in his office or mine. They were in the form of private conversations which would not have been overheard by anyone else.

My working relationship became even more strained when Judge Thomas began to use work situations to discuss sex. . . .

It is only after a great deal of agonizing consideration that I am able to talk of these unpleasant matters to anyone but my closest friends. Telling the world is the most difficult experience of my life. I was aware that he could affect my future career and did not wish to burn all my bridges. I may have used poor judgment; perhaps I should have taken angry or even militant steps both when I was in the agency or after I left it, but I must confess to the world that the course I took seemed to me to be the better as well as the easier approach. I declined any comment to newspapers, but later, when Senate staff asked me about these matters, I felt I had a duty to report. I have no personal vendetta against Clarence Thomas. I seek only to provide the Committee with information which it may regard as relevant. It would have been more comfortable to remain silent. I took no initiative to inform anyone. But when I was asked by a representative of this committee to report my experience, I felt that I had no other choice but to tell the truth.

Glossary

EEOC: Equal Employment Opportunity Commission

jeopardize: to place at risk

"militant steps": legal or public action

vendetta: an effort to destroy someone's social life or career

Short-Answer Questions

1. What reasons does Professor Hill give for not reporting Clarence Thomas's behavior toward her as soon as it happened?

2. Professor Hill says that making her statement about Clarence Thomas was "the most difficult experience of my life." Why might that be the case?

3. The first paragraph of Professor Hill's opening statement is an outline of her personal life. Why might she be stating these facts rather than moving directly to her account of Clarence Thomas's behavior?

"African American Women in Defense of Ourselves"

Author
Elsa Barkley Brown, Deborah King, and Barbara Ransby

Date
1991

Document Type
Essays, Reports, Manifestos

Significance
Objected publicly to the confirmation of Clarence Thomas to the U.S. Supreme Court, confronting both Thomas's sexism and his opposition to affirmative action

Overview

On November 17, 1991, a full-page ad appeared in the *New York Times*. It was in the form of an essay signed by more than 1,600 Black women, and it protested in strong terms the recent appointment of Clarence Thomas to the U.S. Supreme Court. Thomas was a controversial figure, in part because he was a Black man who held decided conservative views. He opposed affirmative action, believing that it perpetuated the "separate but equal" principle that had been overturned in *Brown v. Board of Education of Topeka* almost four decades earlier.

In addition, during Thomas's hearings, allegations were brought by a University of Oklahoma law professor named Anita Hill. In a series of televised hearings, Professor Hill stated that she had been sexually harassed by Thomas some years earlier, when he had been her supervisor. She was subjected to hostile cross-examination, in which her credibility was questioned and her character assaulted. Thomas was finally confirmed on October 15, 1991, in a close vote. The essay "African American Women in Defense of Ourselves" appeared in the *New York Times* about a month later.

The essay was the brainchild of three Black academics: Elsa Barkley Brown, Deborah King, and Barbara Ransby. The three had watched the Thomas confirmation hearings and the Hill testimony closely. They identified with Hill; all of them had had similar experiences in their lives, and they were outraged by the treatment to which Hill was subjected. The three organized a fundraising program that raised fifty thousand dollars toward the cost of the ad within a few weeks.

Document Text
African American Women in Defense of Ourselves

As women of African descent, we are deeply troubled by the recent nomination, confirmation and seating of Clarence Thomas as an Associate Justice of the U.S. Supreme Court. We know that the presence of Clarence Thomas on the Court will be continually used to divert attention from historic struggles for social justice through suggestions that the presence of a Black man on the Supreme Court constitutes an assurance that the rights of African Americans will be protected. Clarence Thomas' public record is ample evidence this will not be true. Further, the consolidation of a conservative majority on the Supreme Court seriously endangers the rights of all women, poor and working class people and the elderly. The seating of Clarence Thomas is an affront not only to African American women and men, but to all people concerned with social justice.

We are particularly outraged by the racist and sexist treatment of Professor Anita Hill, an African American woman who was maligned and castigated for daring to speak publicly of her own experience of sexual abuse. The malicious defamation of Professor Hill insulted all women of African descent and sent a dangerous message to any woman who might contemplate a sexual harassment complaint.

We speak here because we recognize that the media are now portraying the Black community as prepared to tolerate both the dismantling of affirmative action and the evil of sexual harassment in order to have any Black man on the Supreme Court. We want to make clear that the media have ignored or distorted many African American voices. We will not be silenced.

Many have erroneously portrayed the allegations against Clarence Thomas as an issue of either gender or race. As women of African descent, we understand sexual harassment as both. We further understand that Clarence Thomas outrageously manipulated the legacy of lynching in order to shelter himself from Anita Hill's allegations. To deflect attention away from the reality of sexual abuse in African American women's lives, he trivialized and misrepresented this painful part of African American people's history. This country which has a long legacy of racism and sexism, has never taken the sexual abuse of Black women seriously. Throughout U.S. history Black women have been sexually stereotyped as immoral, insatiable, perverse; the initiators in all sexual contacts—abusive or otherwise. The common assumption in legal proceedings as well as in the larger society has been that Black women cannot be raped or otherwise sexually abused. As Anita Hill's experience demonstrates, Black women who speak of these matters are not likely to be believed.

In 1991, we cannot tolerate this type of dismissal of any one Black woman's experience or this attack upon our collective character without protest, outrage, and resistance.

As women of African descent, we express our vehement opposition to the policies represented by the placement of Clarence Thomas on the Supreme Court. The Bush administration, having obstructed the passage of civil rights legislation, impeded the extension of unemployment compensation, cut student aid and dismantled social welfare programs, has continually demonstrated that it is not operating in our best interests. Nor is this appointee. We pledge ourselves to continue to speak out in defense of one another, in defense of the African American community and against those who are hostile to social justice no matter what color they are. No one will speak for us but ourselves.

Glossary

erroneously: wrong or incorrectly

"the legacy of lynching": refers to a statement Clarence Thomas made as part of his defense following the televised Hill hearings, accusing the media of conducting a "high-tech lynching"

"nomination, confirmation, and seating": the three parts of the process of creating a U.S. Supreme Court justice: nomination by the president, confirmation by the Senate, and being seated on the court

trivialized: made to seem insignificant or unimportant

Short-Answer Questions

1. What specifically do the authors of "African American Women in Defense of Ourselves" object to about Clarence Thomas's confirmation to the Supreme Court?

2. How do the authors characterize social justice?

3. The essay identifies sexual harassment as a matter of both race and sex. Why do the authors say this is important?

Alicia Garza: "A Herstory of the #BlackLivesMatter Movement"

Author
Alicia Garza

Date
2014

Document Type
Essays, Reports, Manifestos

Significance
Explained how the Black Lives Matter movement took shape, the issues it seeks to redress, and how attempts to universalize the movement may diminish its impact

Overview

The 2013 acquittal of George Zimmerman, a neighborhood watch coordinator from Florida, for the 2012 shooting death of Trayvon Martin, a Black teenager, set into motion the formation of a political movement called #BlackLivesMatter (BLM). With a strong emphasis on grassroots activism, BLM built a national and then global network of chapters committed to calling attention to the continued inequities and challenges, many of them institutional, faced by Black Americans. BLM's founders sought to better include people from marginalized groups such as women, homosexuals and trans people who have previously been overlooked or excluded from participating in political movements. In this essay excerpt, Alicia Garza, one of BLM's original three founders, explains how the movement came to be formed and its general objectives.

Document Text

I created #BlackLivesMatter with Patrisse Cullors and Opal Tometi, two of my sisters, as a call to action for Black people after 17-year-old Trayvon Martin was posthumously placed on trial for his own murder and the killer, George Zimmerman, was not held accountable for the crime he committed. It was a response to the anti-Black racism that permeates our society and also, unfortunately, our movements.

Black Lives Matter is an ideological and political intervention in a world where Black lives are systematically and intentionally targeted for demise. It is an affirmation of Black folks' contributions to this society, our humanity, and our resilience in the face of deadly oppression. . . .

Alicia Garza is one of the founders of the Black Lives Matter Movement. (Wikimedia Commons)

When we say Black Lives Matter, we are talking about the ways in which Black people are deprived of our basic human rights and dignity. It is an acknowledgement Black poverty and genocide is state violence. It is an acknowledgment that 1 million Black people are locked in cages in this country—one half of all people in prisons or jails—is an act of state violence. It is an acknowledgment that Black women continue to bear the burden of a relentless assault on our children and our families and that assault is an act of state violence. . . . And the fact is that the lives of Black people—not ALL people—exist within these conditions is consequence of state violence. . . .

#BlackLivesMatter doesn't mean your life isn't important—it means that Black lives, which are seen as without value within White supremacy, are important to your liberation. Given the disproportionate impact state violence has on Black lives, we understand that when Black people in this country get free, the benefits will be wide reaching and transformative for society as a whole. When we are able to end hyper-criminalization and sexualization of Black people and end the poverty, control, and surveillance of Black people, every single person in this world has a better shot at getting and staying free. When Black people get free, everybody gets free. This is why we call on Black people and our allies to take up the call that Black lives matter. We're not saying Black lives are more important than other lives, or that other lives are not criminalized and oppressed in various ways. We remain in active solidarity with all oppressed people who are fighting for their liberation and we know that our destinies are intertwined....

When we deploy "All Lives Matter" as to correct an intervention specifically created to address anti-Blackness, we lose the ways in which the state apparatus has built a program of genocide and repression mostly on the backs of Black people—beginning with the theft of millions of people for free labor—and then adapted it to control, murder, and profit off of other communities of color and immigrant communities. We perpetuate a level of White supremacist domination by reproducing a tired trope that we are all the same, rather than acknowledging that non-Black oppressed people in this country are both impacted by racism and domination, and simultaneously, BENEFIT from anti-Black racism.

When you adopt Black Lives Matter and transform it into something else . . . it's appropriate politically to credit the lineage from which your adapted work derived. It's important that we work together to build and acknowledge the legacy of Black contributions to the struggle for human rights. If you adapt Black Lives Matter, use the opportunity to talk about its inception and political framing. Lift up Black lives as an opportunity to connect struggles across race, class, gender, nationality, sexuality and disability.

And, perhaps more importantly, when Black people cry out in defense of our lives, which are uniquely, systematically, and savagely targeted by the state, we are asking you, our family, to stand with us in affirming Black lives. Not just all lives. Black lives. Please do not change the conversation by talking about how your life matters, too. It does, but we need less watered down unity and a more active solidarities with us, Black people, unwaveringly, in defense of our humanity. Our collective futures depend on it.

Glossary

solidarity: agreement and common interest

systematically: part of a fixed system

Short-Answer Questions

1. What circumstances brought about the creation of the Black Lives Matter movement?

2. According to Garza, what are the intended goals of the Black Lives Matter movement?

3. How does Garza contend that the insistence that "all lives matter" undermines the Black Lives Matter movement?

Say Her Name: Resisting Police Brutality against Black Women

Author
Kimberlé Williams Crenshaw, Andrea J. Richie, Rachel Anspach, Rachel Glimer, and Luke Harris

Date
2015

Document Type
Essays, Reports, Manifestos

Significance
Highlighted the omission from social justice narratives of the stories of Black women and girls and their experiences with police brutality, structural violence, and abuse

Overview

The booklet *Say Her Name: Resisting Police Brutality against Black Women* was published in 2015 to outline the purpose and goals of the Say Her Name campaign, promoted by the African American Policy Forum (AAPF) and the Center for Intersectionality and Social Policy Studies at Columbia Law School. The work was authored by Kimberlé Williams Crenshaw and Andrea J. Richie with Rachel Anspach, Rachel Glimer, and Luke Harris.

Violence against people of color is a chronic problem in the United States, and Black communities have rallied for decades to bring this injustice to light. Much of the story, however, is regularly omitted. The AAPF published *Say Her Name* to show how Black women and girls are largely absent from the account. This absence, according to the authors, is the product of structural and institutional bias and inequity and is exacerbated by poverty. Factors compounding the issue are mental health crises, women's relation to known or suspected criminals, and "collateral damage," among others. Black women's and girls' experiences are markedly different in many ways from those of their male counterparts. By including women and girls in the narrative, a more complete picture emerges of the existing problem that allows groups to focus on improving conditions for all and ending these needless killings. The AAPF encourages citizens to attend rallies, to protest, and to "say her name" to shine light on those who are victims of state and structural violence.

A vigil remembering Black women and girls who died from police brutality (Wikimedia Commons)

Document Text

THERE ARE SEVERAL REASONS WHY THE RESURGENT RACIAL JUSTICE MOVEMENT MUST PRIORITIZE THE DEVELOPMENT OF A GENDER INCLUSIVE LENS.

First, including Black women and girls in the narrative broadens the scope of the debate, enhancing our overall understanding of the structural relationship between Black communities and law enforcement agencies. In order to comprehend the root causes and full scope of state violence against Black communities, we must consider and illuminate all the ways in which Black people in the US are routinely targeted for state violence. Acknowledging and analyzing the connections between anti-Black violence against Black men, women, transgender, and gender-nonconforming people reveals systemic realities that go unnoticed when the focus is limited exclusively to cases involving Black non-transgender men.

Second, both the incidence and consequences of state violence against Black women are often informed by their roles as primary caretakers of people of all ages in their communities. As a result, violence against them has ripple effects throughout families and neighborhoods. Black women are positioned at the center of the domestic sphere and of community life. Yet their marginal position with respect to economic and social power relations creates the isolating and vulnerable context in which their struggle against police violence, mass incarceration, and economic marginalization occurs. In order to ensure safe and healthy Black communities, we must address police violence against Black women with equal outrage and commitment.

Third, centering the lives of all segments of our communities will permit us to step away from the idea that to address police violence we must "fix" individual Black men and bad police officers. Moving beyond these narrow concepts is critical if we are to embrace a framework that focuses on the complex structural dimensions that are actually at play. Through inclusion it becomes clear that the problem is not a matter of whether a young man's hands were held up over his head, whether he had a mentor, or whether the police officers in question were wearing cameras or had been exposed to implicit bias trainings. A comprehensive approach reveals that the epidemic of police violence across the country is about how police relations reinforce the structural marginality of all members of Black communities in myriad ways.

Fourth, including Black women and girls in this discourse sends the powerful message that, indeed, all Black lives do matter. If our collective outrage is meant to warn the state that its agents cannot kill Black men and boys with impunity, then our silence around the killing of Black women and girls sends the message that their deaths are acceptable and do not merit repercussions.

Our failure to rally around Black women's stories represents a broader failure to demand accountability for all Black lives targeted by the state. Families who lose Black women to police violence are not regularly invited to speak at rallies and do not receive the same level of community support or media and political attention as families who lose Black men. This leaves the families of Black women killed by the police not only to suffer the loss of their loved ones but also to confront the fact that no one seems to care. Yet the killings of Black women and girls are no less troubling than the killings of their male counterparts. Their families mourn no less for their lost loved ones, and they should not be left to suffer in solitude and silence.

Black women have consistently played a leadership role in struggles against state violence—from the Underground Railroad to the anti-lynching movement to the Civil Rights and Black Power movements to the current Black Lives Matter movement—yet the forms of victimization they face at the hands of police are consistently left out of social movement demands. Black women leaders are often asked to speak only about their fears of losing their sons, brothers, partners, and comrades. Yet as the tragedies that have befallen many Black women who have died at the hands of the police reveal, Black women and girls also face real risks of lethal police violence, which must be contested along with those facing Black men and boys.

Glossary

Black Lives Matter: an international movement for racial justice and against systemic racism and violence toward Black people

state violence: the use of legal, state-sanctioned violence against a group of people, which may include political violence, neglect of prisoners, delayed justice, rape, and genocide

structural marginality: the unequal distribution of goods and resources that benefit one group while harming another, with the result that certain groups do not have the same access to power, influence, or assets of others in society and have poorer health, economic, or mortality outcomes

Underground Railroad: an informal network of routes, guides, and safe houses that worked to help enslaved people flee to non-slave states and to Canada

Short-Answer Questions

1. What are two examples of state violence found in the excerpt from *Say Her Name*?

2. Why do the authors claim that Black women and girls have been left out of the discussion and the movement to end state-sanctioned violence? How can this be changed?

3. List three ways the inclusion of Black women's and girls' stories can benefit the movement to end state violence and abuse of all people?

Kimberlé Williams Crenshaw: "Say Her Name" Speech

Author
Kimberlé Williams Crenshaw

Date
2016

Document Type
Speeches/Addresses

Significance
Drew attention to the multitude of ways women and girls of color are overlooked when issues of racism, sexism, and violence are considered

Overview

Kimberlé Williams Crenshaw is a professor of law at Columbia Law School and the University of California, Los Angeles, School of Law specializing in race and gender studies. She is credited with coining the term *intersectionality* in the 1980s to describe the dual oppression of racism and sexism. As a cofounder of the African American Policy Forum (AAPF) at Columbia Law School, she helped launch the Say Her Name campaign to call attention to police violence against Black women and girls. She was invited to offer the keynote address, "Say Her Name," at the Women of the World (WOW) festival in London, England, on March 12, 2016. In it, she points out that in the discussion of racism, sexism, and violence, social commentators often omit the stories of women and girls of color. Crenshaw proposes new ways to consider the intersectional issues that affect all people of color and asserts that women and girls must be included if solutions are to be found to the problems of state-sponsored violence and inequity.

Document Text

I want to draw attention to an intersectional crisis unfolding today, particularly how many of the battles that we're fighting today are problems that grow out of intersectional failures from yesterday. . . .

Now, when I introduced the term *intersectionality* almost thirty years ago, it was to address multiple failures not only in law but also rhetorical failures, political failures, within feminism and anti-racism.

So first in the context of employment discrimination, intersectionality was meant to draw attention to the many ways that black women were being excluded from employment in industrial plants and elsewhere that were segregated by both gender and race. Specifically, black jobs were available to blacks who were men and women's jobs were available to women who were white. Black women—who were blacks who were not men and women who were not white—were not able to be hired in many of these industries because they didn't fit the kind of woman or the kind of black that was looked for by the employer. . . .

So intersectionality was meant to draw attention to the way that black women's experience, sometimes distinct experience of gender discrimination, was buried under the experiences of white women and black [women's] sometimes distinct experience of race was buried under the experiences of African American men. . . .

Intersectionality is not primarily about identity. It's about how structures make certain identities the consequence of, the vehicle for, vulnerability. So if you want to know how many intersections matter, you've got to look at the context. What's happening? What kind of discrimination is going on? What are the policies? What are the institutional structures that play a role in contributing to the exclusion of some people and not others? . . .

In contemporary politics, significant articulations of anti-racism have been built around the denial

Kimberlé Crenshaw
(Wikimedia Commons)

of black male patriarchy, the denial of leadership in families, in communities and in politics. These limited versions of feminism and anti-racism are not only just incomplete—they've been utterly damaging to the struggles of women and to people of color.

Most problematically, these failures from our past—the failure to interrogate patriarchy in anti-racism, the failure to interrogate racism and feminism—continue to shape modern politics. . . .

I call these intersectional failures of the past Trojan horses of today that import elements of patriarchy with anti-racism and racial power within conceptions of feminisms. These consequences are often invisible to the naked eye, and the naked eye is the eye that's not accustomed to looking at issues through an intersectional prism.

There is, however, a solution, a practice that can heighten our capacity to see the limitations of a nonintersectional feminism or nonintersectional racism so they no longer hold our visions of the possible hostage to the failures of our past. It's invoked in the commitment to see beyond the conventional ways that feminist and anti-racist agendas are built on the narratives of just a few. It requires us to insist on bringing more fully into view, for example, the ways that women of color experience racism, the ways that women of color experience sexism. . . .

[In] President Obama's signature racial justice program called My Brother's Keeper . . . men and boys of color are listed as more likely than their peers to be born into low-income families and to live in concentrated poverty, to have teenage mothers, to live with one or no parent, to attend a high-poverty school, a poor-performing school, to miss out on rigorous classes, to have teachers that are inexperienced or unqualified. I want to ask, more likely than whom?

These data apply to girls who live in the same neighborhoods, attend the same schools, have to navigate the same racialized state practices as their brothers do. Simply looking at the justifications given for this exclusive focus raises the question about where are the girls? Why are girls and women not seen as subjects of racial abuse? The question that it raises is, is this the new picture of intersectional erasure? . . .

What's missing here is all of the ways in which sisters, wives, daughters, mothers are also vulnerable to some of the same structural problems that have created disproportionate outcomes for communities of color. What's missing in this framework is the defunding of public institutions, the asset-stripping of urban landscapes, the unleashing of the police force, diminished oversight of discriminators in federal courts, the shifting of resources from service delivery to group management, the emphasis on individual punishment rather than on institutional and structural reform. . . .

We are a gender- and race-based unequal society and all of those dimensions need to be addressed in an intersectional, anti-racist, anti-poverty program. . . .

So we're looking at a significant racial barrier, a significant mode of racial bias that plays out between women, that plays out between girls but we don't know about it because we have thought about racism primarily as a question having to do with men.

So, our Why We Can't Wait campaign is made up of the clear aspiration for girls and women of color to tell stories about how they've been subjected to race and gender disempowerment, so that first their communities, their families, their stakeholders have an understanding, have an image, have a story about what racism looks like for women or what sexism looks like for blacks.

. . . We talk about all women of color. We talk about cis- and transgender women. We talk about queer women and straight women. We're talking about the variety of ways that our understanding about what sexism, patriarchy, heteronormativity, transphobia, racism looks like when it's embodied in people who are dealing with all of those issues at the same time. . . .

When we look at questions of violence against women, we know black women are more likely to be raped. We know black women are less likely to have their rapists charged. We know that when they are charged, their rapists are less likely to be convicted. . . .

We do have a movement against gender-based violence but the question is, is that movement against gender-based violence sensitive to the racial differences, the class differences that different women confront? . . .

So we're talking about a two-layer problem. You're subject to intersectional discrimination and subordination number one, but then number two, when it comes time to look for your allies, when you want people to show up, when you want people to say your life matters, intersectional failure often means nobody is showing up for you.

That's the kind of intersectional failure that Say Her Name is trying to address. Say Her Name is trying to draw attention to the various ways that black women also experience police abuse. It's trying to pay attention to the fact that black women are killed in many of the same circumstances that black men are killed.

They're killed driving while black—like Mya Hall, transgender black woman who was killed when she accidentally turned down the wrong street and the NSA shot in her car.

They're killed in the war on drugs when police—many times on a mistaken warrant—enter a home, shoot first, ask questions later. People as old as 93 have been killed, people as young as six years old have been killed. Women have been killed. Mothers have been killed holding babies in their arms.

We don't talk about state-sanctioned violence as a consequence of policing poverty. Black women such as Eleanor Bumpurs, killed when the New York police came to evict her for an overdue rent bill—less than a hundred dollars—shotgunned her to death.

We don't talk about Margaret Mitchell, a homeless black woman who was shot in the back by Los Angeles police as she was walking away with a shopping basket.

We don't talk about the fact that when police are called to homes in domestic violence calls, black women are vulnerable to police actually shooting them. Two cases this year alone, weeks after more notable men were killed, black women were killed seconds after the police arrived in their homes. . . .

We believe that this issue is not an issue just in the United States. We believe that if we reach out our hands across these boundaries, we'll find . . . other circumstances that show us that women are subject to private and public violence, that people of color are subject to public and private violence, that women of color are subject to both public and private violence.

So the question we have to ask is, what can we each do about it? We've been saying the first thing you can do about it is say her name. . . .

If we can simply begin to say their names, the invisibility that shrouds their loss will no longer legitimize what happened to them.

Glossary

cisgender: someone whose sex assigned at birth and expressed gender identity match

feminist: supporting and promoting equal rights for women

heteronormativity: the expectation that people are heterosexual and that heterosexuality is the norm or the ideal

intersectionality: the overlapping or combining of multiple forms of discrimination

Glossary

My Brother's Keeper: program implemented by President Barack Obama in 2014 to acknowledge and rectify the inequities that men and boys of color face in America

patriarchy: social and political system that favors men above women

queer: people whose sexuality does not align with the heteronormative ideal

Say Her Name: a political and social campaign started in 2014 to bring attention to police-inflicted violence and death against women and girls of color

sexism: discrimination based on a person's sex or gender

state-sanctioned violence: the government's use of its authority to cause unnecessary violence against a person or group of people

transgender: someone whose gender or sex does not match the one they were assigned at birth

transphobia: fear of people whose gender identity does not match the one they were assigned at birth

Trojan horse: deceptive way to trick an enemy; from a Greek myth in which soldiers hid inside a hollow wooden horse statue presented as a gift to their enemies in Troy

Short-Answer Questions

1. What reasons does Crenshaw list for omitting women and girls of color from discussions of racism, violence, and discrimination? Why should they be included?

2. How does the concept of intersectionality explain people's differing experiences of discrimination?

3. How might the Say Her Name campaign raise awareness of the issues of racism, sexism, violence and the need for social justice?

Judith Heumann:
"Our Fight for Disability Rights—And Why We're Not Done Yet"

Author
Judith Heumann

Date
2018

Document Type
Speeches/Addresses

Significance
Urged the United States to ratify its support for the United Nations' Convention on the Rights of Persons with Disabilities

Overview

Judith Heumann (1947–2023), known as the mother of the disability rights movement, gave this TED Talk to provide an overview of both her activism and the important issues for disability rights in 2018. As an infant, Heumann became infected with polio, which limited her mobility and led to her use of a wheelchair throughout the rest of her life. Part of Heumann's activism also comes from her family background. Heumann's parents were German Jews who fled Europe in the 1930s to come to America. Their experiences with discrimination and inequality shaped both the values they instilled in Heumann and the ways they reacted to unfairness in Heumann's life. Heumann served as the assistant secretary for the Office of Special Education and Rehabilitative Services in the Department of Education for the Clinton administration and as the special advisor for international disability rights in the State Department under the Obama administration. She worked as an advisor for disability inclusion, for special education, and for public health in other governmental and corporate organizations throughout her life.

Heumann delivered her speech to urge the U.S. Congress to ratify its support for the Convention on the Rights of Persons with Disabilities (CRPD), which was drafted by the United Nations in 2006 and went into effect in 2008. U.S. leadership signed the CRPD in 2009, but by 2018 Congress had yet to ratify its support. To make her argument, she tells the story of her life and includes some specific ways she faced discrimination because of her disability. Heumann talks about being denied a teaching license in New York City for failing the medical examination, and how this led to the court case and settlement that granted her teaching license and brought her to prominence as a disability rights advocate. She then describes the ways that disability rights activists used grassroots and collective action to protest during the second half of the twentieth century. At the end of the speech, as she begins her call to action, Heumann also includes a brief overview of the advances in disability legislation and acceptance since the 1970s.

American disability rights activist Judith Ellen Heumann (Wikimedia Commons)

Document Text

I was born in 1947, a long time ago, and when I was eighteen months old, I had polio. I was in an iron lung for three months and in and out of the hospital for three years. Now, we had lots of neighbors in our Brooklyn neighborhood, and some of them were really very helpful for my parents. Some of them were really afraid of contagion, and they wouldn't even walk in front of our house. They would literally walk across the street. I think this was a time when my family really began to realize what disability meant to some people: fear. . . .

I didn't actually get to go to school in a real building until I was nine years old, and then I was in classes only with disabled children in a school that had mainly nondisabled children. And in my classes, there were students up to the age of twenty-one. And then, after twenty-one, they went to something called sheltered workshops with menial work and earning either nothing or below minimum wage. So I understood discrimination. . . .

I had always wanted to be a teacher, and so I minored in education and I took all the appropriate courses, and then when it was time for me to go for my license, I had to take a written exam, an oral exam and a medical exam. At that time, all three of those exams were given in completely inaccessible buildings, so I had friends who carried me up and down the steps for these exams. . . . I passed my oral exam. I passed my written exam.

My medical exam was something completely different. One of the first questions the doctor asked me was, could I please show her how I went to the bathroom. I was twenty-two years old, and you know when you go for any kind of an interview, you think about all the kinds of questions that people could ask you? That was not one of them. . . . I'd been denied my license because I couldn't walk. So, what was I going to do? . . .

It would be the first time that I really would be challenging the system—me—and although I was working with a lot of other friends who had disabilities who were encouraging me to move forward with this, it was nonetheless quite frightening. But I was really very lucky. I had a friend who was a disabled student at Long Island University and was also a stringer at the *New York Times*, and he was able to get a reporter to write a really good piece about what had happened and why he thought what had happened was wrong. The next day there was an editorial in the *New York Times* with the title of "Heumann v. The Board of Education," and the *New York Times* came out in support of my getting my teaching license.

And then the same day, I got a call from an attorney who was writing a book about civil rights. And he was calling me to interview me, and I was interviewing him. He didn't know that. And at the end of our discussion, I said, "Would you be willing to represent me? I want to sue the Board of Education." And he said yes. Now, sometimes I say that the stars were aligned around this court case, because we had an amazing judge: the first African American female federal judge—Constance Baker Motley.

And she knew discrimination when she saw it.

So she strongly encouraged the Board of Ed to give me another medical exam, which they did. And then I got my license. . . .

I was learning—as my friends were, and people I didn't know around the country—that we had to be our own advocates, that we needed to fight back people's view that if you had a disability, you needed to be cured, that equality was not part of the equation. And we were learning from the Civil Rights Movement and from the Women's Rights Movement. We were learning from them about their activism and their ability to come together, not only to discuss problems but to discuss solutions. And what was born is what we call today the Disability Rights Movement. . . .

When the Americans with Disabilities Act, the ADA, our Emancipation Proclamation Act, looked as though it might not in fact be passed in the House or Senate, disabled people from all across the United States came together and they crawled up the Capitol steps. That was an amazing day, and the House and Senate passed the ADA. And then President Bush signed the ADA. . . . It was July 26th, 1990, and one of the most famous statements he had in his speech was, "Let the shameful walls of exclusion finally come tumbling down."

For any of you in the room who are fifty or older, . . . you remember a time when there were no ramps on the streets, when buses were not accessible, when trains were not accessible, when there were no wheelchair-accessible bathrooms and shopping malls, when you certainly did not have a sign language interpreter or captioning or Braille or other kinds of supports. These things have changed, and they have inspired the world. And disabled people around the world want laws like we have, and they want those laws enforced.

And so what we've seen is something called the Convention on the Rights of Persons with Disabilities. It is a treaty that was adopted in 2006. It's celebrating its ten-year anniversary. More than 165 countries have joined this treaty. It is the first international human rights treaty fully focused on disabled people. But I am sad to say that our U.S. Senate has failed to recommend to our president that we ratify the treaty. . . . So we feel really strongly that our U.S. Senate needs to do its job, that our Senate needs to enable us as Americans not only to be able to assist disabled people and governments around the world to learn about the good work that we've been doing, but it's equally important that disabled people have the same opportunities to travel, study, and work abroad as anyone else in our country. And as long as many countries don't have the same laws as we do and don't enforce them if they have them, opportunities for disabled people are more limited.

When I travel abroad, I am always meeting with disabled women, and those women tell me stories about how they experience violence . . . and how in many cases these forms of violence occur from family members and people that they know. . . . We know discrimination when we see it, and we need to be fighting it together.

Glossary

Americans with Disabilities Act: a 1990 civil rights legislation that prohibits discrimination based on disability status

Constance Baker Motley: the first Black woman to argue a case before the Supreme Court, to serve in the New York State Senate, and to serve as a federal judge

Convention on the Rights of Persons with Disabilities: a treaty drafted by the United Nations in 2006, signed in 2007, and enacted in 2008 to protect the human rights of people with disabilities worldwide

Disability Rights Movement: a social movement that began in the 1970s to fight for the civil rights of people with disabilities

Short-Answer Questions

1. Summarize how Heumann received her teaching license. What were her obstacles? Who helped her overcome them, and how?

2. There is one idea that Heumann repeats three times throughout the speech. What is it? What is the effect of Heumann's repetition? How does it relate to her overall message?

3. Based on the text of this speech, what do you think is the relationship between disability rights and women's rights? How does Heumann view them?

Oprah Winfrey: Cecil B. DeMille Award Acceptance Speech

Author
Oprah Winfrey

Date
2018

Document Type
Speeches/Addresses

Significance
Used the prominent forum of the Golden Globe Awards to comment on racial and sexual violence

Overview

In January of 2018, Oprah Winfrey became the first Black woman to be honored with the Cecil B. DeMille Award at the 75th Golden Globe Awards. The award, which is bestowed by the Hollywood Foreign Press Association, recognizes outstanding contributions by entertainers. Winfrey received the award for her work in the motion picture *The Color Purple* (1985) as well as her accomplishments as a talk show host, television producer, and creator across other forms of media. After a tumultuous childhood, Winfrey began her career in news television and radio talk shows before transitioning to television talk shows in Chicago in the early 1980s. *The Oprah Winfrey Show* rose to national prominence in the mid-1980s. Its success enabled Winfrey to conduct celebrity interviews, publish books, produce several television shows and movies, endorse Barack Obama for president in 2008, and use her platform to explore deeper themes for the American public.

Winfrey's acceptance speech opened with her experiences growing up in the late twentieth century, witnessing achievements by Black Americans in the entertainment industry. She highlighted the importance of women from all walks of life being able to share their stories. Winfrey went on to center her speech on sexual harassment and assault of women in Hollywood and Black women in general. She also included the story of one woman's sexual assault in the mid-twentieth century.

Winfrey's speech acknowledges the importance of the free press and the media and entertainment industries' commitment to telling true stories. This framework reflects the growing political discourse around news transparency and accountability after the 2016 presidential election. Winfrey's comments also reflect the larger "Me Too" movement. After women raised allegations against powerful Hollywood directors and producers in 2017, the movement empowered victims of sexual assault to speak up about their experiences. Many attendees of the 75th Golden Globe Awards, including Winfrey, wore black to protest widespread harassment and gender discrimination. Winfrey's insistence to perpetrators that "their time is up" is a reference to the TIME'S UP organization founded to support victims of sexual harassment. The demonstration followed other controversies surrounding major entertainment award shows favoring white male nominees in previous years, like the #OscarsSoWhite controversy in 2015.

Oprah Winfrey
(Wikimedia Commons)

Document Text

In 1964, I was a little girl sitting on the linoleum floor of my mother's house in Milwaukee, watching Anne Bancroft present the Oscar for Best Actor at the 36th Academy Awards. She opened the envelope and said five words that literally made history: "The winner is Sidney Poitier." Up to the stage came the most elegant man I had ever seen. I remember his tie was white, and, of course, his skin was black, and I had never seen a Black man being celebrated like that. And I have tried many, many, many times to explain what a moment like that means to a little girl, a kid watching from the cheap seats, as my mom came through the door bone-tired from cleaning other people's houses. But all I can do is quote and say that the explanation is in Sidney's performance in *Lilies of the Field*: "Amen, amen, amen, amen."

In 1982, Sidney received the Cecil B. DeMille Award right here at the Golden Globes, and it is not lost on me that, at this moment, there are some little girls watching as I become the first Black woman to be given this same award. It is an honor—it is an honor and it is a privilege to share the evening with all of them and also with the incredible men and women who've inspired me, who've challenged me, who've sustained me and made my journey to this stage possible. Dennis Swanson, who took a chance on me for *A.M. Chicago*. Quincy Jones who saw me on that show and said to Steven Spielberg, "Yes, she is Sofia in *The Color Purple*." Gayle, who's been the definition of what a friend is. And Stedman, who's been my rock. Just to name a few.

I'd like to thank the Hollywood Foreign Press Association because we all know that the press is under siege these days, but we also know that it is the insatiable dedication to uncovering the absolute truth that keeps us from turning a blind eye to corruption and to injustice. To tyrants and victims, and secrets and lies. I want to say that I value the press more than ever before as we try to navigate these complicated times, which brings me to this: What I know for sure is that speaking your truth is the most powerful tool we all have. And I'm especially proud and inspired by all the women who have felt strong enough and empowered enough to speak up and share their personal stories. Each of us in this room are celebrated because of the stories that we tell, and this year we became the story.

But it's not just a story affecting the entertainment industry; it's one that transcends any culture, geography, race, religion, politics or workplace. So, I want tonight to express gratitude to all the women who have endured years of abuse and assault because they, like my mother, had children to feed and bills to pay and dreams to pursue. They're the women whose names we'll never know. They are domestic workers and farm workers. They are working in factories, and they work in restaurants, and they're in academia and engineering and medicine and science. They're part of the world of tech and politics and business. They're our athletes in the Olympics, and they're our soldiers in the military.

And there's someone else, Recy Taylor, a name I know and I think you should know too. In 1944, Recy Taylor was a young wife and a mother. She was just walking home from a church service she'd attended in Abbeville, Alabama, when she was abducted by six armed white men, raped and left blindfolded by the side of the road, coming home from church. They threatened to kill her if she ever told anyone, but her story was reported to the NAACP, where a young worker by the name of Rosa Parks became the lead investigator on her case, and together they sought justice. But justice wasn't an option in the era of Jim Crow. The men who tried to destroy her were never persecuted. Recy Taylor died 10 days ago, just shy of her 98th birthday. She lived as we all have lived, too many years in a culture broken by brutally powerful men. For too long, women have not been heard or believed if they dared to speak their truth to the power of those men. But their time is up. Their time is up.

Their time is up. And I just hope—I just hope that Recy Taylor died knowing that her truth, like the truth of so many other women who were tormented in those years, and are even now tormented, goes marching on. It was somewhere in Rosa Parks's heart almost 11 years later when she made the decision to stay seated on that bus in Montgomery, and it's here with every woman who chooses to say "Me too." And every man—every man who chooses to listen.

In my career, what I've always tried my best to do, whether on television or through film, is to say something about how men and women really behave. To say how we experience shame, how we love and how we rage, how we fail, how we retreat, persevere, and how we overcome. I've interviewed and portrayed people who've withstood some of the ugliest things life can throw at you, but the one quality all of them seem to share is an ability to maintain hope for a brighter morning, even during our darkest nights. So, I want all the girls watching here and now to know that a new day is on the horizon! And when that new day finally dawns, it will be because of a lot of magnificent women, many of whom are right here in this room tonight, and some pretty phenomenal men, fighting hard to make sure that they become the leaders who take us to the time when nobody ever has to say "Me too" again. Thank you.

Glossary

Jim Crow: a reference to local and regional legislation passed during the late nineteenth and early twentieth centuries across the United States to enforce racial segregation

Me Too: a twenty-first-century social campaign publicizing experiences of sexual violence and harassment to support the survivors

NAACP: the National Association for the Advancement of Colored People, an American civil rights group founded in 1909 to fight for racial equality through activism, advocacy, and legal counsel

Rosa Parks: civil rights activist known for her pivotal role in the Montgomery bus boycott of 1956

Sidney Poitier: winner of the Academy Award for Best Actor in 1964 for his performance in the motion picture *Lilies of the Field*, the first Black actor to receive the award

Short-Answer Questions

1. Examine the setting and audience of this speech. Why do you think Winfrey chose to give this speech at the Golden Globe Awards ceremony? Is there a reason she structured her acceptance speech around political themes?

2. Why did Winfrey include the story of Recy Taylor? To what extent are Taylor's historical time and place important to the audience and to Winfrey?

3. Considering the text of the speech, analyze how Winfrey talks about race. In what ways does she talk about race explicitly? Implicitly? Why do you think she chose the language she did? Do you think it's effective?

Tarana Burke: "Full Power of Women"

Author
Tarana Burke

Date
2018

Document Type
Speeches/Addresses

Significance
Clarified the goals and intentions of the Me Too movement and foundation to support victims of sexual assault

Overview

Tarana Burke is an American activist focusing on supporting survivors of sexual assault and uplifting Black girls and women. Burke began the Me Too movement (sometimes styled as MeToo) in 2006. Using Burke's own experiences with sexual violence, the Me Too movement used empathy and community as tools of recovery. Activists encouraged survivors to speak openly about their stories to find connections, access resources, and minimize narratives of shame. The hashtag #MeToo rose to prominent usage in 2017, particularly in the entertainment industry. Burke received numerous awards for her work as the movement grew, including being named *Time*'s 2017 Person of the Year along with other "silence breakers" speaking up about sexual harassment. The increased awareness of widespread sexual harassment led to national dialogues and a number of demonstrations across industries. Burke was also honored in *Variety* magazine's 2018 "Power of Women" issue, for which she delivered this acceptance speech.

This speech speaks to Me Too as an organization, clarifying its goals and the intention of its mission. Burke also recounts recent successes and interactions she had within the context of the organization. Finally, she presents a call to action for the audience to join the movement to empower victims of sexual violence and support their healing. Burke and the movement earned multiple accolades and recognitions in 2018, making it an important year for their activism on a national level. Since receiving the Power of Women honor, Burke has continued her activism both in the Me Too movement and supporting Black arts programs and has published books about her experiences.

Tarana Burke started the Me Too movement. (Wikimedia Commons)

Document Text

I want to say I'm excited to be here, but I feel like this moment needs more words. I'm excited, I'm overwhelmed, I'm humbled, but mostly I'm grateful.

When Claudia Eller first emailed me asking if I would accept this honor, I didn't really know what to make of it. And then she said the Me Too movement would get a donation and I said, "Oh!" And then she said we get free ad space in *Variety*, and I said, "Okay." And then she said, "You'll be on the cover," and I was like, "Oh . . . I don't know about that."

These past six months have been like something out of a movie, and every day that I wake up and folks still want to hear what I have to say, I'm really surprised—and motivated. I could have never dreamed that I'd live to see a time where we were having a sustained national dialogue about sexual violence in this country, but here we are.

What this moment has solidified for me more than any other time in my life is that anything is possible even in these gloomy, untenable political times, I still feel like anything is possible.

That's why I'm so desperate to change the narrative about the Me Too movement before it's too late. Right now, the conversation is mired in misconceptions. Folks think that this is about naming and shaming. They think it's about taking down powerful men. But they're wrong.

Even the women who came forward around Harvey Weinstein didn't ask for what happened to him. They didn't even think it was possible. They were simply trying to be heard and trying to be seen and believed. That's all most survivors want—to not be the only one holding on to their truth.

And finally we have a language that provides some space for that. With two words, folks who have been wearing the fear and shame that sexual violence leaves you with like a scarlet letter are able to come out into the sunlight and see that we are a global community.

In my work, we strongly discourage victim language, not only because psychologically it's more empowering to survive something than to fall victim to it, but because it pushes back on the false notion that we need or want sympathy or pity. We have already survived some of the worst things possible and we're still here. It didn't kill us—it made us stronger.

And so we should be engaged from a place of power. We are a constituency, a power base, and we are no longer hiding in the shadows. What started as a simple exchange of empathy between survivors has now become a rallying cry, a movement builder and a clarion call.

And so it is a mistake to think of this as a moment. Movements are long and they are built over time.

This one started over a decade ago and has been building slowly but steadily. Movements are made from moments. There was the moment when I realized that these two words were enough. There was the moment when I saw it change the trajectory of those Black and Brown girls' lives in Selma, Alabama. There was a moment when we realized it was bigger than a small town in Alabama.

And now we are in a moment when the whole world is ready to join us. Let's not squander this moment by allowing others to define it for us. This is a survivors' movement, a people's movement. It's about making sure that survivors of sexual violence have what they need to craft their own healing journey and the skills they need to heal our communities. . . .

A few weeks ago I had breakfast with Billie Jean King, the famous tennis player. She just wanted to, like, hear my plans. If anybody knows Billie Jean King, she's kind of like, "Come on, talk to me, let me know what's going on, let me understand." When I told her, she immediately said, "You need a million dollars, right now." And we laughed about it and I thought, "Yeah, I do need a million dollars."

Well, earlier this week she called me up and she said, "I believe in your vision and I believe in your leadership, so I'm gonna give you $100,000 and I'm gonna try to help you get nine more people to do the same." So once I stopped crying and jumping for joy, I said, "I can't believe you're doing this. I just—I can't believe it," and she said, "You said that you believe anything is possible and I believe you."

And I do believe that, and I know I'm not the only one. I need people to join me, though—join us. This day it means so much to me because of the people who are in this room, and it's been a long time coming and people always ask me, How do you feel now? How do you feel now? And I'm just like, I don't really know how to feel but I know I have to keep going. . . .

I did not get to this place alone by any stretch of the imagination—there's no way possible. The people at that table taught me resiliency and they taught me to speak truth to power and they taught me what being a Black woman is really about. I learned so much from the Black women at that table. I learned about love and I learned about joy and I learned about tenacity and I learned not to give up.

And so I'm asking you all to join me. We can change the world. We've already started. If you are ready to change the world, if you are ready to join this movement, if you are ready to do the work that's necessary to end sexual violence, I can only leave you with these two words: Me Too.

Glossary

Billie Jean King: feminist and former number-one tennis player in the world

Claudia Eller: editor-in-chief of *Variety* magazine

Harvey Weinstein: American film producer accused by dozens of women of sexual abuse; convicted of rape and other assault charges in 2020 (in New York) and 2022 (in Los Angeles)

Me Too: a twenty-first-century social campaign publicizing experiences of sexual violence and harassment to support the survivors

Selma, Alabama: the location of a youth leadership camp where Burke heard girls share their stories of sexual violence, and where she began the work that became the Me Too movement

sexual violence: any sexual activity that happens without consent

Short-Answer Questions

1. What distinction does Burke make between a "moment" and a "movement"? Why does she make that distinction?

2. Describe Burke's tone throughout the speech. Why do you think she presented herself that way? What effect does it have on the audience?

3. Given what you know about the Me Too movement and the text of Burke's speech, what do you think was the aftermath of this address? How do you think people reacted?

Chapter 14

Women's Rights Are Human Rights

The women's rights movement in the United States primarily was primarily focused on securing equality for American females. However, there was always a recognition that the rights and liberties sought in the United States were also applicable to women around the world. By the 1900s, it became increasingly clear that there were deep disparities between the lives and lifestyles of women in the developed world and those in developing nations. By the later years of the twentieth century, female leaders from across the globe embraced the need to link women's rights with the broader struggle to promote human rights. The phrase "Women's rights are human rights" emerged in the 1980s as a call to action by feminists to secure equality and freedom for women everywhere.

Rigoberta Menchú Tum and Indira Ghandi

In 1992 Rigoberta Menchú Tum was awarded the Nobel Peace Prize. Menchú was an advocate for women's rights and equality for indigenous peoples in her native Guatemala. In her acceptance speech, Menchú highlighted the struggles of indigenous peoples in the Western Hemisphere over the past five centuries. She called for reconciliation between the dominant European culture in her native country and the indigenous community through greater rights for native peoples.

While many countries had internal women's rights movements, efforts to fight genderism at the global level were led by a growing number of female political leaders. Indira Gandhi was the third prime minister of India and the nation's first female leader. She was a trailblazer who proved that women could not only lead major nations but lead during times of great crisis. In an address in November 1974 titled "What Educated Women Can Do," Gandhi argued for the need to reform India's educational system to better address the needs of girls. She also contended that her nation needed to move beyond outdated superstitions and customs to fully overcome "imbalances" in Indian society and allow women to better contribute to the future of their country. After serving as prime minister for more than fifteen years in two separate terms, Gandhi was assassinated on October 31, 1984.

The 1995 UN Conference on Women

Then U.S. First Lady, future secretary of state, and future presidential candidate Hillary Rodham Clinton delivered a powerful speech on women's rights to the United Nations World Conference on Women in Beijing, China, in September 1995. Clinton's address called for an end to discrimination against women and a recognition that women's rights and human rights were synonymous. Clinton cited specific examples of female abuse and condemned inequalities in education, pay, and healthcare faced by many women around the globe. The speech was widely credited with reinvigorating efforts to improve women's rights.

Also speaking at the UN Conference on Women in 1995 was Pakistani Prime Minister Benazir Bhutto. Bhutto twice served as prime minister of Pakistan, from 1988 to 1990 and from 1993 to 1996. She was Pakistan's first female prime minister. In her address to the conference, Bhutto stressed the need for action. She defended Pakistan and other Islamic nations against accusations that Muslim women were treated as second-class citizens because of religion. Instead, she argued that Islamic women had a special responsibility to correct misperceptions about their religion that were used to justify gender discrimination. Bhutto also warned attendees of the need for specific actions to dismantle the patterns of discrimination against women. Bhutto was assassinated on December 27, 2007, while campaigning for another term as prime minister.

On the eve of the 1995 UN Conference, American feminist Charlotte Bunch spoke to representatives from non-governmental organizations. She warned of the rise of reactionary forces around the world that embraced discriminatory practices toward women. These forces also supported repressive measures against the lesbian, gay, bisexual, and transgender (LGBT) community. Her solution to the growing threats to equality was to embrace definitions of human rights that were inclusive and broad.

Social Justice Advocates in Kenya and Northern Ireland

For many a new conceptualization of human rights meant integrating issues such as environmental justice into the greater campaign for equality. Wangari Maathai won the Nobel Peace Prize in 2004 for her efforts to improve Africa's environment. She was the first African woman and the first Kenyan to receive the honor. Maathai helped establish the Pan African Green Belt Network, which worked to conserve the environment by planting trees. In her acceptance speech, Maathai described how her organization sought to help impoverished women by enhancing soil quality and providing new resources through reforestation. Her initiative emerged as a means to help empower disadvantaged groups and as a symbol for human rights. The Green Belt Network also survived government efforts to suppress the organization because of its support for democracy in Kenya.

Betty Williams won the Nobel Peace Prize in 1976 for her work in trying to end the religious and political turmoil in Northern Ireland. Ireland had been part of Great Britain, but in 1922, the twenty-six mainly Catholic southern counties became independent. However, the six predominately Protestant counties of Northern Ireland remained part of Britain. In the 1970s, violence broke out in Northern Ireland as Catholic and Protestant groups fought. Catholic organizations such as the Irish Republican Army sought independence, while Protestant groups wanted to remain part of the United Kingdom. The conflict caused a large number of civilian casualties. Williams and fellow Nobel winner Mairead Corrigan Maguire created a group, Women for Peace. Williams later helped establish the Nobel Women's Initiative with five other female recipients of the award, including Maguire, Menchú, and Maathai. The purpose of the group was to promote women's rights within the broader context of human rights. In 2007 Williams gave an address, "Peace in the World Is Everybody's Business." Williams described her background and the history of violence in Northern Ireland. She then related how women in Northern Ireland worked together to try to end the violence. Ultimately, a peaceful solution to the conflict was found through the Good Friday Agreement in 1999.

Further Reading

Books
Allen, Brooke. *Benazir Bhutto: Favored Daughter.* New York: New Harvest, 2016.

Beitz, Charles R. *The Idea of Human Rights.* New York: Oxford University Press, 2009.

Bernstein, Carl. *A Woman in Charge: The Life of Hillary Rodham Clinton.* New York: Alfred A. Knopf, 2007.

Bulbeck, Chilla. *Re-Orienting Western Feminisms: Women's Diversity in a Postcolonial World.* New York: Cambridge University Press, 1998.

Buscher, Sarah, and Bettina Ling. *Mairead Corrigan and Betty Williams: Making Peace in Northern Ireland.* New York: The Feminist Press, 1999.

Calvert, Peter. *Guatemala: A Nation in Turmoil.* Boulder, CO: Westview Press, 1985.

Donnelly, Jack. *Universal Human Rights in Theory and Practice.* Ithaca, NY: Cornell University Press, 2003.

Frank, Katherine. *Indira: The Life of Indira Nehru Gandhi.* New York: HarperCollins, 2010.

Howard, Rhoda E. *Human Rights and the Search for Community.* Boulder, CO: Westview, 1995.

Lerner, Hanna. *Making Constitutions in Deeply Divided Societies.* Cambridge: Cambridge University Press, 2011.

Mwaura, N. *Kenya Today: Breaking the Yoke of Colonialism in Africa.* New York: Algora Publishing, 2005.

Press, Robert M. *Peaceful Resistance: Advancing Human Rights and Democratic Freedoms.* Aldershot, UK: Ashgate Publishing, 2006.

Articles
Akhter, M. Javaiid. "Politics of Reconciliation and Accommodation: A Study of Benazir Bhutto's First Era Democratic Government 1988–1990." *Journal of Political Studies* 16 (2009).

Fester, Gertrude. "Women's Rights Are Human Rights." *Agenda: Empowering Women for Gender Equity* 20 (1994).

Mitchell, George J. "Toward Peace in Northern Ireland." *Fordham International Law Journal* 22 (1998).

Websites
"The Human Rights of Women." UN Population Fund website, accessed September 5, 2023, https://www.unfpa.org/resources/human-rights-women.

"Women's Rights." Human Rights Watch website, accessed September 5, 2023, https://www.hrw.org/topic/womens-rights.

Indira Gandhi:
"What Educated Women Can Do"

Author
Indira Gandhi

Date
1974

Document Type
Presidential/Executive; Speeches/Addresses

Significance
An address given by the first female prime minister of India to commemorate the fiftieth anniversary of the oldest women's college of the University of Delhi

Overview

Indira Gandhi was the first female prime minister of India. She was born in 1917, while India was still under British control. Gandhi's father, Jawaharlal Nehru, was a member of the Indian National Congress, also known as the Congress Party. The Congress Party led the movement for Indian independence from Britain in the twentieth century and gained control when Nehru was elected the first prime minister in 1947. During the 1950s and 1960s, Gandhi helped organize women's organizations within the Congress Party. Her first term of office began in 1966, when she was chosen after the death of the previous prime minister. Gandhi served three terms as prime minister before she was defeated in the 1977 election, but she was reelected to power in 1980. Gandhi's terms of office were characterized by industrialization, a close relationship with the Soviet Union, continued work with women's groups, and increasing attempts at independence by minority groups. After a government strike at a Sikh temple in 1984, Sikh members of Gandhi's bodyguard assassinated her.

While Gandhi's legacy may be complicated by her consolidation of power, violence against minority groups, and accusations of corruption, she stressed the importance of equal opportunities for girls throughout her career. Gandhi delivered her "What Educated Women Can Do" speech to commemorate the fiftieth anniversary of the Indraprastha College for Women, the oldest women's college in Delhi. Using her experience growing up in India before its independence in 1947 as well as her own education, Gandhi highlights the need to support and promote women's education. Gandhi emphasizes that education not only impacts the individual but also has far-reaching effects on communities, countries, and the world. She points out that knowledge alone is not the marker of education but also the ability to think scientifically, analyze problems, and judge the merits of both the past and the present. Education, for Gandhi, is not only about elevating women but also about elevating India.

Document Text

An ancient Sanskrit saying says: Woman is the home, and the home is the basis of society. It is as we build our homes that we can build our country. If the home is inadequate—either inadequate in material goods and necessities or inadequate in the sort of friendly, loving atmosphere that every child needs to grow and develop—then that country cannot have harmony, and no country which does not have harmony can grow in any direction at all.

That is why women's education is almost more important than the education of boys and men. We—and by "we" I do not mean only we in India but all the world—have neglected women's education. . . .

Our own ancient philosophy has taught us that nothing in life is entirely bad or entirely good. Everything is somewhat of a mixture, and it depends on us and our capability how we can extract the good, how we can make use of what is around us. There are people who through observation can learn from anything that is around them. There are others who can be surrounded by the most fascinating people, the most wonderful books, and other things, and who yet remain quite closed in, and they are unable to take anything from this wealth around them. . . . Before anybody does anything, he has to have, of course, knowledge and capability, but along with it he has to have a certain amount of pride in what he or she is doing. He has to have self-confidence in his own ability. If your teacher tells you, "You cannot do this," even if you are a very bright student, I think every time you will find it will be more and more difficult for you to do it. But if your teacher encourages you, saying, "Go along, you have done very good work, now try a little harder," then you will try a little harder and you will be able to do it. And it is the same with societies and with countries. . . .

I do not know how many of you know that the countries of Western Europe and Japan import 41 per cent of their food needs, whereas India imports just under two per cent. Yet, somehow we ourselves

Indira Gandhi
(Prime Minister's Office of India)

project an image that India is out with the begging bowl. . . . We have to see, and you—the educated women, because it is a great privilege for you to have higher education—you have to try and see our problems in the perspective of what has happened here in this country and what is happening all over the world. . . .

As I said, we do have many shortcomings, whether it is the government, whether it is the society. Some are due to our traditions because, as I said, not all tradition is good. And one of the biggest responsibilities of the educated women today is how to synthesize what has been valuable and timeless in our ancient traditions with what is good and valuable in modern thought. All that is modern is not good, just as all that is old is neither all good nor all bad. We have to decide, not once and for all but almost every week, every month what is coming out that is good and useful to our country and what of the old we can keep and enshrine in our society. To be modern, most people think that it is something of a manner of dress or a manner of speaking or certain habits and customs, but that is not really being modern. It is a very superficial part of modernity....

What clothes we wear is really quite unimportant. What is important is how we are thinking.

Sometimes, I am very sad that even people who do science are quite unscientific in their thinking and in their other actions—not what they are doing in the laboratories but how they live at home or their attitudes towards other people. Now, for India to become what we want it to become with a modern, rational society and firmly based on what is good in our ancient tradition and in our soil, for this we have to have a thinking public, thinking young women who are not content to accept what comes from any part of the world but are willing to listen to it, to analyze it and to decide whether it is to be accepted or whether it is to be thrown out.... This is the sort of education which we want, which enables our young people to adjust to this changing world and to be able to contribute to it.

Some people think that only by taking up very high jobs, you are doing something important or you are doing national service. But we all know that the most complex machinery will be ineffective if one small screw is not working as it should, and that screw is just as important as any big part. It is the same in national life. There is no job that is too small; there is no person who is too small. Everybody has something to do. And if he or she does it well, then the country will run well....

So, I hope that all of you who have this great advantage of education will not only do whatever work you are doing keeping the national interests in view, but you will make your own contribution to creating peace and harmony, to bringing beauty in the lives of our people and our country. I think this is the special responsibility of the women of India. We want to do a great deal for our country, but we have never regarded India as isolated from the rest of the world. What we want to do is to make a better world. So, we have to see India's problems in the perspective of the larger world problems.

It has given me great pleasure to be with you here. I give my warm congratulations to those who are doing well and my very good wishes to all the others that they will also do much better. This college has had a high reputation, but we must always see that we do better than those who were there before us. So, good luck and good wishes to you.

Glossary

modernity: the state or appearance of being modern, in particular adapting from a rural to an industrial economy and culture

Sanskrit: a classical language of India and the sacred language of Hinduism

Short-Answer Questions

1. What is the role of globalism in Gandhi's speech? Does Gandhi present globalism as a positive or a negative?

2. Identify one of the analogies Gandhi uses to describe the importance of women's education. How does Gandhi relate it to her central argument? Is it effective? Why or why not?

3. Based on the text of the speech, why do you think Gandhi delivered this when she did? What do you infer was happening in India or the world at that time?

"A Mother's Life in Rural Pernambuco, Brazil"

Author
Unknown

Date
1982

Document Type
Essays, Reports, Manifestos

Significance
Described the realities of life for women in Brazil's sugar-growing northeast, where premature deaths, early marriages, frequent pregnancies, and high child mortality conspired to keep women locked in a state of crushing poverty

Overview

The social roles of women in modern Brazil have been shaped by an enduring legacy of patriarchal culture. Women in the cultures of the Iberian Peninsula and Latin America have traditionally been regarded as inferior to men and subject to male dominance and control. These social norms were developed in Spain and Portugal during the medieval period and transferred into colonial contexts as these two cultures expanded across the globe during the seventeenth century. The exploitative labor systems used by these two imperial societies, coupled with the marginalization of indigenous peoples across Latin America, led to patriarchy becoming an entrenched aspect of modern Brazilian life.

The Brazilian women's movement, which has been regarded as the most organized of its kind on the South American continent, has traditionally been helmed by women from educated, middle-class backgrounds, and its impact has been limited to Brazil's major urban centers. As a result, women in rural Brazil, particularly in the sugar-growing regions of the country's northeast, have struggled to realize the same rights as women in more prosperous parts of the country.

Pernambuco is a state in northeastern Brazil known for its beaches on the Atlantic Ocean. It is a major producer of sugarcane and one of the poorest states in Brazil. Throughout the twentieth century, women in Pernambuco's shanty towns and slums struggled against endemic poverty, malnutrition, abusive male partners, and child mortality. The rural workers of Pernambuco remained trapped in a precarious existence, dependent on sugarcane and numbed to the inevitability of premature death. Research has indicated that in Brazil's Northeast, the infant death rate in 1987 was 76.6 per 1,000. This was more than twice that of the Southeast of the country. Women over the age of forty had an average of more than twelve children; younger women had an average of seven children, half of whom died before they reach adulthood. The account presented here, which was recorded in 1982, reveals the harsh realities faced by women in Brazil's northeastern slums. The conditions described in this excerpt have been alleviated by sustained government investment and public services, but life remains difficult for the women of Pernambuco.

Document Text

I never learned to read or write, although Mama and Auntie tried to make me go to school. It was no use. I learned to sign my name, but not very well, because it is a complicated name and it has a lot of parts to it. When I was about five years old . . . we got divided up. Mama took Biu, Tia took Antonieta, and I stayed at Bela Vista with my godmother, Dona Graças.

My *madrinha* was a real mother to me. Dona Graças raised me with care and great sacrifice. In those days food was scarce, and some days all we had to eat was the coarsest manioc flour, *farinha de roça*. I found it hard to swallow because of a sickness that injured my throat when I was a small baby. It made my grandmother sad to see me getting skinny, so she begged a few spoonfuls of the finest whitest *farinha* every day from her *patroa* so that she could make me a smooth custard. When there was no other food, Madrinha would take an ear of hard Indian corn, and she would roast it and coax me into eating the dried kernels one by one. I was close to dying more than once, but my grandmother fought with me to stay alive. And she won!

When I was fifteen I was married for the first time. I became the legitimate wife of Severino José da Silva. But it was a marriage that wasn't worth much, and it soon fell apart. We lived in a tiny room built onto the side of Tia's house on the Alto do Cruzeiro, so small you could only lie down in it. Severino was miserable the whole time we were together. He never wanted to marry me; it was Mama and Auntie who forced him into it. In those days when a boy ruined a virgin, he was made to marry the girl, and if he refused, the judge could put him behind bars. . . . Finally, he left me to live with his other woman. . . .

I left to work outside of town in a ceramic factory, and that's where I met my second husband, Nelson. Nelson's job was firing roof tiles, and he was very skilled at this. . . .

At first Nelson was good to me. Every Saturday he would climb the Alto to visit, and he always brought a basket of groceries for the week. He never once came empty-handed. . . . But after I got pregnant, everything changed. Nelson began to abuse me. It looked like I was going to follow in my mother's footsteps. I was actually glad my firstborn died right away. Things got better for a little bit, and then I was pregnant again. After Zezinho was born, things went from bad to worse. I was living in a hovel without even a roof over my head. It was worse than living in an outhouse. . . . I began to see that Nelson was abusing me for the fun of it. It was a kind of sport. He wanted to keep making me pregnant just so he could threaten to leave me again and again. . . . I got stronger, and I put him out for good. . . .

I spent three months working in the tomato fields, and that's where I met Milton, my third husband. . . . I was too afraid to say anything when I got pregnant again because Mama and Tia were losing patience with me. So I tried to hide it, and I never told anyone at all about Milton.

I was low and dispirited during this time. It was the only time in my life that I didn't have energy for anything. I didn't have any interest in Zezinho, and I never did anything to prepare for the birth of Wagner. . . . I didn't care about anything. I wanted that baby to die and Zezinho, too. But it turned out to be a pretty baby. Still, they were the cause of my misery! . . .

After Wagner was born there was no reason to hide what was going on. So finally Milton came to visit, carrying a big sack of fresh corn on his head to give as a present to Mãe. He told Mãe and Tia that he was responsible for the baby. And that's how he became my third husband. Well, with Milton I finally had some luck. It worked out, and I wound up living with him for fourteen years. I was pregnant ten more times with him. I had three miscarriages and seven live births, and of those I managed to raise four. So we didn't do badly. The three of his that died all died quickly. The first one died in his hammock while I was away working. One of the older children killed him. He got too close and yelled in his ear. He just frightened that baby to death. He died of *susto* in less than a day, and I didn't suffer very much. The other two were weak and sickly from birth. They had no "knack" for life. The other four came into the world ready to confront [*enfrentar*] hardship and suffering, so naturally they lived.

Glossary

Alto do Cruzeiro: a desperately poor shantytown in Brazil's municipality of Timbaúba, one of many similar towns located in the state of Pernambuco

madrinha: godmother

Mãe: Mother

manioc flour: flour made from cassava root

patroa: female landowner

susto: fright

Tia: Aunt

Short-Answer Questions

1. Describe the challenges faced by the author, and explain how these challenges contributed to her pervasive sense of insecurity, poverty, and desperation.

2. Explain the author's attitudes toward childbearing and maternity. What surprises you about her perspective and her attitudes?

3. The author's attitude toward the mortality of her own children may be shocking to many readers. Such attitudes have been commonly described by sociologists and anthropologists working in northeastern Brazil. What factors might have contributed to the shaping of her seemingly indifferent attitudes toward child mortality? What might her attitude suggest about the connections between mortality, poverty, and childbearing?

Rigoberta Menchú Tum: Nobel Peace Prize Lecture

Author
Rigoberta Menchú Tum

Date
1992

Document Type
Speeches/Addresses

Significance
Described the author's activism for women's and Indigenous rights amid the civil war in Guatemala

Overview

In 1992, Rigoberta Menchú Tum was awarded the Nobel Peace Prize for her peacemaking and racial reconciliation efforts in her native Guatemala. Guatemala entered a civil war in 1960 when poor, rural groups revolted against the land-holding elite, many of whom represented European and American interests. Throughout the war, which ended in 1996, the Guatemalan government carried out various civil rights abuses against the rebels and was accused of genocidal action toward Mayan and other Indigenous communities. This included Tum and her K'iche' Maya family. They were already actively involved in social reform and women's rights through the Catholic Church but became more involved in the resistance movement in the late 1970s. By the mid-1980s, Tum's parents and both of her brothers had been tortured and killed by the Guatemalan government.

Tum faced discrimination in her resistance work because of her gender, but she became such an active leader of anti-government protests that she went into hiding in 1981 and eventually fled to Mexico. From exile, Tum helped found the United Representation of the Guatemalan Opposition and published an autobiography, *I, Rigoberta Menchú*. Since her receipt of the Nobel Peace Prize, Tum has continued to advocate for Indigenous peoples, served as a UNESCO Goodwill Ambassador, and cofounded the Nobel Women's Initiative. She also started the first Indigenous political party in Guatemala, Winaq, in the early 2000s.

The Nobel Foundation awarded Tum the Peace Prize on the 500th anniversary of Christopher Columbus's arrival in the Western Hemisphere. Tum was the first Indigenous woman to receive the Nobel Peace Prize, and at the time of her speech, the United Nations voted to designate 1993 as the International Year of the World's Indigenous Peoples. In of this historical context, Tum focused on the abuses suffered by Indigenous

Guatemalans during the civil war but also spoke more broadly about ways that war harms communities and women and about the general plight of Indigenous peoples around the world. The Guatemalan civil war, for Tum, was a woman's issue because of the targeted violence against Indigenous women, the creation of widows and orphans, and the importance of women's voices in reconciliation.

Rigoberta Menchú Tum
(Wikimedia Commons)

Document Text

I feel a deep emotion and pride for the honor of having been awarded the Nobel Peace Prize for 1992. A deep personal feeling and pride for my country and its very ancient culture. For the values of the community and the people to which I belong, for the love of my country, of Mother Nature. Whoever understands this respects life and encourages the struggle that aims at such objectives.

I consider this prize not as a reward to me personally, but rather as one of the greatest conquests in the struggle for peace, for human rights, and for the rights of the Indigenous people, who, for 500 years, have been split, fragmented, as well as the victims of genocides, repression and discrimination....

As a contrast, and paradoxically, it was actually in my own country where I met, on the part of some people, the strongest objections, reserve and indifference, for the award of the Nobel Peace Prize to this Quiché Indian. Perhaps because in Latin America, it is precisely in Guatemala where the discrimination towards the Indigenous, towards women, and the repression of the longing for justice and peace, are more deeply rooted in certain social and political sectors....

The expressions of great happiness by the Indian organizations throughout the entire continent and the worldwide congratulations received for the award of the Nobel Peace Prize clearly indicate the great importance of this decision. It is the recognition of the European debt to the American Indigenous people; it is an appeal to the conscience of Humanity so that those conditions of marginalization that condemned them to colonialism and exploitation may be eradicated; it is a cry for life, peace, justice, equality and fraternity between human beings.

The peculiarities of the vision of the Indian people are expressed according to the ways in which they are related to each other. First, between human beings, through communication. Second, with the earth, as with our mother, because she gives us our lives and is not mere merchandise. Third, with nature, because we are an integral part of it, and not its owners.

To us Mother Earth is not only a source of economic riches that give us the maize, which is our life, but she also provides so many other things that the privileged ones of today strive for. The Earth is the root and the source of our culture. She keeps our memories, she receives our ancestors, and she therefore demands that we honor her and return to her, with tenderness and respect, those goods that she gives us. We have to take care of her so that our children and grandchildren may continue to benefit from her. If the world does not learn now to show respect to nature, what kind of future will the new generations have?

From these basic features derive behavior, rights and obligations in the American continent, for the Indigenous people as well as for the non-Indigenous, whether they be racially mixed, Blacks, whites or Asian. The whole society has an obligation to show mutual respect, to learn from each other and to share material and scientific achievements, in the most convenient way. The Indigenous peoples never had, and still do not have, the place that they should have occupied in the progress and benefits of science and technology, although they represented an important basis for this development. . . .

The attention that this Nobel Peace Prize has focused on Guatemala should imply that the violation of human rights is no longer ignored internationally. It will also honor all those who died in the struggle for social equality and justice in my country. . . .

The economic, social and political subjection that derived from the Cold War was what initiated the internal armed conflict. The repression against the organizations of the people, the democratic parties, and the intellectuals started in Guatemala long before the war started. Let us not forget that.

In the attempt to crush rebellion, dictatorships have committed the greatest atrocities. They have leveled villages and murdered thousands of peasants, particularly Indians, hundreds of trade union workers and students, outstanding intellectuals and politicians, priests and nuns. Through this systematic persecution in the name of the safety of the nation, one million peasants were removed by force from their lands; 100,000 had to seek refuge in the neighboring countries. In Guatemala, there are today almost 100,000 orphans and more than 40,000 widows. The practice of "disappeared" politicians was invented in Guatemala, as a government policy.

As you know, I am myself a survivor of a massacred family. . . .

In the new Guatemalan society, there must be a fundamental reorganization in the matter of land ownership to allow for the development of the agricultural potential, as well as for the return of the land to the legitimate owners. This process of reorganization must be carried out with the greatest respect for nature in order to protect her and return to her, her strength and capability to generate life.

No less characteristic of a democracy is social justice. This demands a solution to the frightening statistics on infant mortality, of malnutrition, lack of education, analphabetism, wages insufficient to sustain life. These problems have a growing and painful impact on the Guatemalan population and imply no prospects and no hope.

Among the features that characterize society today is that of the role of women, although female emancipation has not, in fact, been fully achieved so far by any country in the world.

The historical development in Guatemala reflects now the need and the irreversibility of the active contribution of women to the configuration of the new Guatemalan social order, of which, I humbly believe, the Indian women already are a clear testimony. This Nobel Peace Prize is a recognition to those who have been, and still are in most parts of the world, the most exploited of the exploited, the most discriminated of the discriminated, the most marginalized of the marginalized, but still those who produce life and riches.

Democracy, development and modernization of a country are impossible and incongruous without the solution of these problems. . . .

Along these same lines, I invite the international community to contribute with specific actions so that the parties involved may overcome the differences that at this stage keep negotiations in a wait-and-see state, so that they will succeed, first of all, in signing an agreement on Human Rights. And then, to re-initiate the rounds of negotiation and identify those issues on which to compromise, to allow for the Peace Agreement to be signed and immediately ratified, because I have no doubt that this will bring about great relief in the prevailing situation in Guatemala.

Glossary

analphabetism: illiteracy

Cold War: the state of tension between the United States and the Soviet Union, fought largely through those nations' proxies, that lasted from the end of World War II to the dissolution of the Soviet Union in 1991

colonialism: the invasion or domination of an area by a foreign power

genocide: a reference to the intentional massacre of Maya people by Guatemalan military governments from the 1960s through the 1990s

Indigenous people: the original inhabitants of a place before its colonization by a foreign power

Peace Agreement: the Agreement on a Firm and Lasting Peace, moderated by the United Nations and signed in 1996, four years after this speech, by the Government of Guatemala and the Guatemalan National Revolutionary Unity, ending the civil war

Quiché: Spanish spelling of K'iche', an Indigenous people of Guatemala and one of the Maya peoples

Short-Answer Questions

1. What does Tum view as the solution for women's and Indigenous empowerment? How might this reflect her identity and context?

2. How does Tum see the relationship between indigeneity and womanhood? How does her wording throughout the lecture connect them?

3. Describe Tum's tone and language choices throughout the piece. What impact do they have? Do you find them effective? What do they reveal about the speech's audience?

Hillary Rodham Clinton: "Women's Rights Are Human Rights"

Author
Hillary Rodham Clinton

Date
1995

Document Type
Speeches/Addresses

Significance
A landmark speech by the First Lady of the United States emphasizing the global importance of women's rights

Overview

Hillary Rodham Clinton, the Democratic Party's candidate for U.S. president in 2016, has had a varied and influential political and legal career. She served as U.S. secretary of state from 2009 to 2013 and before that as U.S. senator from New York from 2001 to 2009. She became the First Lady of the United States in 1993 when her husband, Bill Clinton, was elected to the first of his two terms of office. After working on political campaigns through high school and college, she received a law degree from Yale University in 1973. She moved to Arkansas in 1974, where she would go on to marry Clinton, teach at the University of Arkansas Law School, practice law, work on the board of the Legal Services Corporation under the Carter administration, and serve as the First Lady of Arkansas during her husband's term as governor. When her husband was elected president of the United States in 1992, she became the first First Lady to have a postgraduate degree and a full-time career prior to her husband entering office.

While First Lady, Rodham Clinton used her background in law and politics to advise the president on policy. She remained an influence throughout Clinton's terms of office despite many people criticizing her active role in government. Rodham Clinton had several focuses as First Lady, including her interest in women's and children's issues, particularly through health care. She also brought global women's issues before the public through books and her weekly "Talking It Over" column.

In 1995, Rodham Clinton appeared at the Fourth World Conference on Women in her capacity as First Lady and delivered her "Women's Rights Are Human Rights" speech. Although many groups attempted to get Rodham Clinton to deliver a more diplomatic address, she went ahead as planned. In her speech, Rodham Clinton maintains that although women face many different challenges and realities internationally, they have more commonalities than differences. She references several instances of harm against women and urges the world to take action on behalf of women's rights. The speech became one of the most memorable feminist speeches of the twentieth century, influencing the language of women's organizations while solidifying Clinton's status as a voice for women's rights worldwide.

Hillary Clinton speaking at the United Nations in 1995 (National Archives and Records Administration)

Document Text

This is truly a celebration—a celebration of the contributions women make in every aspect of life: in the home, on the job, in their communities, as mothers, wives, sisters, daughters, learners, workers, citizens and leaders.

It is also a coming together, much the way women come together every day in every country.

We come together in fields and in factories. In village markets and supermarkets. In living rooms and board rooms.

Whether it is while playing with our children in the park or washing clothes in a river, or taking a break at the office water cooler, we come together and talk about our aspirations and concerns. And time and again, our talk turns to our children and our families.

However different we may be, there is far more that unites us than divides us. We share a common future. And we are here to find common ground so that we may help bring new dignity and respect to women and girls all over the world—and in so doing, bring new strength and stability to families as well. . . .

What we are learning around the world is that, if women are healthy and educated, their families will flourish. If women are free from violence, their families will flourish. If women have a chance to work and earn as full and equal partners in society, their families will flourish.

And when families flourish, communities and nations will flourish.

That is why every woman, every man, every child, every family, and every nation on our planet has a stake in the discussion that takes place here. . . .

The great challenge of this conference is to give voice to women everywhere whose experiences go unnoticed, whose words go unheard. . . .

Women are the primary caretakers for most of the world's children and elderly. Yet much of the work we do is not valued—not by economists, not by historians, not by popular culture, not by government leaders.

At this very moment, as we sit here, women around the world are giving birth, raising children, cooking meals, washing clothes, cleaning houses, planting crops, working on assembly lines, running companies, and running countries.

Women also are dying from diseases that should have been prevented or treated; they are watching their children succumb to malnutrition caused by poverty and economic deprivation; they are being denied the right to go to school by their own fathers and brothers; they are being forced into prostitution, and they are being barred from the ballot box and the bank lending office.

Those of us who have the opportunity to be here have the responsibility to speak for those who could not. . . .

Speaking to you today, I speak for them, just as each of us speaks for women around the world who are denied the chance to go to school, or see a doctor, or own property, or have a say about the direction of their lives, simply because they are women.

The truth is that most women around the world work both inside and outside the home, usually by necessity.

We need to understand that there is no formula for how women should lead their lives. That is why we must respect the choices that each woman makes for herself and her family. Every woman deserves the chance to realize her God-given potential.

We also must recognize that women will never gain full dignity until their human rights are respected and protected. . . .

The international community has long acknowledged—and recently affirmed at Vienna—that both women and men are entitled to a range of protections and personal freedoms, from the right of personal security to the right to determine freely the number and spacing of the children they bear. . . .

I believe that, on the eve of a new millennium, it is time to break our silence. It is time for us to say here in Beijing, and for the world to hear, that it is no longer acceptable to discuss women's rights as separate from human rights.

These abuses have continued because, for too long, the history of women has been a history of silence. Even today, there are those who are trying to silence our words.

The voices of this conference and of the women at Huairou must be heard loud and clear:

It is a violation of human rights when babies are denied food, or drowned, or suffocated, or their spines broken, simply because they are born girls.

It is a violation of human rights when women and girls are sold into the slavery of prostitution.

It is a violation of human rights when women are doused with gasoline, set on fire and burned to death because their marriage dowries are deemed too small.

It is a violation of human rights when individual women are raped in their own communities and when thousands of women are subjected to rape as a tactic or prize of war.

It is a violation of human rights when a leading cause of death worldwide among women ages 14 to 44 is the violence they are subjected to in their own homes.

It is a violation of human rights when young girls are brutalized by the painful and degrading practice of genital mutilation.

It is a violation of human rights when women are denied the right to plan their own families, and that includes being forced to have abortions or being sterilized against their will.

If there is one message that echoes forth from this conference, it is that human rights are women's rights—and women's rights are human rights.

Let us not forget that among those rights are the right to speak freely. And the right to be heard.

Women must enjoy the right to participate fully in the social and political lives of their countries if we want freedom and democracy to thrive and endure. . . .

As long as discrimination and inequities remain so commonplace around the world—as long as girls and women are valued less, fed less, fed last, overworked, underpaid, not schooled and subjected to violence in and out of their homes—the potential of the human family to create a peaceful, prosperous world will not be realized.

Let this conference be our—and the world's—call to action.

And let us heed the call so that we can create a world in which every woman is treated with respect and dignity, every boy and girl is loved and cared for equally, and every family has the hope of a strong and stable future.

Glossary

Fourth World Conference on Women: a conference held by the United Nations in Beijing, China, in 1995 to discuss areas of gender inequality around the world and set objectives to advance women's rights

genital mutilation: or female genital mutilation (FGM), a practice that involves the total or partial removal of girls' reproductive organs for non-medical reasons

Huairou: a reference to the Huairou Commission, named for a district in northern Beijing, China, which describes itself as "a women-led social movement of grassroots groups from poor urban, rural and indigenous communities in 45+ countries who collectively work for transformative change that improves the living conditions, status, and quality of life of women, their families and municipalities"

Vienna: a reference to the Vienna Declaration and Programme of Action, adopted in June 1993 by the World Conference on Human Rights in Vienna, Austria, and subsequently endorsed by the United Nations General Assembly in December 1993

Short-Answer Questions

1. What rhetorical device does Rodham Clinton use to emphasize her main point? Explain whether you find it effective and why (or why not).

2. Why is it important for Rodham Clinton to equate women's rights with human rights? How do you think her audience received this argument?

3. Does Rodham Clinton distinguish between the work women do inside the home and outside the home? Why do you think she frames women's responsibilities the way that she does?

Benazir Bhutto: Address at the Fourth World Conference on Women

Author
Benazir Bhutto

Date
1995

Document Type
Presidential/Executive; Speeches/Addresses

Significance
A speech arguing for economic and social equality for women delivered by the first female head of a majority Muslim country

Overview

The first woman to lead a modern Islamic country, Benazir Bhutto (1953–2007) was elected prime minister of Pakistan in 1988. Bhutto became the head of the Pakistan People's Party when her father, Zulfikar Bhutto, who had founded the party and led Pakistan from 1971 to 1977, was executed in 1979. After the death of the previous prime minister, Benazir Bhutto was elected to the first of her two terms in 1988 and served until her defeat in the election of 1990. Her second term lasted from 1993 to 1996. Bhutto represented liberal, secular interests, which put her at odds with more traditional politicians and those who supported increased militarization. She is still regarded as gaining support from both Pakistani Muslims and non-Muslim Westerners, regardless of her policies. Toward the end of her second term, she faced charges of corruption and was forced into exile after a hostile takeover in 1999. Eventually a new administration granted Bhutto amnesty and allowed her to return to Pakistan in October 2007, but she was assassinated soon after, on December 7, at a public appearance there in Rawalpindi, Punjab.

Although she did not pass influential policy on women's rights, Bhutto remained outspoken on gender inequality, particularly within Islamic contexts. The majority of her statements on gender as prime minister related to her own experiences as a woman in politics. In her address at the Fourth World Conference on Women in Beijing, China, she counters popular Western notions about sexism and the treatment of women in Islamic countries. As she argues for expanded opportunities and protections for women through democracy, she also connects Muslim values to women's rights. This speech, along with Bhutto's success in a majority male framework, contributed to her legacy as a figure in the women's rights movement.

Document Text

On this solemn occasion I stand before you not only as a Prime Minister but as a woman and a mother—a woman proud of her cultural and religious heritage, a woman sensitive to the obstacles to justice and full participation that still stand before women in almost every society on earth. As the first woman ever elected to head an Islamic nation, I feel a special responsibility towards women's issues and towards all women. And as a Muslim woman, I feel a special responsibility to counter the propaganda of a handful that Islam gives women a second-class status. . . .

In distinguishing between Islamic teachings and social taboos, we must remember that Islam forbids injustice: injustice against people, against nations, against women. It shuns race, color, and gender as a basis of distinction amongst fellowmen. It enshrines piety as the sole criteria for judging humankind. It treats women as human beings in their own right, not as chattels. A woman can inherit, divorce, receive alimony and child custody. Women were intellectuals, poets, jurists and even took part in war. The Holy Book of the Muslims refers to the rule of a woman, the Queen of Sabah. The Holy Book alludes to her wisdom and to her country being a land of plenty. . . .

Statistics show that men now increasingly outnumber women in more than 15 Asian nations. Boys are wanted. Boys are wanted because their worth is considered more than that of the girl. Boys are wanted to satisfy the ego: they carry on the father's name in this world. Yet too often we forget that for Muslims on the Day of Judgment, each person will be called not by their father's name but by the mother's name. To please her husband, a woman wants a son. To keep her husband from abandoning her, a woman wants a son. . . .

The rights Islam gave Muslim women have too often been denied. And women are denied rights all over the world, whether developed or developing. All over the world women are subjected to domes-

Benazir Bhutto in 1996
(Oliver Mark)

tic violence. Often a woman does not walk out for she has nowhere to go. . . .

It is my firm conviction that a woman cannot ultimately control her own life and make her own choices unless she has financial independence. A woman cannot have financial independence if she cannot work. The discrimination against women can only begin to erode when women are educated and women are employed. If my father had not educated me or left me with independent financial means, I would not have been able to sustain myself or to struggle against tyranny or to stand here before you today as a special guest speaker. . . .

When I visit poverty-stricken villages with no access to clean drinking water, it gladdens my heart to see a lady health visitor, to see a working woman amidst the unfortunate surroundings. For it is my conviction that we can only conquer poverty, squalor, illiteracy and superstition when we invest in our women and when our women begin working:

Begin working in our far-flung villages where time seems to have stood still and where the bullock, not the tractor, is still used for cultivation.

Where women are too weak from bearing too many children.

Where the daughters are more malnourished than the sons for the daughters get to eat the leftovers.

Where villagers work night and day with their women and children to eke out an existence.

Where floods and rain wash out crops and destroy homes.

Where poverty stalks the land with an appetite that cannot be controlled until we wake up to the twin reality of population control and women's empowerment.

And it is here that the United Nations and its Secretary General have played a critical role. . . .

The holding of this conference demonstrates that women are not forgotten, that the world cares. . . .

As women, we draw satisfaction from Beijing Platform for Action which encompasses a comprehensive approach towards the empowerment of women.

But women cannot be expected to struggle alone against the forces of discrimination and exploitation. I recall the words of Dante who reminded us that "the hottest place in Hell is reserved for those who remain neutral in times of moral crisis."

Today in this world, in the fight for the liberation of women, there can be no neutrality. But my dear sisters, we have learned that democracy alone is not enough. Freedom of choice alone does not guarantee justice. Equal rights are not defined only by political values. Social justice is a triad of freedom, of equality, of liberty: Justice is political liberty. Justice is economic independence. Justice is social equality. . . .

The use of rape as a weapon of war and an instrument of "ethnic cleansing" is as depraved as it is reprehensible. The unfolding of this saga in different parts of the world, including Jammu and Kashmir and Bosnia Herzegovina, has shaken the conscience of the entire international community. The enormity of the tragedy dwarfs our other issues—urgent though they are. This conference must, therefore, express its complete solidarity with our sisters and daughters who are victims of armed conflict, oppression, and brutality. Their misfortunes must be our first priority. . . .

We must shape a world free from exploitation and maltreatment of women. A world in which women have opportunities to rise to the highest level in politics, business, diplomacy, and other spheres of life. Where there are no battered women. Where honor and dignity is protected in war and conflict. Where we have economic freedom and independence. Where we are equal partners in peace and development. A world equally committed to economic development and political development. A world as committed to free markets as to women's emancipation.

And even as we catalogue, organize, and reach our goals, step by step by step, let us be ever vigilant. Repressive forces always will stand ready to exploit the moment and push us back into the past.

Let us remember the words of the German writer, Goethe: "Freedom has to be re-made and re-earned in every generation." We must do much more than decry the past. We must change the future.

Remembering the words of a sister parliamentarian, Senator Barbara Mikulski, that "demography is destiny," I believe time, justice and the forces of history are on our side. . . .

Glossary

Barbara Mikulski: Barbara Ann Mikulski (1936–), U.S. senator from Maryland (1987–2017) at the time of the speech

Beijing Platform for Action: a global policy framework adopted by 189 countries in 1995 to realize gender equality through certain policies and programs

Dante: Dante Alighieri, fourteenth-century poet and philosopher; author of the *Divine Comedy*, whose depictions of hell, purgatory, and heaven influenced the Christian religion and Western literature

ethnic cleansing: the systematic expulsion or killing of specific groups to eradicate their people and culture from an area

Goethe: Johan Wolfgang von Goethe (1749–1832), German poet, playwright, and statesman

Holy Book of the Muslims: the Koran

Islamic: related to Islam, the religious faith of Muslims

Muslim: an adherent of Islam

"my father": Zulfikar Ali Bhutto (1928–1979), the fourth president of Pakistan (1971–73) and ninth prime minister of Pakistan (1973–77), and the founder and chair of the Pakistan People's Party

"this conference": the Fourth World Conference on Women, held by the United Nations in Beijing, China, in 1995 to discuss areas of gender inequality around the world and set objectives to advance women's rights

Short-Answer Questions

1. Describe Bhutto's use of quotations in her speech. Are they effective? What do they teach us about Bhutto as a speaker?

2. How does Bhutto see the relationship between international policy and gender equality?

3. Using the text provided, how does Bhutto's Muslim background shape her approach to women's issues and gender inequality? How might this context set her perspective apart from others?

Charlotte Bunch: "Through Women's Eyes: Global Forces Facing Women in the 21st Century"

Author
Charlotte Bunch

Date
1995

Document Type
Speeches/Addresses

Significance
Argued for the necessity of women's perspectives and participation in global policy and human rights activism

Overview

Charlotte Bunch, an American feminist scholar, started several organizations throughout the 1970s and 1980s to connect women and create activist coalitions. She was influenced by her upbringing in the Christian church to pursue social justice into adulthood. Before starting the Women's Institute for Freedom of the Press in 1977, Bunch published *Women's Liberation*, *Quest: A Feminist Quarterly*, and *The Furies*, a short-lived lesbian newspaper, out of Washington, D.C. Bunch also founded the Center for Women's Global Leadership in 1989 at Rutgers University. The center lobbied international bodies, like Amnesty International and the United Nations, to prioritize women's rights as a global issue. Partially due to this activism, the United Nations organized the Fourth World Conference on Women: Action for Equality, Development, and Peace, held in Beijing, China in 1995.

Bunch delivered the address "Through Women's Eyes" at that conference, where she argued for the necessity of women's perspectives in global policy and human rights activism. Bunch also used her speech to criticize the inaction of governments and the United Nations when it came to addressing women's rights before the 1990s. The phrase "through women's eyes" has become a common slogan and title for feminist publications and organizations since 1995.

The Beijing Platform for Action was adopted at the Fourth World Conference, creating a policy blueprint for women's rights that included sections on education, the environment, reproduction, and health but did not authorize new organizations dedicated to women's issues. Bunch continued her activism after 1995, working with the Gender Equality Architecture Reform campaign to urge the United Nations to create a body specifically focused on gender issues. In 2010, the work culminated in the creation of the United Nations Entity for Gender Equality and the Empowerment of Women, commonly known as UN Women.

Charlotte Bunch (Wikimedia Commons)

Document Text

This conference is occurring at a critical juncture in time throughout the world because it is a time of transition—a time when the ways of governing, the ways of living and of doing business, the ways of interacting amongst people and nations are in flux. In my region, Europe and North America, which has a long history of war and domination that has affected the entire globe, we see this transition in what is called the end of the cold war. We have now what I call the hot peace. Rather than a truly peaceful era, we are seeing a shift in power blocs in which the anticipated peace dividend has turned instead into increased racial, ethnic, religious and gender-based conflicts and violence. In this escalation, the role of women—questions of women's human rights and the violation of women as a symbol of their cultures and peoples—has become central.

These global changes are offering both opportunity and danger for women, as in any time of crisis. The opportunity is there for women to offer new solutions, to enter the public policy debate in a way that we have never been able to do before. And the danger is that even those advances we have made in this century will be reversed if we are not able to take this opportunity to move forward. When I talk about women entering the global policy debates and influencing those discussions, I don't see this as totally separate from, but rather building on, the work that women are already doing. Women are usually the leaders at the local community level. Women are the leaders who have held families and communities together in times of crisis. Women have managed budgets that were inadequate to raise children and have managed to keep people together in times of war and other conflicts. And yet, as power moves up the ladder from that local community to national and international policy making, women's voices and women themselves disappear. . . .

The challenge in terms of human rights is to find a model that shows one can have respect for the common humanity and universality of the human rights of every person regardless of gender, race, ethnicity, religion, sexual orientation, age, disability, etc., while also respecting and creating space for the incredible multicultural diversity that exists among us so that everyone doesn't have to become like the dominant group in order to have rights. Human rights is not static but is an evolving concept that responds to how people see their human needs and dignity over time. Thus as people exercise their human right to self-determination there will always be a dynamic process of both expanding the concept and ensuring that the exercise of rights does not allow for domination over others. . . .

Seeing the importance of the recognition of women's human rights and the need of all these nationalistic and fundamentalist movements to control women's sexuality, reproduction, and labor helps us understand why this conference and the Cairo conference are under so much attack. These events represent women's efforts to move into the global arena, to have a voice, to become a global force that must be reckoned with. When I look at the list of the global forces that we are to speak about today, I realize the one most important to me is the global force of women in movement around the world today. This global force of women around the world has many different names—call it feminist, call it womanist, call it women in development, call it women's rights or women's human rights. Call it many different things, because each of us has found different terms that describe best for us that reality of domination and change. Women are the most important new global force on the horizon in the world today with the potential to create a more humane future and a humane global governance.

For women to be such a force, however, carries great responsibility. We cannot be a movement that thinks and speaks only from our own experiences. We began our movement in this past few decades with the concept that the personal is political and with the need to put women's experiences on the agenda because these were missing. Women's issues, women's perspectives, women's experiences were and still often are left out of policy deliberations. But if we don't want to be simply an added-on dimension, we must also bring in all those whose voices are not heard—all the diverse women and men whose voices have been muted—so that we show it is possible for this world to hear from all its peoples. . . .

Finally, at this conference, we must take one step further into the global arenas of this decade. I think of these UN world conferences as global town meetings. They are opportunities where we meet and talk to each other across the lines of nationality, across lines that we don't often have other opportunities to cross. But as global town meetings, they are also occasions for us to show the world our visions. Looking at the world through women's eyes is an excellent slogan for this forum because this is the place where we can demonstrate the visions of possibility that come from women. . . . We are participating now, we are watching, we are demanding, and we are here to see if this can become the arena of real participation where global governance and policies can be created with a human face that is both male and female and where all the diversity of both male and female can emerge. And if this does not prove possible, women must say to the United Nations and to all of our governments that we have a vision for the future and that is where we are going. We hope that they will allow us to participate and to lead. If they don't, we will take leadership anyway and show that the world can be better for all in the twenty-first century.

Glossary

cold war: a state of tension between the United States and the Soviet Union, along with those nations' allies, that lasted from the end of World War II to the dissolution of the Soviet Union in 1991

self-determination: the process by which a person, group, or state controls their own decision making without coercion

"the Cairo conference": the International Conference on Population and Development (ICPD), held by the United Nations in Cairo, Egypt, in September 1994

"this conference": the Fourth World Conference on Women, held by the United Nations in Beijing, China, in 1995 to discuss areas of gender inequality around the world and set objectives to advance women's rights

Short-Answer Questions

1. How does Bunch define or describe seeing the world "through women's eyes"?

2. Does Bunch propose a concrete plan for women's empowerment into the twenty-first century? Use specific examples from the text to explain how she does or does not give detailed objectives.

3. Bunch writes that the "personal is political" in the fifth paragraph of the text. What do you think this means? What examples can you think of that illustrate Bunch's point?

Charlotte Bunch: "Through Women's Eyes: Global Forces Facing Women in the 21st Century"

Queen Noor of Jordan: Remarks at the National Organization for Arab-American Women Banquet

Author
Queen Noor of Jordan

Date
1995

Document Type
Presidential/Executive; Speeches/Addresses

Significance
Encouraged Arab-American and other women to work for international women's empowerment

Overview

Queen Noor of Jordan was born and raised in the United States to a father of Syrian-Lebanese descent and a mother of Swedish descent. She studied architecture and urban planning before taking a series of jobs designing cities in Australia, Iran, and the United Kingdom. Drawn to the Middle East because of her heritage, Queen Noor started working for Royal Jordanian Airlines in the late 1970s, where she met King Hussein of Jordan. She married King Hussein in 1978 and converted to Islam. Queen Noor was accepted for her conversion and her Arabic ancestry and became an active public figure involved in urban planning, economic development, and women's empowerment in Jordan.

The United Nations hosted a banquet in 1995 for the National Organization for Arab-American Women, a grassroots group that seeks to connect Arab-American women to fight for social justice. As an Arab-American woman, Queen Noor gave a speech on the evolving status of women in the Middle East, the importance of democracy, and the need to fight for women's empowerment. She includes statistics that counter popular Western ideas about instability in the Middle East and show areas of both growth and opportunity. Queen Noor finishes by stressing the importance of cross-cultural collaboration for women's rights.

After King Hussein's death in 1999, his first son took power, and Queen Noor stepped away from the crown. She remains a prominent figure in Jordan and around the world due to her continued philanthropic and activist work across the Middle East and the globe since being widowed. Her work continues to revolve around women, children, and the family, but she has also started organizations and initiatives focusing on the arts, environmentalism, and community growth.

Document Text

I am delighted to join you here today at the United Nations, and I am honored to accept this international award for the promotion of development, democracy and peace. Had my life's journey not taken me to Jordan, I might still have been here with you tonight—perhaps not as the recipient of this award, but very possibly as an active Arab-American, pledged to the personal and professional advancement of women and to inter-cultural understanding. Throughout my life, I have shared your sense of pride in the extraordinary achievements of both the Arab and American cultures. I also share your commitment to promote constructive communication, and mutual respect between the United States and the Arab world....

If we are to advance beyond the futile rivalries, inequities and violence, we must reassess our past differences and look towards reinforcing national achievements and strengths with the immeasurably greater forces of regional integration and economies of scale; and we must develop a common vision of our future based on our shared history and strong cultural bonds. For the past half century, we have suffered the debilitating military and economic constraints of the armed conflict with Israel. And we have failed to generate adequate popular participation in socio-economic development and political affairs. The new Middle East that we seek to pass on to our children offers the promise of peace, development and stability. But it is impossible to speak credibly of these, without speaking of social justice, political participation and fundamental human rights. Our countries of the Middle East face the common challenge to mobilize the talents and energies of all their members to achieve economic and political development that is sustainable, equitable and responsive to real needs.

The development experience of many nations in the past decades has highlighted the primacy of the role of women and the importance of their education and participation in local and national affairs in the attainment of these goals.

Queen Noor in 1996
(Wikimedia Commons)

While in all Arab societies, women still face varying degrees of legal and social obstacles to their personal development professional fulfillment and participation in public and political life, large numbers of women have nevertheless contributed to and benefited from the development momentum of recent decades. Unlike their prevalent portrayal in the West, many Arab women are educated, deeply involved in family and local community decisions, and increasingly active in political, professional and economic life at the national level. The rising level of education of Arab girls and women has been one of the most profound and positive forces of change in our region.

It is a tribute to Arab women that in the past decade, the Middle East registered the world's fastest decline in the under-five mortality rate . . . while simultaneously registering the world's worst economic performance. . . . While Arab economies were generally regressing, the health of Arab children actually improved—primarily because a better educated generation of young women were able to translate their education and knowledge into good family health practices.

The greatest gains for women and for society as a whole have been achieved in those countries where women have improved their legal, educational and social status, but have not precipitously abandoned their traditional role as the strong anchor of the family unit.

Empowerment of women encourages a new regard for human rights and equitable social and political development. The empowerment of women cannot, however, be isolated from the empowerment of the entire community through more democratic and participatory decision-making. Local communities whose members are educated and self-reliant will be able to tap their own resources and dynamism to devise appropriate strategies to assure their well-being. Democratic participation has generated a dynamic that has energized entire societies. . . .

As a result, women have increased their participation in local community, economic and social affairs; family incomes have risen; female school enrollment rates have increased and drop-out rates have declined; migration to the cities has slowed; and we are beginning to notice a decline in fertility rates. The key to our success is the close collaboration of the men and women of local communities to determine their own goals and to devise strategies to achieve them. There has been a quantifiable improvement in the quality of life of individual families and entire communities, which have become more dynamic and self-reliant. I am particularly proud that these projects are considered national and regional development models by several international agencies, including the United Nations Population Fund and the World Health Organization. We have been asked to support their implementation in other Arab countries.

The two essential factors—gender equity and democracy—are anathema in many countries, but this successful combination has often been the difference between development that tangibly improves the quality of life of each new generation of infants, and unsustainable, inconsistent progress which relies heavily on subsidies and directives from central government. . . .

The world now has an exciting and historic opportunity to work together for human development goals which are deeply rooted in a common moral legacy of justice, humanism and peace. Yet this new momentum of hope and cooperation is threatened by disquieting predictions, appearing in the discourse of Western analysts, of an inevitable and violent clash of cultures, particularly between the Islamic and Western worlds. At this moment of global change and hope, it would be a great tragedy and a tremendous waste to allow the ideological polarization that characterized the Cold War era to be replaced by a civilizational confrontation, based on ignorance and unfounded fears. Our shared ethic and our interdependence for solving global challenges should naturally compel us to forge a promising new partnership based on understanding, mutual respect and cooperation.

The National Organization of Arab-American Women is particularly well placed to further better and clearer communication between our two worlds. Your understanding of the Arab and American cultures entails a special responsibility to promote a meaningful and constructive dialogue between our peoples. The cross-cultural activities and developmental aims of individuals and groups such as yourselves are pivotal to our hopes for a new world of tolerance, peace and development.

Thank you all again. I wish the conference much success and urge you to continue to pursue with enthusiasm your worthwhile endeavors. I remain your partner, always ready to contribute to the advancement of Arab women and women everywhere.

Glossary

Cold War era: the state of tension between the United States and the Soviet Union, along with those nations' allies, that lasted from the end of World War II to the dissolution of the Soviet Union in 1991

interdependence: the state of having one's success or failure connected to or reliant on the success or failure of another person or group

National Organization of Arab-American Women: a grassroots organization to connect American women of Arab descent toward a common goal of social justice

Short-Answer Questions

1. What does Queen Noor argue is the role of family in women's empowerment? Why do you think she frames it that way?

2. Does Queen Noor emphasize initiatives in Jordan or initiatives across the Middle East? How might this change the way the audience receives her message?

3. Based on the contents and tone of the speech, why do you think this address was given to Arab-American women? Why was this speech not addressed to Arab women instead?

Wangari Maathai:
Nobel Peace Prize Acceptance Speech

Author
Wangari Maathai

Date
2004

Document Type
Speeches/Addresses

Significance
Described environmentalism as a tool for human rights and women's empowerment

Overview

Born in a small Kenyan town, Wangari Maathai excelled in Catholic primary school and earned degrees in the United States and Germany before earning her Ph.D. at the University of Nairobi. Although she did not witness it personally, Maathai lived through the Mau Mau uprising (1952–60) and the end of British colonialism in Kenya. Her background in biology and anatomy helped her identify the importance of environmental conservation as a success factor for Kenya due to the opportunities and resources it brought to communities and families, particularly in the unrest and instability after Kenya declared independence in 1963. In 1976, Maathai joined the National Council of Women of Kenya and began promoting the idea of planting trees to rural women—an idea that became the Green Belt Movement in 1977.

Maathai attended the Third World Conference on women held by the United Nations in Nairobi in 1985, where she made connections and gained funding that expanded the Green Belt Movement to other African countries. While the international attention led to many accolades for Maathai, the Kenyan government criticized her. The repressive government ordered the Green Belt Movement to separate from the National Council of Women of Kenya because governmental officials viewed the two organizations as having different causes, and they criticized Green Belt meetings and activities for the movement's advocacy of democracy. Maathai and the Green Belt Movement continued to plant trees both for their environmental impact and as a form of peaceful protest.

In 2002, Maathai was elected to the Kenyan parliament. She established the Mazingira Green Party of Kenya in 2003 as an outgrowth of the existing Liberal Party of Kenya, and she served as assistant minister for environment and natural resources between 2003 and 2005. In 2004, Maathai became the first African woman and the first environmentalist to receive the Nobel Peace Prize. Her acceptance speech gives an overview of the organization's history and the impacts of tree planting on rural communities. She specifically focuses on the ways that both the act and environmental effect of planting trees empower women.

Document Text

As the first African woman to receive this prize, I accept it on behalf of the people of Kenya and Africa, and indeed the world. I am especially mindful of women and the girl child. I hope it will encourage them to raise their voices and take more space for leadership. I know the honour also gives a deep sense of pride to our men, both old and young. As a mother, I appreciate the inspiration this brings to the youth and urge them to use it to pursue their dreams.

Although this prize comes to me, it acknowledges the work of countless individuals and groups across the globe. They work quietly and often without recognition to protect the environment, promote democracy, defend human rights and ensure equality between women and men. By so doing, they plant seeds of peace. I know they, too, are proud today. To all who feel represented by this prize, I say use it to advance your mission and meet the high expectations the world will place on us. . . .

In 1977, when we started the Green Belt Movement, I was partly responding to needs identified by rural women, namely lack of firewood, clean drinking water, balanced diets, shelter and income.

Throughout Africa, women are the primary caretakers, holding significant responsibility for tilling the land and feeding their families. As a result, they are often the first to become aware of environmental damage as resources become scarce and incapable of sustaining their families.

The women we worked with recounted that unlike in the past, they were unable to meet their basic needs. This was due to the degradation of their immediate environment as well as the introduction of commercial farming, which replaced the growing of household food crops. But international trade controlled the price of the exports from these small-scale farmers, and a reasonable and just income could not be guaranteed. I came to understand that when the environment is destroyed,

Photograph of Wangari Maathai
(Wikimedia Commons)

plundered or mismanaged, we undermine our quality of life and that of future generations.

Tree planting became a natural choice to address some of the initial basic needs identified by women. Also, tree planting is simple, attainable and guarantees quick, successful results within a reasonable amount time. This sustains interest and commitment.

So, together, we have planted over 30 million trees that provide fuel, food, shelter, and income to support their children's education and household needs. The activity also creates employment and improves soils and watersheds. Through their involvement, women gain some degree of power over their lives, especially their social and economic position and relevance in the family. This work continues.

Initially, the work was difficult because historically our people have been persuaded to believe that because they are poor, they lack not only capital, but also knowledge and skills to address their challenges. Instead they are conditioned to believe that solutions to their problems must come from "outside." Further, women did not realize that meeting their needs depended on their environment being healthy and well managed. They were also unaware that a degraded environment leads to a scramble for scarce resources and may culminate in poverty and even conflict. They were also unaware of the injustices of international economic arrangements.

In order to assist communities to understand these linkages, we developed a citizen education program, during which people identify their problems, the causes and possible solutions. They then make connections between their own personal actions and the problems they witness in the environment and in society. They learn that our world is confronted with a litany of woes: corruption, violence against women and children, disruption and breakdown of families, and disintegration of cultures and communities. They also identify the abuse of drugs and chemical substances, especially among young people. There are also devastating diseases that are defying cures or occurring in epidemic proportions. Of particular concern are HIV/AIDS, malaria and diseases associated with malnutrition.

On the environment front, they are exposed to many human activities that are devastating to the environment and societies. These include widespread destruction of ecosystems, especially through deforestation, climatic instability, and contamination in the soils and waters that all contribute to excruciating poverty.

In the process, the participants discover that they must be part of the solutions. They realize their hidden potential and are empowered to overcome inertia and take action. They come to recognize that they are the primary custodians and beneficiaries of the environment that sustains them. . . .

Those of us who have been privileged to receive education, skills, and experiences and even power must be role models for the next generation of leadership. In this regard, I would also like to appeal for the freedom of my fellow laureate Aung San Suu Kyi so that she can continue her work for peace and democracy for the people of Burma and the world at large.

Culture plays a central role in the political, economic and social life of communities. Indeed, culture may be the missing link in the development of Africa. Culture is dynamic and evolves over time, consciously discarding retrogressive traditions, like female genital mutilation (FGM), and embracing aspects that are good and useful.

Africans, especially, should re-discover positive aspects of their culture. In accepting them, they would give themselves a sense of belonging, identity and self-confidence. . . .

I would like to call on young people to commit themselves to activities that contribute toward achieving their long-term dreams. They have the energy and creativity to shape a sustainable future. To the young people I say, you are a gift to your communities and indeed the world. You are our hope and our future.

The holistic approach to development, as exemplified by the Green Belt Movement, could be embraced and replicated in more parts of Africa and beyond. It is for this reason that I have established the Wangari Maathai Foundation to ensure the continuation and expansion of these activities. Although a lot has been achieved, much remains to be done.

Glossary

Green Belt Movement: a Kenyan grassroots organization that both empowers women and fights deforestation through tree planting

sustainable: able to maintain a particular culture, set of resources, and population effectively over time

"this prize": the 2004 Nobel Peace Prize

Short-Answer Questions

1. How does Maathai connect environmental protection, democracy, and women's rights? Are they separate issues, or does Maathai describe a relationship between them?

2. How does Maathai define culture? How does culture play a role in empowerment and development?

3. Using what you know about this speech and its context, how was Maathai influenced by the process of decolonization? How explicitly does Maathai discuss this aspect of her work?

Betty Williams: "Peace in the World Is Everybody's Business"

Author
Betty Williams

Date
2007

Document Type
Speeches/Addresses

Significance
Depicted the beginning of one woman's grassroots activism for peace in Northern Ireland that grew to pursue peace around the world

Overview

Peace activist Betty Williams, the recipient of the 1976 Nobel Peace Prize, delivered the address "Peace in the World Is Everybody's Business" on September 20, 2007, at Soka University of America. In her speech, she spoke about the anti-Catholic sentiment in Northern Ireland that led to the incident that inspired her to become a reluctant activist.

The 1960s brought the fight for civil and human rights to the forefront worldwide. In the United States, the fight for civil rights focused on the rights of African Americans, who were discriminated against based on race, perpetuated by white Americans. In Northern Ireland, the fight for civil and human rights focused on the rights of Catholics, who were discriminated against based on religion, perpetuated by Protestants. Both groups battled against institutional discrimination, including segregation, voter suppression, and inequalities in education, employment, and housing. In her speech, Williams spoke of being one of only fifteen Catholics at Queens University of Belfast, Northern Ireland, out of a student body of 4,000.

Williams described in detail the senseless murder in 1976 of three children, John, Joanne, and Andrew MacGuire, on a street in Belfast, an event that became the catalyst of her activism. After witnessing the shooting, she created a movement to end the violence between Protestants and Catholics in Northern Ireland. She began collecting signatures from the community, spoke to the media, and organized peace marches with the deceased children's aunt, Mairead Corrigan. Shortly after the fourth and final march, attended by a quarter million people, the pair created a peace organization called the Community of Peace People in 1976 to end the violence in Northern Ireland. The mission of the organization expanded globally when Williams visited regions of conflict in Asia and Africa. At the conclusion of her address, Williams includes a short poem that promotes the pursuit of peace around the world.

A scene from the Troubles in Northern Ireland, which ignited Williams's activism
(Wikimedia Commons)

Document Text

I was born and brought up in Belfast, Northern Ireland; I'm the daughter of a wonderful father who was a butcher, and my mother, who was a waitress. I was brought up in a poor area of the city of Belfast called Andersonstown, which is commonly known as Catholic Ghetto. And I know of all my life being brought up, the injustices that were perpetrated upon the Catholic people of Northern Ireland were absolutely gross. We can make similarities between what happens to the Black people of the United States and what happened to the Catholic Irish people. It was really bad. We couldn't vote, we couldn't own property, we had to take the most menial of jobs, and we certainly hadn't got access to education. But my father pushed us: "Education, education, education. The only way forward, is if you're educated." And so, I became educated. And when I went to university in Northern Ireland, Queens University of Belfast, in a student body of 4,000, there were fifteen Catholics. . . .

But something happened to me on August 10, 1969, when I was driving home from my mother's house. And my daughter was in the back of the car, in her little car seat, and I heard shots from outside. And I suddenly realized how sick I was because I could distinguish gun fire. Imagine being able to distinguish gun fire. And I heard shots from an ArmaLite rifle, which was the rifle of choice used by Provisional IRA. And I heard a return fire from an SLR, which is the "self-loading rifle," used by the British army. And as I turned off the main road, down onto the avenue where I lived, a car came careening out of control, round the corner, right to the pavement, and slammed into a woman and her children. I was the first one on the scene. I had never seen, and I hope you'll never witness, the carnage like I did. You don't see my little angels, but I will never leave home without them. Their names are John, Joanne, and

Andrew MacGuire—those of the three children who were killed that day, slaughtered that day, on a Belfast street. And I remember sitting in my car and looking at the scene, thinking, "Well, what can I do?" . . . And I remember holding little Joanne in my arms, in shock. Covered in her blood and whispering in her ear "I love you." And saying to myself, "I've got to do something to make sure that this doesn't happen to any more children in Northern Ireland."

I remember going home. I remember taking my little girl out of her car seat. I remember my sister coming in and making me a cup of tea. . . . I remember coming back into my living room with my son sitting, doing his homework. And I lifted the page he was writing on, and I jumped in my car, and I went up into what was Provisional IRA territory and I began banging on doors. And I wasn't very nice about it, believe me; I was yelling, screaming at the women: "We can't live like this anymore. We've got to do something to change this society." And I had the piece of paper in my hand, and I said to the woman: "Sign this!" She said, "What I am signing?" And I wrote across the top of it, "Petition for Peace." And that's how it began. And then, it was rather like being the Pied Piper of Hamelin.

All the women who had held these feelings that I was feeling—I only gave voice to what they were feeling. And they were coming out in the hundreds, and we started collecting signatures for peace. Within six hours—not two days, *six hours*—we had 5,000 signatures for peace. . . .

And we marched to the graveyard, to say goodbye to the children, Joanne, John, and Andrew. And then I planned a series of rallies. "Oh, thank you God, *somebody came*!" Ten thousand, you know! If you don't believe in miracles, trust me, miracles happen because I witnessed one that day. So, I called a series of rallies, twelve in all. And I called them all over Northern Ireland, Republic of Ireland, England, Scotland, and Wales. So every time we marched in Northern Ireland, there would be a coinciding march somewhere on the mainland England, Wales, or Scotland, or the New Republic. The second march, 35,000. The third march, 40,000. And up and up and up they went every week, until our final rally in Trafalgar square—we had a quarter million people at that rally. . . .

I then began to write the Declaration of the Community of the Peace People, and we had signatures on that, 250,000 signed up on that, so I knew we'd have a little more than ten workers, and then we went on to get on with the reality of what we've got to do. Northern Ireland had a population of 1.5 million people, with an unemployment problem of fourteen and a half percent. And pocket areas where that went up as high as 93 percent without a job, social violence of the worst kind. We had the worst housing conditions in Western Europe. . . .

Second thing we set about doing was rebuilding, rehousing. . . . And then I think one of the most important things that we did, we opened the first integrated school in Ireland's history. Now integration here [in the United States] meant Black and White. Integration in Northern Ireland was Catholic and Protestant.

Mairead and I got the Nobel Peace Prize, which is a pretty vague—you know, I personally don't think that there are any famous people in the world. There are just people who *think* they are, you know, which is totally different. . . .

We received the Nobel Peace Prize and I've said, from that day forth, "The Nobel Peace Prize is not given for what one has done but, hopefully, for what one will do." And because the Peace Movement of Ireland started with the death of the children, I would be sent to go around countries all over the world, where children were in dire need and where children were suffering beyond belief. . . . It was the most incredibly painful way to learn about how much suffering goes on when children are neglected, abused, and punished, in wars that they do not declare and haven't a say in. . . .

And I'd like to finish by saying to you, this is my little dream. And hopefully, if I've managed to reach one of you in this audience, I will have done a great day's work. If I reached more than one, halleluiah! But really, one is all I'm looking for, because that one will change twenty on their way.

> I dreamt of a world without sorrow,
> and I dreamt of a world without hate,
> I dreamt of a world rejoicing,
> And I walked to find Christ at my gate.
>
> I dreamt of a world without hunger,
> and I dreamt of a world without war,
> I dreamt of a world full of loving,
> And I walked to find Allah at my door.
>
> I dreamt of a world without anger,
> And I dreamt of a world without pride,
> I dreamt of a world of compassion,
> And I walked to find Buddha at my side.
>
> I dreamt of this world of tomorrow,
> And I dreamt of this world set apart,
> I dreamt of this world full of glory,
> And I walked to find my Creator in my heart.

Glossary

ghetto: a portion of a city occupied by a minority group, particularly due to social, racial, or economic pressure

pavement: the word for "sidewalk" in British English

Provisional IRA: the Provisional Irish Republican Army, a militia that sought to end British rule in Northern Ireland and reunify all of Ireland into a republic

Trafalgar Square: a public square in central London, England, and a common site for celebrations and political demonstrations

Short-Answer Questions

1. What does the excerpt reveal about traditional attitudes toward Catholics in Northern Ireland? How does the author compare it to the treatment of African Americans in the United States?

2. Describe how the loss of life, especially among children, galvanized a community.

3. Analyze how the short poem at the end of the speech promotes inclusivity in the pursuit of peace.

"Elena's Story"

Author
Elena; Zara Marselian

Date
2010

Document Type
Essays, Reports, Manifestos

Significance
Demonstrates the perseverance and resilience of women and the ways their lives are shaped by access to education, immigration, and economic opportunities

Overview

An oral history is when someone tells the story of their life and experiences, and another person records them or writes them down. This is Elena's story of her life, published in a collection of such stories titled *The Soul Speaks* and compiled by Zara Marselian, the cofounder of an immigrant and refugee support center in San Diego, California, called La Maestra Community Health Centers. Elena immigrated from Belize to the United States in 1969. In subsequent decades, she traveled between the two countries, and her life was shaped by ongoing family relationships in both places. Her story revolves around her hope and aspirations for better education and job opportunities. She first moved to New Orleans to further her education. She started off in New Orleans not knowing anyone and with only $125. Through grit, determination, and hard work, she managed to provide for herself, but she encountered numerous obstacles to achieving her educational and professional goals.

She persisted in spite of two marriages in which she described her husbands as abusive and unsupportive of her work and career ambitions. Throughout her career, she gravitated toward work that helped women, immigrants, and low-income communities by providing resources like job placement and translation services. She had to navigate her career aspirations with her challenging personal circumstances, including abusive husbands, a cancer diagnosis and treatment, and caring for her children.

Elena is not a famous woman, and she did not have great wealth or political power. Her story is included as one of the many "ordinary" women who, throughout time, did extraordinary things in an effort to seek safety for themselves and their children, to pursue an education, and to secure a more stable economic future for their families.

In this passage, Elena recounts the poverty her family experienced in her childhood but also the skills and resilience she learned from her parents. Throughout this oral history, she points to the hard work she saw her mother and other women perform against great odds to provide for their children. In the opening paragraph when she says "this country," she is talking about the United States and the women she works with who are immigrants and refugees there.

Document Text

I have arrived at a point in my life where I am doing things that are really important to me. I work with women. Not just any women, but truly destitute women—women who have been forced to leave their countries behind for the sake of their children. One of the things I saw while growing up was that women were the best managers. Women could make do with almost nothing. My mother was a great example of this. Even when it seemed like there was nothing to eat, she would figure something out. My mother raised chickens and she would barter, trading the chickens for supplies for our family. I remember thinking then that if a woman could do so much with nothing, how much better could she do if she had even a little bit of money? Everything my mother did was for her children—nothing was for her. When I wanted things for myself, she would call me selfish. Thinking back, I know my mother was right. I also know that that I am where I am today because of my mother's upbringing. She helped me to understand why the women I work with are here in this country, why they put their own needs and desires aside. It is all for their children.

It was July 1969 when I first came to the United States. I was in the states on a visitor's visa from Belize. A friend of mine, a fellow teacher from Belize, convinced me that I could study at Tulane University....

I was a stranger in a strange land with only 125 dollars cash. I found a phone book and worked my way through until I found a boarding house with a vacancy. The weekly rate was 35 dollars and included two daily meals....

I came from an extremely poor family, and a culture that did not believe in divorce....

As a child, it was difficult getting up each morning to see how my mother and father struggled to put food on the table. My mother would get up early every morning to cook and bake so that it would be ready in time for us to go out and sell it, bringing home just enough money for breakfast. Her pots were smoke-stained black because she cooked over an open fire. The fire would be lit each morning, and stoked throughout the day so that she could keep cooking and keep baking. I knew there had to be an easier way of life. My father would purchase sacks of pumpkin seeds for my mother to toast. Then my siblings and I would go out at night, with cans on our heads, to sell them. We would measure out a penny's worth of seeds using an empty match box. When we had sold all of our seeds, we would come home. My parents always sent the same three of us, because we had the best sales skills of all the children. We would strategically place ourselves at the ticket counter just outside the theater. I would tell the ticket buyers, "You will want to snack on these seeds while you are enjoying the movie." There were other sales people as well, and we would sometimes get in fights over territory. My sisters and brothers who did not excel in sales as well as the three of us were sent out to deliver orders of cakes and other food. My mom would make bean fritters with sauce and we would take them to school to sell during morning recess so that we could bring the money home at lunchtime. Then we would take something else to sell during the afternoon recess. My parents were very strict about homework, so we had to hurry and finish that before we were allowed to go out at night to sell....

Life presently [in the United States] seems to consist of a series of tragedies. Sometimes I lie awake at night, thinking about the events of the past two years. But a voice deep inside reminds me of the principle that has guided my life for as long as I can remember—the gifts that God granted me are not for my own good, but for the good of my fellow man. Along with these words comes the consolation that I am still in obedience, and that good things are in store for me.

1 am reminded of the women that I work with, of how their lives have been a struggle not for just two years, but forever. I think of Lidia, a refugee from Cuba, [who] came to this country in a boat. She risked her life to get here, and the fact that she is legally blind did not deter her. She says that death and life in Cuba are the same thing. To her, being in Cuba was a form of death. If she died at sea, at least her suffering would be over. Lidia and I met in 1998 when I was teaching English as a Second Language. She wanted to start a business of her own, but she had no money and no idea how to conduct business in America. La Maestra Community Health Centers partnered with a local foundation to initiate a microcredit program. . . .

Lidia presented her idea, and on the surface it seemed impossible because of her blindness. She proposed going to Los Angeles to buy surplus merchandise and reselling it at the swap meet. I asked how she would get to Los Angeles, and she replied, "*Hermana, si vine de Cuba y estoy viva coma no voy a ir a Los Angeles que es aqui mismo.*" (Sister, if I made it all the way from Cuba and I'm alive, how would I not be able to get to Los Angeles which is just nearby?) Her loan for $250 was approved. Lidia travels to Los Angeles by train, buys her merchandise and then transports it to the swap meet on the trolley or bus. The bus drivers all know her, and help her to get on the bus with her bags of merchandise and table. She does not limit her sales to the swap meet, but instead moves from person to person on the trolley. She tells them that she is on her way to the swap meet, but can sell them anything they'd like right then and there.

The microcredit program has a savings component built in. When Lidia paid off her loan, she was given proprietorship over her savings. She opened a bank account, and you would have thought that it had a million dollars. Lidia is now a US citizen with a bank account. She boasts about having achieved the American Dream. Lidia is on her third loan, and has hired two women to work for her. She supplies them with merchandise, and tells them how much money she expects back. If they sell it at a profit, then the profit is for them to keep.

Glossary

La Maestra Community Health Centers: an organization that provides health care and social services to immigrants and refugees in San Diego, California

microcredit program: a program in which small loans are given to individuals (particularly those with low incomes who may not have a credit history or collateral) who are looking to start businesses

refugee: according to the United Nations, "someone who has been forced to flee his or her country because of persecution, war or violence"; unlike some other types of immigrants, a refugee cannot return home, having been forced to flee, often without being able to bring anything with them

Short-Answer Questions

1. What kind of daily work did Elena do as a child, in addition to attending school?

2. What does Elena believe women will do if they have access to education and economic opportunities?

3. What is the benefit of preserving the oral histories of "ordinary" people?

"Fabienne's Story"

Author
Fabienne; Zara Marselian

Date
2010

Document Type
Essays, Reports, Manifestos

Significance
Illustrates the ways a woman's life is shaped by culture, religion, gender roles, legislation, and access to education

Overview

Fabienne grew up in the 1970s in Bangui, the capital of the Central African Republic. This document is an excerpt from the oral history of her life, in which she recounted her struggles growing up and her eventual decision to escape an abusive husband and move to the United States. Her account was recorded by Zara Marselian and published in *The Soul Speaks,* an anthology of real-life stories from around the world. Marselian is the cofounder of La Maestra Community Health Centers, which provides healthcare and social services to immigrants and refugees in San Diego, California.

Fabienne's story illustrates many of the issues that have faced—and continue to face—women and girls around the world. Although she is not a famous person, her story is a "milestone document" because it demonstrates the similarities in life circumstances that many ordinary women throughout time have experienced. Fabienne's story describes her struggle to access higher education, her lack of legal equality, her husband's control over her finances, children, and career, and a high level of physical violence.

Fabienne's childhood contained a marked educational disparity from her brother's. She was allowed to go to school, where she proved to be smart and successful. However, her mother did not fully support her education and would give away her schoolbooks, emphasizing that a girl's primary responsibility was to learn how to be a wife and mother. Her brother and, later, her husband would criticize and physically abuse her for seeming too smart, mocking her derisively with the name "Miss Education." Fortunately, she had a supportive high school principal who helped her achieve her goal of becoming a doctor.

When Fabienne was ten, she was sent to "circumcision camp" to undergo what the United Nations now calls female genital mutilation (FGM). Her best friend, Marianne, died at the camp as a result of the FGM procedure. For six weeks the girls were beaten, whipped, and taught how to be "good" women. Although her mother was a devout Christian, this was a cultural practice that members of their community practiced regardless of religious belief. Fabienne describes how the girls were made to lay outside in a row while adult women held them down and an older woman with a bloody knife performed the procedure. Marianne bled to death afterward. Fabienne had recurring urinary infections for the rest of her life as a result, and she later realized that she knew other women with very severe, even fatal, medical complications that resulted from the FGM.

In this passage, Fabienne describes how she was assigned an arranged marriage after returning from circumcision camp and was routinely physically inspected by her future mother-in-law. The man she was forced to marry as a teenager turned out to be violent and abusive, and he controlled Fabienne's career and took the money she made. He openly had mistresses while they were married. When Fabienne tried to leave, he would not allow her any access to her young children and moved other women into his house instead. A combination of law and custom severely limited Fabienne's ability to seek a divorce or gain access to her children. She made the painful decision to flee her husband by moving to a graduate program in the United States. Although Fabienne was a doctor in the Central African Republic, she faced a problem common to many immigrants to the United States: her professional qualifications did not transfer to the United States. She essentially had to start her medical career over again and began working at the community health center in San Diego, where she told this story of her life. After many years of separation, she was able to reunite with her children and bring them to the United States to be with her. Her story demonstrates the universal need for women and girls to have access to basic human rights like safety, education, and equality under the law. It also demonstrates the remarkable perseverance and fortitude of women like Fabienne who have survived and thrived despite so many obstacles.

Document Text

... Meanwhile, I continued to go to school as usual. The only problem was, I had two families to work for. I still had my chores and other duties in my original household. Additionally, I now belonged to the family of my future husband, so they wanted to know what I was capable of accomplishing as a wife. His relatives would call on me to go fetch water for them, cook for them, do grocery shopping, write or read letters for them—all kinds of things.

They also checked on me often to make sure that I was well-behaved. They paid a respected lady in the neighborhood to check on my virginity. Every month, the lady would come. She would meet with my mother and my future mother-in-law. They would say, "Go wash and come back. It's time." So I would quickly splash my parts to clean off any urine drops, take off my undies, come back and lie down. They would part my legs and each of them would check: first Auntie Lucia, then my mother-in-law, then my mother. They would look, touch, and say, "Just as we saw last month; still good." I'd wait until all three agreed; then I'd get up and get dressed. My mother felt especially proud and happy after these sessions. Several times, my mother-in-law requested that I be checked out between sessions because she said she had heard rumors. She would tell my mother, "Let's just do it, you and me, and if we see something suspicious, I will call Lucia."

When I got my period, it was a big catastrophe because the conventional wisdom was that virgins could not possibly "see the moon," as we call it. We were taught in camp that we should be "tight" with no hole for blood to come out. You get your period when you have been with a man and he has opened the way for blood to flow out. Girls who showed holes after the circumcision were suspected of being "loose" and referred to be sewn further. I was still a virgin when I got my first period. But again, I was not your typical girl. All my campmates had become mothers by the time I got married, although I was much older than most of them when we went to camp. My mother knew I was a virgin. Yet, I knew what she believed with regard to first menstruations. I could not tell her. We never discussed these kinds of things. I could not ask my sister. She had so many problems of her own that I doubted she could keep a secret. I suspected she would use this information as a chip to try to extort her freedom or some other concession from my mother or her family-in-law. I had to hide it. But how could I? I had a heavy flow right on my first cycle; blood smells and blood stains. Additionally, the way our communities were set up, the washrooms were usually located at the far end of the properties. When we went to wash, we would carry a bucket of water across the yard to the washroom. So if you carried a bucket to the bathroom three to four times a day, people would notice and start to talk. And your mother-in-law-to-be would certainly order a check-up. I was mortified. It was a very messy few days. It was humiliating. Not just that first cycle, but other cycles after that as well. Not just at home, but at school as well.

It was one of the most traumatic times in my life. I had not completely recovered from the shock of the camp yet and this happened. . . .

After I got married, my family responsibilities increased with the birth of my children. My responsibility to my mother's household increased because my siblings were also beginning to have children and I needed to help my mother care for my siblings and their children. My responsibilities in school increased when I entered medical school.

My life was quite unusual. I was initiated and betrothed at ten, but I did not marry until I was fifteen. . . .

I did not bear my first child until I was eighteen. . . .

My husband wanted me to be the perfect wife: a completely independent woman when it came to keeping the house, yet a completely submissive woman when it came to making decisions and spending money. We argued often. I felt crushed, I felt bullied. I had been bullied a lot by my brother growing up, so I resented my husband even more when he ridiculed me into submitting to his will.

I was unhappy in my early adult life. I was restless and angry. I started to join student marches and teachers who were picketing for their salaries. I felt close to underdog groups. I felt like I understood the problems of oppressed groups everywhere.

I resented that my husband was allowed to control my schedule in school. I was upset that he had easier access to the dean in my school than I did. I hated that he would beat me up for the smallest thing. First my brother, then my initiators, and now my husband. I resented that he and his family or friends knew about every move I made, and yet I didn't know how he spent his days. I did not like it that each time people talked to me they started with "if your husband agrees . . ." or "if it's OK with your husband . . ." Even my teachers! Even my family! I was miserable. I cried a lot—I still can't remember a day during my marriage when I did not shed a tear.

Glossary

circumcision: the term used in Fabienne's community for female genital mutilation (FGM), defined by the United Nations as "all procedures involving partial or total removal of the external female genitalia or other injury to the female genital organs for cultural or other non-medical reasons"

initiated and betrothed: sent to circumcision camp to endure genital mutilation and six weeks of beatings, and then promised to a husband in an arranged marriage

Short-Answer Questions

1. What did Fabienne's community think about the cause of menstruation? What does that tell you about the age at which girls were usually forced to marry?

2. What role did Fabienne's husband have in her life?

3. What responsibilities did Fabienne have outside of school?

Chapter 15

Justice Movements in the Twenty-first Century

On January 20, 2001, George W. Bush was inaugurated as president of the United States after one of the most contentious elections in U.S. history. It had come down to the electoral votes in the state of Florida, which Bush won by 537 votes after a recount was stopped and the result upheld by the Supreme Court in the case of *Bush v. Gore*. Less than nine months later, on September 11, 2001, Al-Qaeda militants hijacked airliners and launched suicide terrorist attacks that claimed 2,996 lives. The twenty-first century thus began in controversy and violence, while the tide of justice and women's rights movements ebbed and flowed.

Women's Rights in Afghanistan

In the United States, one reaction to the 9/11 attacks was the passing and signing of the USA Patriot Act on October 26, 2001, which considerably broadened the government's power of surveillance, policing, and prosecution of terrorist groups and arguably reflected a global tone for stronger governmental centralization, which in certain cases, as in Russia, devolved into autocracy. On the other hand, however, there was a greater realization of the plight of women and other persecuted groups living under repressive regimes—and the initial focus was on Taliban-ruled Afghanistan. After the Taliban, which had allowed Al-Qaeda to set up bases in Afghanistan, refused to hand over Al-Qaeda leader Osama Bin-Laden, American troops attacked, overthrew the Taliban, and established a government under which Afghan women enjoyed greater freedom and autonomy than they previously had. However, in August 2021, as U.S. troops withdrew, the Taliban reinstated their dominance, reversing much of the progress made in women's rights.

During the early months of 2020 the COVID-19 pandemic caused massive economic disruption, millions of deaths and hospitalizations (straining to the limits, and in some cases breaking, health care facilities and networks), and setting the stage for massive social upheavals. The most notable of these upheavals were the Black Lives Matter (BLM) protests. The murder in Minneapolis, Minnesota, on May 25, 2020, of a Black man, George Floyd, by white police officer Derek Chauvin ignited a series of nationwide protests and rioting. In some southern cities, notably Richmond, Virginia, the demonstrations against police brutality conjoined with attempts to destroy confederate statues and monuments. The increasing number of mass shootings generated a number of protests urging stricter gun control legislation—one of the most eloquent calls for reform came from eighteen-year-old Emma Gonzalez, a survivor of the horrific Parkland School shooting in 2018, in her speech "We Call B.S."

Women and the Rise of Social Justice Movements

These were years that social justice movements further solidified and developed around issues like global warming, transgender rights, and abortion rights, and these were countered by backlash. The administration of President Donald Trump (2017–2021) marked a pendulum swing away from U.S. governmental support for justice movements, while those of Barack Obama (2009–2017) and Joe Biden (2021–) saw greater advocacy. Women of all ages and backgrounds were at the forefront of environmental justice activism in these years: ranging from younger women like African American student Mari Copeny, a victim of the water contamination crisis in Flint, Michigan; the famed young Swedish climate change activist Greta Thunberg; and the Native American clean-water advocate Autumn Peltier. Women with a long-established public profile were also notable, including former First Lady Michelle Obama and Nigerian novelist Chimamanda Ngozi Adichie. In 2015 a milestone was reached when the United Nations established Women's Rights as its fifth Sustainable Development Goal.

Women in Africa and the Middle East

Women made visible progress in several spheres and even at times changed the direction of governments. In Liberia in 2003 massive protests by the Women of Liberia Mass Action for Peace movement led to the peace negotiations that ended the Second Liberian Civil War. This in turn paved the way for Ellen Johnson Sirleaf to be elected president of Liberia in 2006, the first woman in Africa to hold a presidential position. Sirleaf and one of the 2003 movement leaders, Leymah Gbowee, were awarded the Nobel Peace Prize in 2011 for their work in fostering women's rights. On June 24, 2018, the Women to Drive Movement in Saudi Arabia won a significant concession when the government lifted its ban on female drivers.

Another Nobel Peace Laureate (awarded for 2014, and at seventeen the youngest so honored), Malala Yousafzai, had almost been assassinated in Pakistan on October 12, 2012, for her advocacy of universal female education. She survived to continue her work and the publish her autobiography, *I Am Malala: The Girl Who Stood Up for Education and Was Shot by the Taliban*. Sirin Ebadi in Iran, Luisa Diogo and Josina Machel in Mozambique, and English actress Emma Watson have all contributed articulate and influential voices on the issues of female educational equality, the need to address violence by men against women and—in the case of Watson—the necessity of encouraging male involvement in women's rights causes.

The election of Donald Trump to the U.S. presidency sparked the Women's March on Washington, DC, on January 21, 2017, the day after his inauguration, in protest at his statements opposing reproductive and other women's rights. Featuring a noteworthy speech by Carmen Perez, it drew the largest single-day crowd of any prior protest in U.S. history.

New Female Heads of State and Government

A record number of women, in fact, became either heads of state, heads of government, or high-level officials between 2001 and 2023: in 2007 Nancy Pelosi became the first female Speaker of the U.S. House of Representatives; Michelle Bachelet served for two terms (2006–2010 and 2014–2018) as Chile's first woman president; Joyce Banda became the first female president of Malawi (2012–2014); Atifete Jahjaga was the first female president of Kosovo (2011–2016); and Kamala Harris was in 2016 elected as the United States's first woman vice president.

Further Reading

Books

Adichie, Chimamanda Ngozi. *Dear Ijeawele, or a Feminist Manifesto in Fifteen Suggestions.* New York: Anchor Books, 2018.

Al-Sharif, Manal. *Daring to Drive: A Saudi Woman's Awakening.* New York: Simon & Schuster, 2017.

Gbowee, Leymah, with Carol Mithers. *Mighty Be Our Powers: How Sisterhood, Prayer, and Sex Changed a Nation at War.* New York: Beast Books, 2011.

Kendall, Mikki. *Hood Feminism: Notes from the Women that a Movement Forgot.* New York: Penguin, 2020.

Morain, Dan. *Kamala's Way: An American Life.* New York: Simon & Schuster, 2021.

Obama, Michelle. *The Light We Carry: Overcoming in Uncertain Times.* New York: Crown, 2022.

Sirleaf, Ellen Johnson. *This Child Will be Great: Memoires of a Remarkable Life by Africa's First Woman President.* New York: HarperCollins Publishers, 2009.

Thunberg, Greta. *No One Is Too Small to Make a Difference.* New York: Penguin, 2019.

Washington, Harriet A. *A Terrible Thing to Waste: Environmental Racism and its Assault on the American Mind.* Boston: Little, Brown Spark, 2020.

Women's March Organizers. *Together We Rise: The Women's March: Behing the Scene at the Protest Heard Around the World.* New York: Dey Street Books, 2018.

Yousafzai, Malala. *I Am Malala: The Girl Who Stood Up for Education and Was Shot by the Taliban.* New York: Little, Brown, 2013.

Websites

"HeForShe." UN Women USA website, accessed September 12, 2023, https://unwomenusa.org/advocacy-3.

"Josina Z. Machel." One Billion Rising 2023, accessed September 12, 2023, https://www.onebillionrising.org/46423/josina-z-machel-mozambique/.

"Women's Role in Liberia's Reconstruction." United States Institute of Peace. May 1, 2007, https://www.usip.org/publications/2007/05/womens-role-liberias-reconstruction.

Shirin Ebadi:
"Iran Awakening: Human Rights, Women, and Islam"

Author
Shirin Ebadi

Date
2008

Document Type
Speeches/Addresses

Significance
Called for women to be treated equally under Iranian law and to end the violence against women and children

Overview

Shirin Ebadi, an Iranian lawyer, author, human rights activist, and winner of the Nobel Peace Prize in 2003, gave an address at the University of San Diego's Institute for Peace and Justice in San Diego, California, on February 7, 2008. In her address, Ebadi discussed the feminist movement in Iran and provided examples of the treatment of women and girls there as second-class citizens. The legal age of marriage for boys, she said, was fifteen years old and for girls was thirteen, but with permission from the girl's father or grandfather through the court system, a girl could be married at an earlier age. As another example, the judicial system disproportionately punished women and girls, as the criminal liability age was designated to be nine for girls and fifteen for boys.

Ebadi also spoke about the power the feminist movement was gaining in Iran and provided an example of a petition circulating asking for a review of laws against women in Iran that had signatures from both men and women. The purpose of her speech was to bring awareness of the continued suppression of human rights in Iran and to be a voice for those who were unsatisfied with the current situation.

Ebadi completed her law degree in 1969 and passed the qualifying exams to become the first woman judge in Iran, and in 1971 she earned a doctorate in law. She served as a judge until the Islamic Iranian Revolution in 1979, which prohibited women judges. She was subsequently downgraded to various positions in the courts and justice department until, in protest, she took early retirement. She worked writing books and articles until, in 1993 after years of trying, Ebadi was granted a license to practice law. Most of her clients were people unjustly persecuted by the government, and in 2000 she was arrested and imprisoned for criticizing the government by promoting the separation of religion and state ideology. In 2003, Ebadi was awarded the Nobel Peace Prize for her efforts to promote human rights for women, children, and political prisoners in Iran. Since 2009, Ebadi has lived in exile in the United Kingdom.

Shirin Ebadi
(Wikimedia Commons)

Document Text

Unlike the 20th century when peace was defined as the absence of war, in the 21st century, the absence of war alone does not define peace; rather, peace is a collection of conditions that provides for the basic needs of human beings, upholds human dignity, and rids human life from any threat. Hence, living on the brink of poverty, facing continuous violations of human rights, lacking the freedom to express belief or religion, and having the fear of unfair punishment are all contributors to the lack of peace in the 21st century.

I would like to seize this opportunity to report on the status of human rights in the past year in Iran. Iranian law is discriminatory against women. I would like to bring a few examples. The value of the life of a woman is considered half that of a man. Therefore, if a man and a woman run into a car accident on the street, the damage paid to the woman would be half that paid to a man. By the same token, it takes two women witnesses to substitute for one male witness before the courts. A man can have up to thirty-five wives simultaneously and divorce his wife without any prior reason, but it would be very difficult, and at times impossible, for a woman to seek divorce. Interestingly, these discriminatory laws are implemented in a society where over 65 percent of university students are female. In other words, if we look at the situation, there are more educated women in Iran than there are educated men. It is exactly because of this level of education that the feminist movement in Iran is very powerful. This movement does not have a leader; it does not have an office or a branch; rather, it resides in the hearts of every Iranian family that values equal rights for men and women and is against discriminatory laws.

As a result of the feminist movement in Iran there has been a recent initiative, a petition requesting a review of discriminatory laws against women in Iran. We are seeking to collect one million signatures from Iranian men and women, and there is a website that has gone up to collect the signatures as well, at www.we-change.org. Collecting one million signatures will help show that these discriminatory laws are incompatible with the culture of Iranian women. And since we know that there is a chance that the site could be filtered, we have also collected signatures on paper from Iranian men and women.

The reason I insist on revising discriminatory laws against women is that I believe that the rights of women and democracy present two sides of a scale. History has shown to us that women are the last group that benefits from democracy, as if concepts such as freedom and equality were created for men and if there is any left over, then the women can take them.

I think in speaking of human rights, it is necessary to also speak of the high number of executions in Iran. Some of these executions have been carried out even in public areas and on the street. Unfortunately, in the last year capital punishment was also carried out for juveniles. According to the regulations laid down in the penal code, the criminal liability age is designated to be nine for a girl and fifteen for a boy. That is to say that if a ten-year-old girl, or say a sixteen-year-old boy, commits a crime, she or he will be treated before the law the same way as a forty-year-old person would. It is on this very basis that child executions are considered legal, and in the past year such sentences were carried out.

I have spoken about the feminist movement in Iran with you tonight. After the revolution, the number of educated women increased compared to before the revolution. Before the revolution, many traditional families were against sending their daughters to universities to seek higher education, to work in offices or in factories with men. In the name of Islam—under the pretext of Islam, rather—they prevented women from studying and leaving the house. After the revolution, because the government claimed that universities and work environments are now supposedly Islamic, it took away the opportunity from the patriarchal society, the father figures in those families, to prevent their daughters from leaving the house. So, they no longer could use Islam as an excuse to prevent their daughters or sisters from continuing their education. Slowly the number of women who went to universities increased. And today it has reached over 65 percent. During the shah, it was at most 25 percent female students in the higher educational system.

After the revolution, to gain more legitimacy, the government realized it needed the votes of the women. So, women who had stayed in their homes until then decided to go to the polls with the encouragement of the government itself. Let us not forget that women often constitute half the society, so their vote is very important in giving legitimacy to a system and a government. In the early years, women who went to vote really were not sure what they were voting for and what results their votes would have. Women coming from traditional families especially were unaware. But gradually they understood the power of their votes. It gave confidence to the Iranian woman. Before the revolution, during the shah, when we spoke of equality of rights, it did not really resonate with society. There were very few women intellectuals, and they only spoke with each other. But, given the larger number of educated women in society today, these demands for our rights resonate much stronger in society today. As a result, the feminist movement is very powerful, and it has also arrived at the doors of those traditional families, too. It is for this reason that I think this movement will succeed.

Glossary

feminist: an advocate of women's rights based on the equality of the sexes

patriarchal society: a culture organized to support the supremacy of men

revolution: the Iranian Revolution of 1978–79, which overthrew the Pahlavi dynasty and replaced the Imperial State with the Islamic Republic of Iran

shah: ruler of Iran; specifically, Mohammad Reza Pahlavi, the shah of Iran from 1941 until the Iranian Revolution of 1979

Short-Answer Questions

1. Describe the strategies that Iranian women are taking to achieve equality.

2. Describe how the criminal liability age gap between girls and boys negatively affects girls.

3. Analyze how the role of education contributes to the advancement of the feminist movement in Iran.

Luisa D. Diogo: "Women for a Better World"

Author
Luisa D. Diogo

Date
2008

Document Type
Speeches/Addresses

Significance
An illustration of the positions of leadership, power, and influence women hold in Africa

Overview

Mozambique's first female prime minister, Luisa D. Diogo, addressed the second Spain-Africa International Meeting on March 7, 2008, in Madrid, Spain, with her International Women's Day speech "Women for a Better World." Diogo reflects that the challenges faced on the continent of Africa are the same as those seen elsewhere around the globe: domestic violence, sexual abuse, low levels of employment and educational opportunities, increased levels of poverty, a lack of adequate housing options, food insecurity, slow economic development, and the effects of climate change. Diogo stresses that the empowerment of women and gender equality in Africa contributes to a better society and directly affects the health and well-being of women and children. Diogo uses Mozambique as an example, stating that there has been an increase in the number of women who hold public office, and consequently bills have been drafted to combat violence against women, particularly domestic violence, and the groundbreaking Family Act was passed by the country's parliament in 2004. The act raises the minimum age of marriage for girls to eighteen, allows widows to inherit land and other property, and grants women the right to seek divorce in the case of domestic violence or infidelity, to create and enforce prenuptial agreements, to work outside the home without the permission of a husband or other male relative, and to buy and own property and other financial assets, among other measures.

Diogo earned a bachelor's degree in economics from Eduardo Mondlane University in Maputo in 1983 and a master's degree in financial economics from the School of Oriental and African Studies at the University of London in 1992. She made history in Mozambique, becoming the first woman minister of finance and then the first woman prime minister of Mozambique, serving from 2004 to 2010. Her mission was to continue the effort to heal and repair the nation after years of colonialism and civil war, specifically focusing on economic reform. Diogo was named one of the 100 most influential people in the world by *Time* magazine and the finance minister of the year by *The Banker,* both in 2004, and was listed as one of the most powerful women in the world by *Forbes* magazine in 2006 and 2008.

Luisa D. Diogo
(World Economic Forum)

Document Text

The meeting which begins today coincides with the celebration on 8 March of International Women's Day, a symbol of homage and of solidarity with all the world's women, through various public actions and demonstrations constituting and continuing to make history in the fight for women's human rights. March 8 is not just a day to claim and demand, but also one to celebrate the successes we have achieved, which strengthen and inspire us to confront tomorrow's challenges. The motto of International Women's Day is "Ending impunity for violence against women and girls," confirming the efforts which have been made worldwide to eliminate any form of discrimination against women and girls. I would like to emphasize that in Mozambique awareness is constantly increasing of the need to combat all forms of violence, specifically domestic violence, and the sexual abuse of minors. We are engaged in debate on a draft bill against domestic violence involving civil society, and, in parallel, action is under way to respond to cases of such violence.

Your Majesty, Ladies and Gentlemen, where women have no rights, there are no human rights. We note with satisfaction that African governments successfully adopted action plans for the application of the Beijing Platform and approved the Protocol of the Charter of African Human and Peoples' Rights on the Rights of Women in Africa and the Solemn Declaration on Gender Equality in Africa. The practical application of these instruments has led us to create legislation on gender equality so that women are represented in significant realms of government and are able to access health services, and girls are able to receive primary education.

In relation to the participation of women in political leadership, we can refer with considerable pride to the case of the Rt. Hon. Ellen Johnson-Sirleaf, President of Liberia, who is here with us. She is an illustrious woman, an outstanding daughter of Mother Africa, and we would like to congratulate her very specially. At the same time, the Speaker of the Pan-African Parliament is a notable woman, the honorable Gertrude Mongella. In our region, in southern Africa, we have two Vice-Presidents, in Zimbabwe and in South Africa, my beloved sisters Joyce Mujuru and Phumzile Mlambo. In the field of activity on gender, Mozambique has been involved in a drive to enhance girls' access to education, and I wish to highlight the following results: a significant reduction of gender disparity in all indicators relative to access, frequency and completion of education; increased numbers of women in training and primary teacher courses (64 percent in 2006), and the preparation of new school texts which include feminine models.

Access to healthcare is a right of women and one of the priorities of African governments. In 2005, African Union Member States approved the continental sexual and reproductive health policy, designed to reduce maternal, neonatal, and infant mortality. The following year, African Union Health Ministers drew up the plan for the operation of that policy. National policy on health and sexual and reproductive rights began to be implemented in Mozambique, its results reflected in cuts in maternal mortality rates, from 900 to 408 per 100,000 live births; in fact, in addition to the maternal deaths, many women are left with after-effects like fistulas, urinary incontinence or sterility. There was also a reduction in infant mortality, from 147 to 124 per thousand live births, and a significant improvement in family planning and maternal-infant health indicators. Despite everything, these successes are threatened by the challenge of the prevalence of the AIDS virus in our country, affecting 16.2 percent of the population. Your Majesty, Ladies and Gentlemen, this New Economic Partnership for Africa's Development (NEPAD) assigns special importance to women's full participation in national development agendas. In this context, particular attention is given to access to information and financial resources, indispensable conditions for women's involvement in the fight against poverty and to secure their economic empowerment. We must reach the Millennium Development Goals, which form a component of gender equality and the empowerment of women in the world in which we live.

In Mozambique, the results of empowerment are visible and yet insufficient. In the field of women's status and their ratio in all legislative and executive bodies at the level of the public administration, significant efforts have been made to ensure gender balance. The Mozambique Parliament is one example of that, 36 percent of its 250 members women, making our chamber a point of reference not just in Africa but worldwide. We know that Ruanda is well ahead, and I must congratulate them for that.

Apart from the Prime Minister, 26 percent of our Executive comprises women ministers and deputy-ministers. We have progressed, because all these ministers and deputy-ministers hold portfolios with power, such as Justice, Foreign Affairs, Labor, etcetera. We have also made great strides forward at the provincial level, with two provincial governors and a considerable number of women in various district administrations and in the Mozambican judicial system. These modest data assume great scope when it is remembered that, until quite recently, in our society women occupied a secondary position.

Considerable successes have been won in other spheres of society such as the law, the economy and social affairs, the result of uniting the forces of government, civil society, and communities to promote and give more power to women. So, in August 2004, our Parliament passed the Family Act, according to the Republic's Constitution, adapted to the remaining instruments of international law, of course with respect for the culture and identity of the Mozambican people, eliminating the base provisions underlying inequality in the treatment of family relations. There remains, however, a long path to the attainment of the objectives set.

Glossary

Beijing Platform: the Beijing Declaration and Platform for Action, a United Nations resolution adopted in 1995 to pursue equality between men and women

civil society: a society considered as a community of citizens linked by common interests and collective activity

discrimination: the unjust treatment of distinct categories of people, especially on the grounds of ethnicity, age, sex, or disability

Family Act: legislation passed in Mozambique in 2004 that reforms marriage law and grants numerous rights to women

human rights: standards that recognize and protect the dignity of all human beings

Millennium Development Goals: goals adopted by the United Nations in September 2000 to combat poverty, hunger, disease, illiteracy, environmental degradation, and discrimination against women

New Economic Partnership for Africa's Development (NEPAD): adopted by the African Union Assembly in July 2001 to accelerate economic cooperation

Protocol of the Charter of African Human and Peoples' Rights on the Rights of Women in Africa: also called the Maputo Protocol; adopted in Maputo, Mozambique, in July 2003 to augment the rights and protections afforded to women by the African Charter on Human and Peoples' Rights

Solemn Declaration on Gender Equality in Africa: adopted by the African Union Assembly in 2004 to pledge continual action toward gender equality

Your Majesty: Queen Sofía of Spain

Short-Answer Questions

1. Summarize why access to health care for women is a priority in Africa, using examples from the speech.

2. Analyze how the increased number of women in positions of power improves the lives of women and girls in Africa.

3. Analyze what Luisa D. Diogo meant when she stated, "Where women have no rights, there are no human rights."

Ellen Johnson Sirleaf: "A Voice for Freedom"

Author
Ellen Johnson Sirleaf

Date
2011

Document Type
Speeches/Addresses

Significance
A call for governmental stability, democracy, social justice, and education for women, from the first woman democratically elected as head of state of an African country after years of civil war

Overview

Ellen Johnson Sirleaf accepted the Nobel Prize for Peace on December 10, 2011. In her acceptance speech, "A Voice for Freedom," Sirleaf focuses on peace and women's rights. She acknowledges the conflicts and political struggles in her native Liberia, in Yemen, and in other countries and warns against going back to the dark days of war and uncertainty. She asserts that stability would bring new opportunities and change for everyone, especially women.

She points out that the state of women in the world remains brutal and unequal. Global and domestic conflicts disproportionately affect the lives and well-being of women and girls. Crimes against women are largely underreported, and the laws created to protect women are often not enforced. Sirleaf stresses that where educating women and girls is often seen as unnecessary, receiving a quality education is a social justice issue.

Sirleaf, the first woman democratically elected head of state of an African country, served as the twenty-fourth president of Liberia from 2006 to 2018. Rebuilding Liberia, strengthening its democratic process by holding free and fair presidential and legislative elections, and maintaining peace were paramount after years of civil war. Before becoming president, Sirleaf was imprisoned twice for sedition, was sentenced to death, and spent a combined twelve years in exile in Kenya, Côte d'Ivoire, and the United States. She ran for president in 1997 and again in 2005, winning the latter election. As a fierce advocate for women's rights, in 2018 Sirleaf founded the Ellen Johnson Sirleaf Presidential Center for Women and Development, with the goal to inspire, encourage, and support women interested in leadership positions.

Ellen Johnson Sirleaf in 2015
(Flickr)

Document Text

My life was safeguarded when thousands of women mobilized around the world to free me from imprisonment, and my life was spared by individual acts of compassion by some of my captors.

My life was forever transformed when I was given the privilege to serve the people of Liberia—taking on the awesome responsibility of rebuilding a nation nearly destroyed by war and plunder. There was no roadmap for post-conflict transformation. But we knew that we could not let our country slip back into the past. We understood that our greatest responsibility was to keep the peace.

There is no doubt that the madness that wrought untold destruction in recent years in the Democratic Republic of Congo, in Rwanda, in Sierra Leone, in Sudan, in Somalia, in the former Yugoslavia, and in my own Liberia, found its expression in unprecedented levels of cruelty directed against women.

Although international tribunals have correctly declared that rape, used as a weapon of war, is a crime against humanity, rapes in times of lawlessness continue unabated. The number of our sisters and daughters of all ages brutally defiled over the past two decades staggers the imagination, and the number of lives devastated by such evil defies comprehension.

Through the mutilation of our bodies and the destruction of our ambitions, women and girls have disproportionately paid the price of domestic and international armed conflict. We have paid in the currencies of blood, of tears, and of dignity.

However, the need to defend the rights of women is not limited to the battlefield, and the threats to those rights do not emanate only from armed violence. Girls' education, seen far too often as an unnecessary indulgence rather than the key investment it is, is still underfunded and understaffed. Too often girls are discouraged from pursuing academic training, no matter how promising they may be.

We are mindful of the enormous challenges we still face. In too many parts of the world, crimes against women are still under-reported, and the laws protecting women are under-enforced. In this 21st century, surely there is no place for human trafficking that victimizes almost a million people, mostly girls and women, each year. Surely there is no place for girls and women to be beaten and abused. Surely there is no place for a continuing belief that leadership qualities belong to only one gender.

Yet, there is occasion for optimism and hope. There are good signs of progress and change. Around the world, slowly, international law and an awareness of human rights are illuminating dark corners, in schools, in courts, in the marketplace. The windows of closed chambers where men and women have been unspeakably abused are being opened, and the light is coming in. Democracies, even if tentatively, are taking root in lands unaccustomed to freedom.

As curtains are raised and as the sun shines upon dark places, what was previously invisible comes into view. Technology has turned our world into one interconnected neighborhood. What happens in one place is seen in every corner, and there has been no better time for the spread of peace, democracy and their attending social justice and fairness for all.

Today, across the globe, women and men from all walks of life are finding the courage to say, loudly and firmly, in a thousand languages, "No more." They reject mindless violence and defend the fundamental values of democracy, of open society, of freedom, and of peace.

So, I urge my sisters, and my brothers, not to be afraid. Be not afraid to denounce injustice, though you may be outnumbered. Be not afraid to seek peace, even if your voice may be small. Be not afraid to demand peace.

If I might thus speak to girls and women everywhere, I would issue them this simple invitation: My sisters, my daughters, my friends, find your voices! Each of us has her own voice, and the differences among us are to be celebrated. But our goals are in harmony. They are the pursuit of peace, the pursuit of justice. They are the defense of rights to which all people are entitled.

Throughout our political campaign, we heard the cry of our young population that they are impatient for their lives to improve. They want to make up for the time and opportunities lost during years of conflict and deprivation. They want better education, useful skills, and jobs. They want to contribute to the rebuilding of their country. They have found their voices, and we have heard them.

Glossary

Liberia: a West African country on the Atlantic coast bordering Sierra Leone, Guinea, and Côte d'Ivoire

post-conflict: referring to the period after Liberia's two civil wars, the first from 1989 to 1997 and the second from 1999 to 2003

safeguarded: protected

Short-Answer Questions

1. Describe how technology has turned the world into one interconnected neighborhood.

2. Describe the long-lasting positive effects of educating girls.

3. Finding and using your voice is a central theme in this speech. Analyze how finding your voice can bring progressive change.

Michelle Bachelet: "Time to Make the Promise of Equality a Reality"

Author
Michelle Bachelet

Date
2011

Document Type
Speeches/Addresses

Significance
Reflected upon the mission, goals, and values of International Women's Day one hundred years after its establishment

Overview

Michelle Bachelet, the former president of Chile and the first executive director of the United Nations Entity for Gender Equality and the Empowerment of Women (better known as UN Women), gave an address in Liberia on March 8, 2011, to mark the 100th anniversary of International Women's Day. The day provides an opportunity annually to honor the achievements of women, promote empowerment, and advocate for gender equality worldwide. In her speech, Bachelet discussed the progress that had been made in the previous 100 years. For example, more women globally have the right to vote, women have been elected to lead governments in every continent, women hold positions of leadership in professions from which they were once banned, two-thirds of countries have laws that penalize domestic violence, and the United Nations Security Council recognizes sexual violence as a deliberate tactic of war. Bachelet also discussed the work that still needed to be done to improve, for example, the high illiteracy rates among women and girls, the low school attendance for girls, the mortality rate of pregnant women and new mothers, and the pay gap between women and men. She stressed that making progress in these areas must be a global effort.

Bachelet has a diverse educational background, having studied medicine at the University of Chile, attended Humboldt University of Berlin, and studied military affairs at Chile's National Academy of Strategy and Policy and at the Inter-American Defense College in Washington, D.C. Bachelet was the first woman to become the president of Chile, serving one term from 2006 to 2010 and another from 2014 to 2018. As president, she dealt with serious issues, including the large student protests in 2006 pushing for better education, an earthquake in 2010, and a host of reforms, including tax, education, and constitutional measures. During her tenures, she strived to provide equal opportunities for women and men, including proposing a cabinet that had an equal number of men and women. In 2010, Bachelet became the first head of UN Women, and she was the United Nations High Commissioner for Human Rights from 2018 to 2022.

Document Text

A hundred years ago today, women across the world took an historic step on the long road to equality. The first ever International Women's Day was called to draw attention to the unacceptable and often dangerous working conditions that so many women faced worldwide. Although the occasion was celebrated in only a handful of countries, it brought over one million women out onto the streets, demanding not just better conditions at work but also the right to vote, to hold office and to be equal partners with men.

I suspect those courageous pioneers would look at our world today with a mixture of pride and disappointment. There has been remarkable progress as the last century has seen an unprecedented expansion of women's legal rights and entitlements. Indeed, the advancement of women's rights can lay claim to be one of the most profound social revolutions the world has seen.

One hundred years ago, only two countries allowed women to vote. Today, that right is virtually universal, and women have now been elected to lead governments in every continent. Women, too, hold leading positions in professions from which they were once banned. Far more recently than a century ago, the police, courts and neighbors still saw violence in the home as a purely private matter. Today two-thirds of countries have specific laws that penalize domestic violence, and the United Nations Security Council now recognizes sexual violence as a deliberate tactic of war.

But despite this progress over the last century, the hopes of equality expressed on that first International Women's Day are a long way from being realized. Almost two out of three illiterate adults are women. Girls are still less likely to be in school than boys. Every ninety seconds of every day, a woman dies in pregnancy or due to childbirth-related complications despite us having the knowledge and resources to make birth safe.

2014 portrait of Michelle Bachelet
(Wikimedia Commons)

Across the world, women continue to earn less than men for the same work. In many countries, too, they have unequal access to land and inheritance rights. And despite high-profile advances, women still make up only 19 percent of legislatures, 8 percent of peace negotiators, and only twenty-eight women are heads of state or government.

It is not just women who pay the price for this discrimination. We all suffer for failing to make the most of half the world's talent and potential. We undermine the quality of our democracy, the strength of our economies, the health of our societies and the sustainability of peace. This year's focus of International Women's Day on women's equal access to education, training, science, and technology underscores the need to tap this potential.

The agenda to secure gender equality and women's rights is a global agenda, a challenge for every country, rich and poor, north and south. It was in recognition of both its universality and the rewards if we get this right that the United Nations brought together four existing organizations to create UN Women. The goal of this new body, which I have the great privilege to lead, is to galvanize the entire UN system so we can deliver on the promise of the UN Charter of equal rights of men and women. It is something I have fought for my whole life.

As a young mother and a pediatrician, I experienced the struggles of balancing family and career and saw how the absence of childcare prevented women from paid employment. The opportunity to help remove these barriers was one of the reasons I went into politics. It is why I supported policies that extended health and childcare services to families and prioritized public spending for social protection.

As President, I worked hard to create equal opportunities for both men and women to contribute their talents and experiences to the challenges facing our country. That is why I proposed a Cabinet that had an equal number of men and women.

As Executive Director of UN Women, I want to use my journey and the collective knowledge and experience all around me to encourage progress towards true gender equality across the world. We will work, in close partnership, with men and women, leaders and citizens, civil society, the private sector and the whole UN system to assist countries to roll out policies, programs and budgets to achieve this worthy goal.

I have seen myself what women, often in the toughest circumstances, can achieve for their families and societies if they are given the opportunity. The strength, industry and wisdom of women remain humanity's greatest untapped resource. We simply cannot afford to wait another 100 years to unlock this potential.

Glossary

discrimination: the unjust treatment of distinct categories of people, especially on the grounds of ethnicity, age, sex, or disability

entitlements: government benefits to a specified group

"four existing organizations": four UN subdivisions that were merged to create UN Women in July 2010: the Division of the Advancement of Women (DAW), the International Research and Training Institute for the Advancement of Women (INSTRAW), the Office of the Special Adviser on Gender Issues and Advancement of Women (OSAGI), and the United Nations Development Fund for Women (UNIFEM)

United Nations Security Council: a United Nations organization responsible for the maintenance of international peace and security

UN Women: also called the United Nations Entity for Gender Equality and the Empowerment of Women, an international organization that advocates for women's rights and the rights of LGBTQ+ individuals

Short-Answer Questions

1. Describe how women in leadership positions promote women's empowerment.

2. Describe how providing equal access to education and training to girls and women have the potential to change the world.

3. Analyze why Michelle Bachelet stated, "I suspect those courageous pioneers would look at our world today with a mixture of pride and disappointment."

Chimamanda Ngozi Adichie: "We Should All Be Feminists"

Author
Chimamanda Ngozi Adichie

Date
2012

Document Type
Speeches/Addresses

Significance
Illustrates the extent to which the treatment, opportunities, and experiences of women and men worldwide are based on gender and cultural expectations

Overview

"We Should All Be Feminists" was a speech delivered by Chimamanda Ngozi Adichie for a TEDxEuston conference in London, England, in December 2012; she later adapted it for publication as a brief book. In her address, Adichie, a self-proclaimed feminist, creative writer, and essayist, discusses how gender and the roles associated with gender hold women and men to different standards and different expectations that may not fit their aspirations. Adichie speaks specifically about Nigeria but observes that the message can be applied globally. She provides an example of a woman with the same educational level and job as her husband but completes most of the housework and childcare and often thanks her husband when he helps. Adichie goes on to question why girls are taught to aspire to marriage but boys are not, and the ramifications of this practice. She discusses how raising boys to be "hard men," as is the phrase in Nigeria, suppresses their humanity and teaches them to hide their authentic selves.

Adichie explains that deeply rooted culture practices play a role in gender inequality, yet culture is made by people, and people must make it an essential part of culture to provide women and girls the same opportunities as men and boys. She uses her grandmother as an example, wondering how her life would have progressed differently if she had been afforded the same opportunities as men.

Adichie was born in Enugu, Nigeria, and was raised in the college town of Nsukka. As a child, she was an avid reader and wrote short stories that were influenced by British literature. Her writing dramatically changed when she discovered literature by the Nigerian author Chinua Achebe at age ten, whereupon she began to write about her own lived experiences as an African. Adichie came to the United States in 1997 to study communication and political science first at Drexel University and then at Eastern Connecticut State University, receiving her bachelor of arts degree in 2001. She earned a master's degree in creative writing from Johns Hopkins University in 2004, was granted a fellowship at Princeton in 2006, and studied African history at Yale.

Adichie has authored novels, short stories, and nonfiction. Her first novel, *Purple Hibiscus*, won the 2004 Hurston/Wright Legacy Award for Best Debut Fiction and the Commonwealth Writers' Prize in 2005 for the best first book overall and in Africa. Her second novel, *Half of a Yellow Sun*, was awarded the Orange Broadband Prize for Fiction in 2007.

Document Text

Gender as it functions today is a grave injustice. We should all be angry. Anger has a long history of bringing about positive change; but, in addition to being angry, I'm also hopeful. Because I believe deeply in the ability of human beings to make and remake themselves for the better.

Gender matters everywhere in the world, but I want to focus on Nigeria and on Africa in general, because it is where I know, and because it is where my heart is. And I would like today to ask that we begin to dream about and plan for a different world, a fairer world, a world of happier men and happier women who are truer to themselves. And this is how to start: we must raise our daughters differently. We must also raise our sons differently. We do a great disservice to boys on how we raise them; we stifle the humanity of boys. We define masculinity in a very narrow way, masculinity becomes this hard, small cage and we put boys inside the cage. We teach boys to be afraid of fear. We teach boys to be afraid of weakness, of vulnerability. We teach them to mask their true selves, because they must be, in Nigerian speak, "hard man!" . . .

I'm expected to aspire to marriage; I'm expected to make my life choices always keeping in mind that marriage is the most important. A marriage can be a good thing; it can be a source of joy and love and mutual support. But why do we teach girls to aspire to marriage and we don't teach boys the same? . . .

It's easy for us to say, "Oh, but women can just say no to all of this." But the reality is more difficult and more complex. We're all social beings. We internalize ideas from our socialization. Even the language we use in talking about marriage and relationships illustrates this. The language of marriage is often the language of ownership rather than the language of partnership. We use the word "respect" to mean something a woman shows a man but often not something a man shows a woman.

The problem with gender is that it prescribes how we should be rather than recognizing how we are.

Now imagine how much happier we would be, how much freer to be our true individual selves, if we didn't have the weight of gender expectations. Boys and girls are undeniably different biologically, but socialization exaggerates the differences and then it becomes a self-fulfilling process. . . .

Chimamanda Ngozi Adichie
(Wikimedia Commons)

I used to look up to my grandmother who was a brilliant, brilliant woman, and wonder how she would have been if she had the same opportunities as men when she was growing up.

Now today, there are many more opportunities for women than there were during my grandmother's time because of changes in policy, changes in law, all of which are very important. But what matters even more is our attitude, our mindset, what we believe and what we value about gender. What if in raising children we focus on ability instead of gender? What if in raising children we focus on interest instead of gender? . . .

I know a woman who has the same degree and the same job as her husband. When they get back from work, she does most of the housework, which I think is true for many marriages. But what struck me about them was that whenever her husband changed the baby's diaper, she said "thank you" to him. Now, what if she saw this as perfectly normal and natural that he should, in fact, care for his child? . . .

That many men do not actively think about gender or notice gender is part of the problem of gender. That many men say, like my friend Louis, that everything is fine now. And that many men do nothing to change it. If you are a man and you walk into a restaurant with a woman and the waiter greets only you, does it occur to you to ask the waiter, "Why haven't you greeted her?" . . .

Gender and class are different forms of oppression. I learned quite a bit about systems of oppression and how they can be blind to one another by talking to Black men. I was once talking to a Black man about gender and he said to me, "Why do you have to say 'my experience as a woman'? Why can't it be your experience as a human being?" Now, this was the same man who would often talk about his experience as a Black man.

Gender matters. Men and women experience the world differently. Gender colors the way we experience the world. But we can change that. . . .

Some people will say that a woman being subordinate to a man is our culture. But culture is constantly changing. I have beautiful twin nieces who are fifteen and live in Lagos. If they had been born a hundred years ago, they would have been taken away and killed. Because it was our culture, it was our culture to kill twins. . . .

Culture does not make people; people make culture. So, if it is in fact true that the full humanity of women is not our culture, then we must make it our culture.

I am a feminist. And when I looked up the word in the dictionary . . . this is what it said: "Feminist: a person who believes in the social, political and economic equality of the sexes."

My great grandmother, from the stories I've heard, was a feminist. She ran away from the house of the man she did not want to marry, and ended up marrying the man of her choice. She refused, she protested, she spoke up whenever she felt she was being deprived of access, of land, that sort of thing. My great grandmother did not know that word "feminist," but it doesn't mean that she wasn't one. More of us should reclaim that word. The best feminist I know is my brother Kene. He's also a kind, good-looking, lovely man, and he's very masculine.

My own definition of a feminist is a man or a woman who says, "Yes, there's a problem with gender as it is today, and we must fix it. We must do better."

Glossary

feminist: a person who supports the social, political, and economic equality of the sexes

gender: the behavioral, cultural, or psychological traits typically associated with one sex

masculinity: qualities or attributes regarded as characteristic of men or boys

Short-Answer Questions

1. What does the excerpt reveal about how gender expectations harm both girls and boys?

2. Explain how Chimamanda Ngozi Adichie's statement "Culture does not make people, people make culture" has the potential to change the reality of girls and boys.

3. Explain the significance of Adichie's statement "The problem with gender is that it prescribes how we should be rather than recognizing how we are."

Michelle Obama: Remarks at the 2012 International Women of Courage Awards

Author
Michelle Obama

Date
2012

Document Type
Speeches/Addresses

Significance
Highlighted the work of women who risked their lives for change, including Zin Mar Aung, Shad Begum, Jineth Bedoya Lima, Şafak Pavey, and Pricilla de Oliveira Azevedo

Overview

First Lady Michelle Obama delivered an address at the 2012 International Women of Courage Awards ceremony at the White House on International Women's Day, celebrated annually on March 8. Her address celebrated the women who have committed to fighting for a world where everyone is heard, valued, and protected. In her speech, Obama highlighted the work of women who risked their lives for change, including Zin Mar Aung, who was imprisoned for eleven years for writing a letter demanding that the elected civilian government take power in Burma; Shad Begum from Pakistan, who won a district council position but was not treated equally with the men on the council; Colombian investigative journalist Jineth Bedoya Lima, who was kidnapped and assaulted for writing about an arms smuggling network; Şafak Pavey, who traveled the world to bring awareness of the challenges of persons with disabilities; and Pricilla de Oliveira Azevedo, who is one of the few women to rise through the ranks of the Rio de Janeiro military police. The women selected for the award demonstrated sacrificial leadership, courage, and originality. There have been over 180 recipients of the award from about eighty countries since its inception.

A native of Chicago, Obama is a lawyer, an author, and the wife of the forty-fourth president of the United States, Barack Obama. She served as the first African American First Lady in the United States from 2009 to 2017. Obama earned a bachelor of arts degree in sociology with a minor in African American studies from Princeton University in 1985 and a Juris Doctor from Harvard Law School in 1988. After graduation, Obama worked at the corporate law firm Sidley & Austin, the city of Chicago's Department of Planning, and the University of Chicago.

During her first term as First Lady, Obama's Let's Move initiative focused on ending childhood obesity, and in her second term, the Reach Higher initiative focused on providing students with the education and skills necessary for employment. Obama is the author of *American Grown: The Story of the White House Kitchen Garden and Gardens across America* (2012), *Becoming* (2018), and *The Light We Carry: Overcoming in Uncertain Times* (2022).

Document Text

I want to recognize most of all the ten Women of Courage that we're honoring here today. These women come from all different corners of the globe. They have taken very different journeys to this moment. But they are all here today because somewhere along the line, they decided they could no longer accept the world as it is. And they committed themselves to fighting for the world as they know it should be. They saw corruption, and they worked to expose it. They saw oppression, and they worked to end it. They saw violence, poverty, discrimination, and inequality, and they decided to use their voices, and risk their lives, to do something about it.

And day after day, these women have stood up and said the things that no one else could say or would say. Year after year, they endured hardships that few of us could bear.

At the age of twenty-two, Zin Mar Aung was imprisoned for eleven years simply for writing a letter demanding that the elected civilian government take power in Burma. When she was freed, she went right back to work, fighting for the rights of women and ethnic minorities and political prisoners.

Shad Begum founded a women's NGO in Pakistan, and she ran for district council. When she won, she intended to use her position to improve health care and education. But when the council met, she was forced to sit in a separate side room, behind a locked door. The microphone that was supposed to allow her to participate never worked. But undeterred, she decided to run for an even higher elected office, saying—and this is her quote—"Whatever it takes, I will make them hear me."

And then there is Jineth Bedoya Lima, an investigative journalist in Colombia. Back in 2000, when she was writing about an arms-smuggling network, she was kidnapped, brutally assaulted for hours by those who wished to silence her. But instead of backing down, she moved from her regional newspaper to

Official portrait of First Lady Michelle Obama
(Library of Congress)

a national one, and despite continued threats to her life, she kept reporting. She became a spokeswoman for a global campaign against sexual violence. And for 12 years, she's fought to hold her attackers responsible for their crimes. She has even taken her case all the way to the Inter-American Commission on Human Rights, seeking justice not just for herself, but for women across her country.

And that is why, despite the risks they face, despite the hardships they endure, these women carry on—because they know that they are fighting not just for their own rights and freedoms, but for the rights and freedoms of so many others. That is why, despite daunting physical obstacles, Şafak Pavey didn't just win a seat in parliament in her own country; she traveled to countries across the globe, winning support for the U.N. Convention on the Rights of Persons with Disabilities. She lives her life by a simple motto—these are her words: "Whatever you experience is an example to others." Whatever you experience is an example to others.

The same can be said of Pricilla de Oliveira Azevedo. Despite being one of just a few women in the Rio de Janeiro military police, she has risen through the ranks, commanding more than 100 male officers—we love that—working in one of the toughest communities in the city and even arresting a gang of criminals who kidnapped her. Women of all ages have been inspired by her leadership, and of them she says—again I quote—"They see me as an example of the fact that any woman can work in any type of activity. It's just a question of wanting to do it."

And that is why each year we invite young people to join us at this event. It is so important because we want them to learn from and be inspired by the example of these women of courage.

We invite them because we want them—we want to say to them and to boys and girls across America that if, despite all the obstacles these women of courage face, if they are still running for office and running organizations and serving their communities and their countries, then surely you can find a way to follow your dreams. Surely, you can find a way to give back to your community and to your country. If these ten women can endure death threats and horrifying violence and years behind bars to stand up for what they believe in, then surely our young people can find a way to stand up for what they believe in. Surely, all of you can overcome the obstacles you face in your own life.

And I'm thinking particularly of Jineth Bedoya Lima and what she endured on that day twelve years ago. As her attackers assaulted her, they said to her, "Pay attention. We're sending a message to the press in Colombia." Well, today, with every story she writes and with every public appearance she makes, Jineth is sending her own message that she will not back down, that she will not give up, and she will never, ever allow her voice to be silenced.

And it is the same message that all these women are sending with every act of courage they commit—the message that injustice will not stand, that inequality will not be tolerated, and that they will not stay silenced in the face of evil.

And to all of those who are oppressed and abused and left out and left behind, they are saying: I am standing with you. I am fighting for you. You are not alone.

Glossary

ethnic minorities: groups that have different national or cultural traditions from the main population

Inter-American Commission on Human Rights: created in 1959 to promote and protect human rights in the Americas

NGO: non-governmental organization; a group that operates independent of the government, often with a national or international social mission

oppression: the state of being subject to unjust treatment or control

Short-Answer Questions

1. Describe how the actions of the women featured in the speech promote women's empowerment.

2. Analyze how Zin Mar Aung's imprisonment is an example of oppression.

3. Based on your reading of the document, analyze how the women's treatment motivated them to find and use their voice.

Malala Yousafzai: Nobel Peace Prize Acceptance Speech

Author
Malala Yousafzai

Date
2014

Document Type
Speeches/Addresses

Significance
Announced the dedication of Malala Yousafzai's Nobel Peace Prize money to the Malala Fund, intended to build schools in Pakistan and to fund and promote education for girls worldwide

Overview

On December 10, 2014, seventeen-year-old Pakistani activist Malala Yousafzai was awarded the Nobel Prize for Peace. She was the youngest recipient and the first Pashtun to receive the prize. In her acceptance speech, Yousafzai told her harrowing survival story while focusing on the prioritization of children's and women's rights, particularly in receiving a quality education.

As a result of her outspoken activism on the right of girls to an education, Yousafzai received public and private death threats. An assassination attempt was made on her life on October 9, 2012, by a member of the Pakistani Taliban who shot Yousafzai and two of her friends on their way home on a school bus in her homeland, Swat. Yousafzai was shot in the left side of her head and transported to a hospital in Birmingham, England, where she gained consciousness ten days after the attack. The assassination attempt placed an international spotlight on the Taliban's opposition to educating girls and the overall treatment of women in the region.

Yousafzai is well known for her advocacy in attaining equal, free, and quality education for the world's children, especially girls. In her address she spoke about the 66 million girls around the world who are not receiving an education and the void that leaves in society. She provided an example of her twelve-year-old friend who aspired to become a doctor but, because she was a girl, was forced into marriage as a child and was unable to continue her education.

In 2014, Yousafzai and her father created the Malala Fund with the goal to provide girls an opportunity to select and pursue their own goals. In 2020, at age twenty-two, Yousafzai graduated from Oxford University with a bachelor of arts degree in philosophy, politics, and economics.

Malala Yousafzai (Flickr)

Document Text

This award is not just for me. It is for those forgotten children who want education. It is for those frightened children who want peace. It is for those voiceless children who want change.

I am just a committed and even stubborn person who wants to see every child getting quality education, who wants to see women having equal rights, and who wants peace in every corner of the world. Education is one of the blessings of life, and one of its necessities.

We had a thirst for education because our future was right there in that classroom. We would sit, learn, and read together. We loved to wear neat and tidy school uniforms, and we would sit there with big dreams in our eyes. We wanted to make our parents proud and prove that we could also excel in our studies and achieve those goals, which some people think only boys can.

But things did not remain the same. When I was in Swat, which was a place of tourism and beauty, [it] suddenly changed into a place of terrorism. I was just ten [when] more than 400 schools were destroyed. Women were flogged. People were killed. And our beautiful dreams turned into nightmares.

Education went from being a right to being a crime.

Girls were stopped from going to school.

When my world suddenly changed, my priorities changed too.

I had two options. One was to remain silent and wait to be killed. And the second was to speak up and then be killed. I chose the second one. I decided to speak up. . . .

The terrorists tried to stop us and attacked me and my friends, who are here today, on our school bus in 2012, but neither their ideas nor their bullets could win. We survived. And since that day, our voices have grown louder and louder. I tell my story, not because it is unique, but because it is not. It is the story of many girls. Today, I tell their stories too.

I have brought with me some of my sisters from Pakistan, from Nigeria and from Syria, who share this story. My brave sisters Shazia and Kainat were also shot that day on our school bus. But they have not stopped learning. And my brave sister Kainat Soomro who went through severe abuse and extreme violence, even her brother was killed, but she did not succumb.

Also my sisters here, whom I met during my Malala Fund campaign. My sixteen-year-old courageous sister, Mezon from Syria, who now lives in Jordan as a refugee and goes from tent to tent encouraging girls and boys to learn. And my sister Amina, from the North of Nigeria, where Boko Haram threatens and stops girls and even kidnaps girls, just for wanting to go to school.

Though I appear as one girl, one person, who is five foot two inches tall, if you include my high heels—it means I am five foot only—I am not a lone voice, I am many. . . . I am those 66 million girls who are deprived of education. And today I am not raising my voice; it is the voice of those 66 million girls.

Sometimes people like to ask me, Why should girls go to school? Why is it important for them? But I think the more important question is, Why shouldn't they? Why shouldn't they have this right to go to school?

Today, in half of the world, we see rapid progress and development. However, there are many countries where millions still suffer from the very old problems of war, poverty, and injustice.

We still see conflicts in which innocent people lose their lives and children become orphans. We see many people becoming refugees in Syria, Gaza, and Iraq. In Afghanistan, we see families being killed in suicide attacks and bomb blasts.

Many children in Africa do not have access to education because of poverty. And as I said, we still see girls who have no freedom to go to school in the north of Nigeria.

Many children in countries like Pakistan and India, as Kailash Satyarthi mentioned, many children, especially in India and Pakistan, are deprived of their right to education because of social taboos, or they have been forced into child marriage or into child labor.

One of my very good school friends, the same age as me, who had always been a bold and confident girl, dreamed of becoming a doctor. But her dream remained a dream. At the age of twelve, she was forced to get married. And then soon she had a son, she had a child when she herself was a child only fourteen. I know that she could have been a very good doctor.

But she couldn't because she was a girl.

Her story is why I dedicate the Nobel Peace Prize money to the Malala Fund, to help give girls quality education, everywhere, anywhere in the world, and to raise their voices. The first place this funding will go to is where my heart is, to build schools in Pakistan, especially in my home of Swat and Shangla.

In my own village, there is still no secondary school for girls. And it is my wish and my commitment, and now my challenge to build one so that my friends and my sisters can go there to school and get a quality education and to get this opportunity to fulfill their dreams.

This is where I will begin, but it is not where I will stop. I will continue this fight until I see every child—every child—in school.

My great hope is that this will be the last time—this will be the last time we must fight for education. Let's solve this once and for all.

It is not time to tell the world leaders to realize how important education is. They already know it; their own children are in good schools. Now it is time to call them to act for the rest of the world's children. We ask the world leaders to unite and make education their top priority.

Glossary

flogged: beaten with a whip or stick as punishment

injustice: unfair treatment

Kailash Satyarthi: Indian social reform worker for children's education and against child labor, and co-recipient of the Nobel Peace Prize in 2014 with Malala Yousafzai

Nobel Peace Prize: started by Alfred Nobel, the weapons maker who invented dynamite and then became interested in peace and, upon his death, funded a series of prizes, which have been awarded since 1901

Pakistan: a country in South Asia, officially the Islamic Republic of Pakistan, that borders Iran, Afghanistan, China, and India

Swat: a district in the Khyber Pakhtunkhwa province of northern Pakistan named for the Swat River and known for the natural beauty of its mountains, forests, meadows, and river valley

Short-Answer Questions

1. Summarize how world leaders can prioritize education for all children.

2. Describe how providing children with a quality education is essential for the betterment of the world.

3. Analyze how Malala Yousafzai's experience can empower and motivate children in developed and developing countries.

Emma Watson: "HeForShe" Speech to the United Nations

Author
Emma Watson

Date
2014

Document Type
Speeches/Addresses

Significance
Asserted the importance of including men and boys in the movement to end gender inequality

Overview

The United Nations (UN) addressed gender inequality in 1945 by making it a core tenet in its charter, yet decades later gender inequality remains prevalent in many areas, including education, health care, politics, leadership, and the economy. Progress has been slow toward gender equality in part because many see gender inequality as a women's issue; however, gender inequality affects both men and women, so it is essential to include everyone in the movement.

To that end, on September 21, 2014, Emma Watson, as goodwill ambassador for the United Nations Entity for Gender Equality and the Empowerment of Women (also known as UN Women), delivered an address to the UN General Assembly in New York City launching the HeForShe initiative. Watson addressed the importance of men and boys joining the fight to end gender inequality and explained how the HeForShe initiative would encourage such involvement.

An actor since childhood, Watson became well known for her role as Hermione Granger in the eight Harry Potter films spanning from 2001 to 2011 and has won numerous awards. In 2014, she received a bachelor of arts degree in English literature from Brown University. That same year, she was named a UN goodwill ambassador. Her activism focuses on women's rights, fair trade clothing, and promoting education for girls worldwide. In 2015, Watson was named one of the 100 most influential people in the world by *Time* magazine.

Document Text

I was appointed as goodwill ambassador for UN Women six months ago, and the more I've spoken about feminism, the more I have realized that fighting for women's rights has too often become synonymous with man hating. If there is one thing I know for certain, it is that this must stop. For the record, feminism is the belief that men and women should have equal rights and opportunities. It is the theory of the political, economic, and social equality of the sexes.

I started questioning gender-based assumptions a long time ago. When I was eight, I was confused at being called bossy because I wanted to direct the plays that we would put on for our parents, but the boys were not. When I was fourteen, I started to be sexualized by certain elements of the media. When at fifteen, my girlfriends started dropping out of their beloved sports teams because they didn't want to appear muscly, and when at eighteen, my male friends were unable to express their feelings, I decided that I was a feminist. And this seemed uncomplicated to me, but my recent research has shown me that feminism has become an unpopular word. Women are choosing not to identify as feminists. I am among the ranks of women whose expressions are seen as too strong, too aggressive, isolating, and anti-men, unattractive even. Why has the word become such an uncomfortable one?

I am from Britain, and it is right that I am paid the same as my male counterparts. I think it is right that I should be able to make decisions about my own body. I think it is right that women be involved on my behalf in the policies and the decisions that will affect my life. I think it is right that socially I am afforded the same respect as men. But sadly, I can say that there is no one country in the world where all women can expect to receive these rights. No country in the world can yet say that they have achieved gender equality.

These rights I consider to be human rights, but I am one of the lucky ones. My life is a sheer privi-

Emma Watson
(David Shankbone)

lege because my parents didn't love me less because I was born a daughter. My school did not limit me because I was a girl. My mentors didn't assume that I would go less far because I might give birth to a child one day. These influences were the gender inequality ambassadors that made me who I am today. They may not know it, but they are the inadvertent feminists who are changing the world today. We need more of those, and if you still hate the word, it is not the word that is important; it's the idea and the ambition behind, it because not all women have received the same rights that I have. In fact, statistically, very few have done.

In 1997, Hillary Clinton made a famous speech in Beijing about women's rights. Sadly, many of the things that she wanted to change are still true today. But what stood out for me the most was that less than 30 percent of the audience were male. How can we effect change in the world when only half of it is invited or feel welcome to participate in the conversation?

Men, I would like to take this opportunity to extend your formal invitation. Gender equality is your issue too. Because to date, I've seen my father's role as a parent being valued less by society despite my needing his presence, as a child, as much as my mother's. I've seen young men suffering from mental illness, unable to ask for help for fear it would make them less of a man. In fact, in the UK, suicide is the biggest killer of men between twenty to forty-nine, eclipsing road accidents, cancer and coronary heart disease. I've seen men made fragile and insecure by a distorted sense of what constitutes male success. Men don't have the benefits of equality either.

We don't often talk about men being imprisoned by gender stereotypes, but I can see that they are and that when they are free, things will change for women as a natural consequence. If men don't have to be aggressive to be accepted, women won't feel compelled to be submissive. If men don't have to control, women won't have to be controlled. Both men and women should feel free to be sensitive. Both men and women should feel free to be strong.

It is time that we all perceive gender on a spectrum instead of two sets of opposing ideals. If we stop defining each other by what we are not and start defining ourselves by who we are, we can all be freer, and this is what HeForShe is about. It's about freedom. I want men to take up this mantle so that their daughters, sisters, and mothers can be free from prejudice, but also so that their sons have permission to be vulnerable and human, to reclaim those parts of themselves they abandoned and, in doing so, be a more true and complete version of themselves.

You might think, "Who is this Harry Potter girl? What is she doing at the UN?" And it's a really good question—I've been asking myself the same thing. All I know is that I care about this problem, and I want to make it better. And having seen what I've seen and given the chance, I feel my responsibility to say something.

Statesman Edmund Burke said, "All that is needed for the forces of evil to triumph is for good men and women to do nothing." In my nervousness for this speech, and in my moments of doubt, I've told myself firmly, "If not me, who? If not now, when?" If you have similar doubts when opportunities are presented to you, I hope that those words will be helpful, because the reality is that if we do nothing, it will take seventy-five years—or for me to be nearly a hundred—before women can expect to be paid the same as men for the same work.

Fifteen point five million girls will be married in the next sixteen years as children, and at current rates, it won't be until 2086 before all rural African girls can have a secondary education. If you believe in equality, you might be one of those inadvertent feminists that I spoke of earlier, and for this, I applaud you. We are struggling for a uniting word, but the good news is that we have a uniting movement. It is called HeForShe.

Glossary

ambassador: a person who acts as a representative or promoter of a specified activity

Edmund Burke: an eighteenth-century Anglo-Irish politician and philosopher

feminism: the belief that men and women should have equal rights and opportunities

Hillary Clinton: former U.S. secretary of state, U.S. senator, First Lady, and presidential candidate

inadvertent: unintentional

inequality: the phenomenon of unequal or unjust distribution of resources and opportunities among members of a given society

"take up this mantle": assume this responsibility

Short-Answer Questions

1. Summarize the gender-based assumptions Emma Watson mentioned.

2. Describe how the inclusion of men and boys in the movement to end gender inequality benefits everyone.

3. How does Edmund Burke's quote "All that is needed for the forces of evil to triumph is for good men and women to do nothing" apply to ending gender inequality?

Atifete Jahjaga: Support of Women's Property Rights in Kosovo

Author
Atifete Jahjaga

Date
2015

Document Type
Speeches/Addresses

Significance
Established the importance of property rights for women as part of universal human rights

Overview

The Kosovo War provides a background for understanding the international status of the Republic of Kosovo. Before the breakup of Yugoslavia following the end of the Cold War, Kosovo was a very cosmopolitan city with a large population of ethnic Albanians and ethnic Serbs. After Yugoslavia collapsed, however, violence spread throughout the region, resulting in thousands of civilian deaths, the vast majority of them occurring among Albanian Kosovars. In 2008 Kosovo declared itself an independent republic, effectively breaking away from Serbia. Although not all of Kosovo's fellow states recognize the republic's independence, most—including the United Sates—do.

Atifete Jahjaga (1975–) is the first woman to have been elected president of the Republic of Kosovo, an office she held from 2011 to 2016. She delivered this speech on December 10, 2015, to launch a national campaign in favor of women's property rights. At the end of the Kosovo War (1998–1999), she attended the city's Police Academy and was appointed an officer. During the years she served with the agency, she rose through the ranks to become Deputy Director of the Kosovo police. Later she went on to graduate from the University of Pristina's law school and then received a certificate in police management and criminal law from the University of Leicester in the United Kingdom in 2007. Jahjaga's political career began in 2011, when she emerged as consensus candidate for the office of president of the republic. Her goal, she said, was to prepare Kosovo for eventual membership in the United Nations and the European Union. So far, that goal remains unrealized.

Document Text

Honourable representatives of the institutions of Kosovo,
Honourable Mr. Kuçi,
Honourable Members of the Parliament of the Republic of Kosovo,
Honourable Mr. Delawie,
Honourable Mr. Hope,
Honourable participants,

I am glad that we have gathered here today to mark December 10th, the international day of human rights, by launching a national campaign of a special importance, which is dedicated to one of the basic human principles, that of the right to property.

This universal right, also incarnated in the laws and the Constitution of our country, is guaranteed to all citizens regardless. But in practice, it is often implemented as a privilege reserved for men, which in an unjust manner denies the enjoyment of this right to women.

Human rights are not a special privilege of a particular group of society, and unfortunately they rarely are realized as such. And whenever it happens, it turns this into a civic and institutional obligation, the undertaking of necessary measures for the protection and full realization of equal rights for all citizens regardless.

Today we are recognizing one of the difficulties faced by women, one of realization of their property rights. At the same time, we are also reflecting the readiness to undertake steps towards changing this reality, determined—as institutions, and seeking the support of all citizens—to address the challenges and to recognize the importance of the guaranteeing of this right.

One year ago, we commenced with the "For Our Own Good" campaign, with many partners from all layers of the society, with the support of the German GIZ, focusing on an important aspect of the realization of the right to property, the one of

Portrait of Atifete Jahjaga
(Wikimedia Commons)

registration of the property in the name of both spouses, as foreseen by law.

Today, with the incessant support of the USAID, we are taking a step further, by asking for full realization of the full property rights of women, asking for their right to inherit, their right for access to economic and financial resources, and their right for equal opportunities.

We are dedicated to the protection of these rights, as women are half of the society and their economic potential can be converted into the catalyzer of an all-encompassing well-being of the society and sustainable economic growth.

I would like to thank USAID and the American people for their continuous support for the strengthening of our state, especially for their support for the protection of equal rights of women, which guarantees an advanced society and a strong state.

Dear friends,
Ladies and Gentlemen,

This day also marks the crowning of the 16 days of global activism against gender-based violence. We are often witnesses of a negative binom of violence exercised upon women and girls and their economic status.

The denied rights to property also deny them the right to financial and economic independence, thus not allowing women to end abusive relationships, which as we have seen, can lead to denial of their right to life.

The right to property is an undeniable right, but we are faced every single day with a multitude of histories of women, such as that of Shyhrete Berisha, whose right is denied at the time when she is also carrying the great pain of the loss of her family.

It is histories like this one and similar ones which we must address, which we must change, to turn them into histories unacceptable for us, which do not belong in our society.

It is true that social discourse is still lagging in reflecting the economic, social and political empowerment of women, which will then impact the whole society.

We are aware that we still have a lot to do, to sense the positive and multiple effects of the economic empowerment of women, which not only brings individual well-being to women but also to the whole family and society, and the importance which access to property plays in this aspect.

But it is very clear that guaranteeing of the right to property is also the respecting of the economic, social and cultural right of all our citizens, the guaranteeing of which contributes to rule of law, economic development of the country and general well-being of the society.

For this reason, initiatives like the one today must find wide support from all of us.

I would also like to congratulate the initiative undertaken by the Ministry of Justice, with the support of the USAID, to compile the national strategy on property rights, by attaching special focus on the property rights of women and the addressing of the problems which women face in realization of this right, from which I expect that it will reflect concrete measures in more efficient guaranteeing of women's rights to property.

Dear friends,

A right denied to women is a right which is denied to the whole society. I call upon all of you to work together, for our own good and for the good of the future generations, for a society which respects and protects the rights of all its citizens regardless.

Thank you.

Glossary

binom: the Croatian word for binomial, the sum of two numbers or terms

German GIZ: the Deutsche Gesellschaft für Internationale Zusammenarbeit, or German Agency for International Cooperation, which works to support sustainable development

"Honourable Mr. Kuçi . . . Honourable Mr. Delawie, Honourable Mr. Hope": dignitaries present at President Jahjaga's speech: Hajredin Kuçi (1971–), who was at the time the Deputy Prime Minister of Kosovo, and an important part of President Jahjaga's own government; Greg Delawie (1957–), the United States Ambassador to Kosovo at that time; and James M. Hope, mission director of USAID in Kosovo at the time incarnated: literally, "made flesh"; embodied; in this case, indicating that the right to property is written into Kosovo's constitution

Shyhrete Berisha: a Kosovar woman whose husband and young children were murdered in 1999 during the Kosovo War, and who was blocked by her own in-laws from claiming her husband's property

USAID: the United States Agency for International Development, created under President John F. Kennedy as a way of distributing U.S. funds to foreign countries in a way that promoted economic and social development

Short-Answer Questions

1. Why does President Atifete Jahjaga say that property rights are also human rights?

2. Why are property rights important for women, and particularly important for women in Kosovo?

3. What is the basis of Jahjaga's argument that women's property rights have to be respected?

Joyce Banda: Wheelock College Commencement Address

Author
Joyce Banda

Date
2015

Document Type
Speeches/Addresses

Significance
Called for programs to address poverty and disease among women through education in Africa

Overview

Joyce Hilda Banda (1950–) was the fourth president of the state of Malawi and the second woman to hold the executive office in that nation (after Queen Elizabeth II, who ruled Malawi while it was a British colony). Banda was also only the second female head of state in all of Africa. She came into office when the previous president, Bingu wa Mutharika, died suddenly in 2012; Banda, as his vice president, assumed the office and held it until the next presidential elections in the spring of 2014.

In the 1980s, Banda built a reputation as a successful female entrepreneur and business owner, starting businesses in the clothing and food preparation industries. In the late 1990s she took the skills she learned in those businesses and began to help other women break free of poverty, abuse, and depression.

Banda ran for parliament in 1999, winning a seat in parliament. Her skillset led then-president Bakili Mulizi to offer her the position of minister for gender and community services. In 2006, after winning reelection, Banda was offered the office of minister of foreign affairs by President Bingu wa Mutharika. She maintained that office, despite Mutharika's attempts to remove her from office, until his death in 2012.

In this speech, delivered at Wheelock College in Boston, Massachusetts, May 15, 2015, Banda is speaking during a self-imposed exile following her loss in the 2014 presidential elections in Malawi to Mutharika's brother. Three years after delivering the commencement address, she returned to Malawi and resumed her work in politics.

Joyce Banda (UK Department for International Development)

Document Text

Distinguished ladies and gentlemen, I am . . . privileged today to share my story. . . .

I was born in a very small village in Malawi. They had just established a little clinic in that village—a British midwife had come to establish that clinic. The morning after I was born, she came around and found my grandmother carrying me on her lap, and asked, "What is the name of this child going to be?" My grandmother looked back at her and asked her what her name was. She said, "My name is Joyce." She [grandmother] said, "Yeah, yeah, that's the name of this child. . . . Because I want this child to grow up to be as important as you are and to build clinics."

What she forgot at that moment was that she was denying me my traditional right to assume her name, because my tradition says that your grandmother will give you her name if you're the first grandchild. What you lose when she doesn't, is you don't become the matriarch of the family when she dies. So [I] ended up being Joyce, but I should have been Hilda.

Number two tradition demands that the grandmother shall bring up the first grandchild. Unfortunately for my grandmother, my father had just joined the Malawi police band and was living 15 kilometers away. So therefore, she had to live in town and I had to go and live with her. My father argued with my grandmother, "I'm going to bring up my daughter, because I want to send her to school." My grandmother said, "No way. It won't be necessary. It is my right to bring her up to grow up to be a very good housewife." So they agreed, we might as well just train her to do both. "I'll keep her on Monday through Friday, and on Saturday and Sunday she'll come home to the village so you can teach her all you want."

And so, indeed, every Friday I would go home by bus, and without fail, a friend of mine from the village named Chrissie would be waiting at the roadside to walk me home, and she would tell me about what had happened in the village during the week and I would tell her what I had seen in town. She went to the village school and I went to the urban school. She was brighter than me. We got to the end of primary school. We were both selected to [go to] the best girls secondary schools. She went one time, and the next time I came back, Chrissie wasn't standing by the roadside. My grandmother told me she wasn't going to be coming back. She had dropped out of school because the family would not raise $6 for her to go back. I am still talking about social justice.

So Chrissie had dropped out of school and I went on . . . and on. And went all the way to the State House and became my country's president. But Chrissie was brighter than me. . . . Chrissie is where I left her. Chrissie didn't go to school, so at 15 she got married and the child she had at 15 died at two months old, of AIDS. That's how unfair the world is. And I got angry then, and I used that anger throughout my life to send as many girls as possible to school so they don't end up like my best friend, Chrissie. . . .

The statistics show that 97 million primary school children are not going to school, right now, in the world. Statistics show that 226 million girls and boys are not going to school in secondary school in the world, as we speak. . . .

In this world, we are leaving a whole generation behind. And that's a time bomb, and we shouldn't be surprised about what we see in the Mediterranean Sea—people leaving Africa, going over to find green pastures. If we empowered them, they would stay at home and work at home. The choice is ours. . . .

Distinguished ladies and gentlemen, allow me to especially give a message about women, because when we speak about justice and education, [we speak] more or less about women and children. Because where I come from, they are the face of poverty. . . .

Whether we like it or not, there are two things. One, we [women] are the majority. We are the majority and so therefore the world needs to know that we are the majority. Number two, I also want the world to know and to remember always that we brought the other half into this world.

But isn't it sad, that [despite] that as it may be, we live in patriarchal societies—most of us. And so whether we like it or not, we have to co-exist. And whether we like it or not, when we draw our action plans as women to empower women, we shall need our men to help us implement those action plans. . . . And so, it would be naive for us to think we can do it on our own. And I have seen . . . champions, gender experts, that have really goofed and ended up failing because they were confrontational and thought they could do it without men. . . .

Sadly, childbirth is a leading cause of death for teenage girls around the world. Many more suffer fistula, and the social stigma that comes along with it. Ensuring those extra years of education can protect girls from early marriage and pregnancy, also giving them the skills and knowledge to earn income and later empower them in life.

Distinguished ladies and gentlemen, these problems may seem far from your challenges—but we need women to be at the policy setting and leadership table to bring this agenda forward. For this, we need women and men to believe in the importance of a joint fight against injustice. We need women and men to commit to be equal partners in service, in decision making and in leadership. . . .

I see my life's work as five pillars: income generation for women, education, women's health, women's leadership, and [women's] rights. These ideas are key to empowering women, and ultimately children. When we empower women with education, small businesses, and allow them to actively participate in society, and provide them reproductive health rights, we can lift an entire nation. . . .

Are you tough enough to change the world? . . .

Glossary

AIDS: acquired immunodeficiency syndrome, a disease that attacks the immune system and remains prevalent in African nations

Malawi: a small nation in southeastern Africa; Banda served as Malawi's president from 2012 to 2014

midwife: a medical professional who works with pregnant women and women in labor, and are often—as in Banda's story—the only medical professionals available in some regions

Wheelock College: a small independent women's college in Boston, Massachusetts, that merged with Boston University in 2018, three years after Banda delivered her commencement speech

Short-Answer Questions

1. What, according to Banda, is the relationship between education, poverty, disease, and the status of women internationally?

2. What does Banda propose as a solution to the problems she describes?

3. Why does Banda propose that it is necessary for women to work with men to solve the problems she outlines?

Carmen Perez: Address at the Women's March on Washington

Author
Carmen Perez

Date
2017

Document Type
Speeches/Addresses

Significance
Established the basis on which women would resist the detrimental policies of the Trump administration

Overview

Carmen Perez (1977–) is an activist for women's rights and the rights of Hispanic Americans. A graduate of Oxnard College and the University of California–Santa Cruz, she served as one of the co-chairs of the Women's March on Washington, where she delivered this speech on January 21, 2017.

The Women's March on Washington was the most prominent of several hundred marches across the United States and worldwide. All the marches were dedicated to expressing opposition to the policies of newly inaugurated President Donald Trump. They were meant to signal the widespread anger over Trump's outright misogyny and other policy positions that threatened women. More than 470,000 participants marched in the Washington event alone—far more than had attended Trump's inauguration, much to his annoyance. Worldwide, somewhere between 3.26 and 5.24 million people participated in the marches. Overall, organizers declared, there were 408 planned marches in the United States and an additional 198 overseas.

The organizers of the Women's March released a broad slate of policies that they urged the marchers to adopt. The policies included positions on health care, reproductive rights, LGBTQ+ rights, workers' rights, and environmental issues, thus linking several disparate issues that had long been pursued piecemeal under one umbrella organization.

The 2017 Women's March in Washington, DC (Wikimedia Commons)

Document Text

Good afternoon, family!

My name is Carmen Perez and I am the executive director of The Gathering for Justice. I am truly humbled to join and serve you as one of the national co-chairs of the Women's March alongside my sistren Tamika Mallory, Linda Sarsour and Bob Bland, as well as the many many people who have worked so hard to make today happen. Thank you.

I stand here as a Chicano Mexican-American woman, as a daughter and granddaughter of farmworkers, as a family member of incarcerated and undocumented people, as a survivor of domestic violence, as a woman who knows pain and who has transformed her pain into gifts, gifts that have allowed me to see light in the darkest places.

For twenty years, I have worked in America's prisons. I have seen families being torn apart, locked up in cages, many stripped of their rights, their freedoms, and ultimately, their lives. And the majority are black and brown, including women, women who I call my sisters. This has to end. This will end because of *you*, because of *us*.

Today I join you all and raise my voice, loud and clear, to say we have had enough. We know what the problems are. We know who our enemy is. We know what the injustices have done to us and those we love.

But to overcome them we have to stand in solidarity. We have to listen to each other and know that we always have more to learn. To protect each other, we don't always have to agree. But we have to organize and stand together. We must remember that unity of action does not mean that we have to be unanimous in thought, but that injury to one is injury to all.

I am reminded of the words of my mentor and boss, Harry Belafonte, "Those who are working for the liberation of our people are only subject to friendship and support. Those who are being divisive are playing the enemy's game."

And so our responsibility is to find our way. There is an entry point for all of us to be involved in this movement, so get involved, stay involved and keep your eyes on the prize.

Know that those closest to the problem are also closest to the solution. Trust them, stand with them in your action. Because I believe what Fannie Lou Hamer said, "When I liberate myself, I liberate others. And if you don't speak, ain't nobody going to speak on behalf of you."

And to those threatening us and our livelihood, I say, "Si no nos dejan soñar, no los vamos te dejar dormir." If they don't let us dream, we won't let them sleep.

We stand here on day one of the new administration, refusing to let them sleep—not for one second. We will hold all our officials, whether elected or appointed, accountable.

There are some in this country who say we should adjust to work with and adjust to hatred. But Dr. Martin Luther King spoke of the power of being maladjusted to an unjust society.

We will not adjust to hatred and bigotry. We will resist Islamophobia, xenophobia, white supremacy, sexism, racism, misogyny, and ableism. We will be brave, intentional and unapologetic in addressing the intersections of our identities, and collectively we will stand up for the most marginalized among us, because they are us.

We will not wait for some magical being to rise up and save us. We are not helpless. We are the ones we've been waiting for. We are who we need.

When I see my liberation bound in your liberation, and you in mine, together we will get free.

So remember, when you go back home think about why you marched and organize, organize, organize. ¡*Si se puede*!

Thank you!

Glossary

Fannie Lou Hamer: a Black activist for rights for women and for African Americans, and one of the seminal figures organizing the "Freedom Summer" movement to enroll Black voters in Mississippi in 1964; inducted into the National Women's Hall of Fame in 1993

Gathering for Justice: an organization founded by the late actor and singer Harry Belafonte dedicated to reducing juvenile imprisonment and lobbying to eliminate racial discrimination in the U.S. justice system

"Islamophobia, xenophobia, white supremacy, sexism, racism, misogyny, and ableism": a series of abuses that Perez associates with the incoming administration, which had demonstrated during the 2016 campaign its willingness to embrace all these forms of abuse

Si se puede: a Spanish phrase meaning "Yes, you can" or "Yes, we can"; since 1972 the motto of the United Farm Workers movement, a pro-union movement whose constituency is largely Hispanic

sistren: close female friend or comrade

Tamika Mallory, Linda Sarsour, Bob Bland: three of the organizers of the March on Washington

Short-Answer Questions

1. What does Perez say that the organizers hope to accomplish through the March on Washington?

2. What kind of change does Perez see as necessary?

3. Where does Perez suggest that the power for change will come from? Why does she suggest this?

X González: "We Call BS"

Author
X González

Date
2018

Document Type
Speeches/Addresses

Significance
Called for tighter regulation on gun sales following a deadly mass shooting at a Florida high school

Overview

X González (born Emma González, 1999) was attending at Marjory Stoneman Douglas High School in Parkland, Florida, on February 14, 2018, when a former student, Nikolas Cruz, opened fire in the building, killing seventeen students and wounding seventeen more. In response to the shooting, González and other students organized a series of protests calling for public officials to pass more restrictions on gun sales. They also co-organized Never Again MSD, a political action committee that advocates for stricter gun regulations.

This speech was delivered by González at a rally for gun control only three days after the shooting. They delivered it in front of the Broward County courthouse to a group of anti-gun activists. In the speech, González stated their disgust with the inaction of public officials toward gun control and pledged that the survivors of the Marjory Stoneman Douglas High School massacre would continue to protest and lobby for changes to state and national gun laws. A month after the speech was delivered, González and fellow Parkland shooting survivors David Hogg, Cameron Kaskey, and Sarah Chadwick organized and participated in a nationwide March for Our Lives protest in Washington, D.C. González delivered a second speech at March for Our Lives in which they listed all the dead by name. González's actions have inspired other activists, including environmentalist Greta Thunberg.

X Gonzalez speaking at the February 17, 2018, gun control rally (Wikimedia Commons)

Document Text

Every single person up here today . . . should be home grieving. But instead we are up here, standing together because if all our government and President can do is send thoughts and prayers, then it's time for victims to be the change that we need to see. . . . Since the time of the Founding Fathers and since they added the Second Amendment to the Constitution, our guns have developed at a rate that leaves me dizzy. The guns have changed and the laws have not.

We certainly do not understand why it should be harder to make plans with friends on weekends than to buy an automatic or semi-automatic weapon. . . . In Florida, to buy a gun you do not need a permit, you do not need a gun license, and once you buy it you do not need to register it. . . . You can buy as many guns as you want at one time.

I read something very powerful to me today. It was from the point of view of a teacher. And I quote: "When adults tell me I have the right to own a gun, all I can hear is my right to own a gun outweighs your student's right to live. All I can hear is mine, mine, mine, mine." . . .

The students at this school have been having debates on guns for what feels like our entire lives. . . . The people involved right now, those who were there, those posting, those tweeting, those doing interviews and talking to people, are being listened to for what feels like the very first time about this topic that has come up over 1,000 times in the past four years alone.

I found out today there's a website: shootingtracker.com. Nothing in the title suggests that it is exclusively tracking the USA's shootings and yet does it need to address that? Because Australia had one mass shooting in 1999 in Port Arthur [and after the] massacre introduced gun safety, and they haven't had one since. . . . Japan has never had a mass shooting. . . . Canada has had three and the UK had one and they both introduced gun control and yet here we are, with websites dedicated to reporting these tragedies so that they can be formulated into statistics at your convenience.

I watched an interview this morning and noticed that one of the questions was, do you think your children will have to go through other school shooter drills? And our response is that our neighbors will not have to go through other school shooter drills. When we've had our say with the government—and maybe the adults have gotten used to saying "it is what it is," but if us students have learned anything, it's that if you don't study, you will fail. And in this case if you actively do nothing, people continually end up dead, so it's time to start doing something. . . .

We are going to be the kids you read about in textbooks. Not because we're going to be another statistic about mass shootings in America, but because . . . we are going to be the last mass shooting. . . . Just like *Tinker v. Des Moines*, we are going to change the law. That's going to be Marjory Stoneman Douglas in that textbook and it's all going to be due to the tireless effort of the school board, the faculty members, the family members and most importantly, the students. . . . The students who are dead, the students still in the hospital, the students who are now suffering from PTSD, the students who had panic attacks during the vigil because the helicopters wouldn't leave us alone, hovering over the school 24 hours a day. . . .

If the President wants to come up to me and tell me to my face that it was a terrible tragedy and how it should never have happened and maintain telling us how nothing is going to be done about it, I'm going to happily ask him how much money he received from the National Rifle Association. . . .

You want to know something? It doesn't matter, because I already know. Thirty million dollars. And divided by the number of gunshot victims in the United States in the one and one-half months in 2018 alone, that comes out to being $5,800. Is that how much these people are worth to you, Trump? If you don't do anything to prevent this from continuing to occur, that number of gunshot victims will go up and the number that they are worth will go down. And we will be worthless to you.

To every politician who is taking donations from the NRA, shame on you. . . .

The people in the government who were voted into power are lying to us. And us kids seem to be the only ones who notice and . . . call BS. Companies trying to make caricatures of the teenagers nowadays, saying that all we are self-involved and trend-obsessed and they hush us into submission when our message doesn't reach the ears of the nation, we are prepared to call BS. . . . Politicians who sit in their gilded House and Senate seats funded by the NRA telling us nothing could have been done to prevent this, we call BS. They say tougher guns laws do not decrease gun violence. We call BS. They say a good guy with a gun stops a bad guy with a gun. We call BS. They say guns are just tools like knives and are as dangerous as cars. We call BS. They say no laws could have prevented the hundreds of senseless tragedies that have occurred. We call BS. That us kids don't know what we're talking about, that we're too young to understand how the government works. We call BS.

If you agree, register to vote. Contact your local congresspeople. Give them a piece of your mind.

Glossary

National Rifle Association (NRA): an organization founded in 1871 to promote the safe handling of firearms that grew into a lobbying group working to prevent restrictions on ownership of firearms

Port Arthur shooting: the mass murder of thirty-five people, the worst shooting in Australian history, which took place on April 28, 1996 (not 1999, as González says), in the state of Tasmania, in response to which the government of Australia passed a series of restrictions on the ownership of automatic and semi-automatic weapons, established a waiting period for the sale of firearms, and created a national gun registry to track weapons nationwide

Tinker v. Des Moines: a 1969 Supreme Court case that upheld the right of students to exercise free speech

Short-Answer Questions

1. What are the main points that González makes in their speech? Do they see the problem as stemming more from gun ownership or from government inaction?

2. What is González's ultimate aim? Do they set out a program in their speech?

3. González calls for the victims of the shooting to "be the change that we need to see." What do they want the victims to do?

Autumn Peltier: Address at the UN World Water Day

Author
Autumn Peltier

Date
2018

Document Type
Speeches/Addresses

Significance
Reminded the world of the absolute necessity of clean fresh water to all people

Overview

Autumn Peltier (2004–), an Indigenous activist and member of the Anishinabek Nation, one of the First Nations of Canada, delivered this speech at the United Nations World Water Day before the UN General Assembly when she was only thirteen years old. Peltier was already a committed environmental warrior who came from ancestors who also revered the environment. She had begun speaking for environmental causes when she was eight, and by the time she stood before the UN on March 22, 2018, she had already addressed the Assembly of First Nations, a representative group made up of chiefs from the Indigenous peoples of Canada.

In 2019, Peltier was named the Anishinabek Nation chief water commissioner following the death of the previous holder of the office: Josephine Mandamin, who also happened to be Peltier's great-aunt. A survivor of the Canadian Indian residential school system, Mandamin drew attention to the importance of protecting water from pollution by participating in a series of water walks that circled the Great Lakes. Following Mandamin's death in 2019, only a few months after this speech was delivered, Peltier took up her cause. In that year, Peltier went on to address the United Nations Global Landscapes Forum. In recognition of her activism, Peltier has been nominated for the International Children's Peace Prize three times.

Document Text

I'm doing this work as we can't just pray anymore—we must do something, and we need to do it now. I need to get right into this message, so you feel where I'm coming from. I can't stress enough what I have learned about the water from my elders in our ceremonies. Many people don't think water is alive or has a spirit. My people believe this to be true—there are studies now that prove this. We believe our water is sacred because we were born of water and live in water for nine months. When the water breaks, new life comes, but even deeper than that we come from our mother's water and her mother's water and so on. All the original water flows through us from the beginning and all around us.

Where I come from, I'm so fortunate I can still drink the water from the lake, but sometimes I question it. Not far from where I live there are communities that have lived through boil water advisories. I ask myself, why is it this way and why in my province? Why in my country? I didn't really understand this because I always hear of the problems in other countries around the world having no water or very polluted water. I really started to think, my mind wondered and thought, what if we ran out of water?

I didn't really understand this because I always hear the problems in other countries around the world having no water or very polluted water. What will happen? Then I got scared. This is serious and it's all over the world. Water is the lifeblood of Mother Earth. Whether it's frozen, in the form of rain or clouds, in rivers, lakes, and oceans, water is around us and sustains us all.

Everything is connected to this issue of clean water, and this impacts our health and well-being. These thoughts bring me to a story shared by my grandfather about the word in our language that says "ode nid." We use this word when we say we are going to town or the city, but it really means where your heart is. My heart is in our land, in our water. My heart is where I come from—ask yourself where your heart is. Where is your spirit? My heart and spirit is where my community is and where my ancestors are buried, where the water is fresh and I can drink from the lake. My grandfather told me to remind everyone where your heart is, as we need our land to live, and we can't be here without the land and the water. We are all connected. My heart is not for sale, and neither is our water and our lands.

So now, here we are, all together, on March 22nd on a World Water Day at the United Nations. We are here to launch the International Decade for Action "Water for Sustainable Development." My first thought is, I will be 23 years old in 2028—in my mind I have taken a photo of where we are today, where we are at with various issues surrounding our water. My snapshot doesn't feel good in terms of pollution, climate change, pipelines breaking, recycling, sanitation, poverty, hunger, and illnesses related to these issues. All I can do is keep helping my auntie educate others and share a story of how we need to respect Mother Earth and need to honor our sacred water.

One day I will be an ancestor and I want my great-grandchildren to know I tried hard to fight so they can have clean drinking water. Our water deserves to be treated as human with human rights. We need to acknowledge our waters with personhood so we can protect our waters. Our water should not be for sale; we all have a right to this water as we need it—not just rich people, all people. No one should have to worry if the water is clean or if they will run out of water. No child should grow up not knowing what clean water is, or never knowing what running water is.

Mr. President, we need to work together. Now is the time to warrior up and empower each other to take a stand for our planet. We need to sustain the little we have now and develop ways not to pollute the environment, and sustain relationships with Mother Earth and save what we have left. I hope to keep my heart in a good place so it can come back and see how much we all have improved with our promise to Mother Earth. Let's not let water and Mother Earth down. Meegwetch. Thank you.

Glossary

meegwetch: "thank you" in Algonquin

"Mr. President": a reference to the president of the United Nations General Assembly, who in February 2018, at the time Peltier spoke, was Miroslav Lajčák, minister of foreign and European affairs for the Slovak Republic

"my auntie": a reference to Josephine Mandamin (1942–2019), an environmental activist, a member of the Anishinaabe First Nation, and Peltier's great-aunt

"where my community is . . . I can drink from the lake": an Anishinaabe community on Manitoulin Island, an island in Lake Huron that is part of Canada

Short-Answer Questions

1. What is the nature of the relationship Peltier and her community have with fresh water? Why is it so important to them?

2. What does Peltier see as the goal of the UN World Water Day?

3. Peltier refers often to members of her community, past, present, and future, as members of her family. How does this shape the rhetoric of her argument?

Greta Thunberg: "Our House Is on Fire"

Author
Greta Thunberg

Date
2019

Document Type
Speeches/Addresses

Significance
Stated in plain language the dangers posed by climate change and pinned the responsibility on the representatives at Davos

Overview

Greta Thunberg is a Swedish environmental activist known for her role in promoting the need for action to mitigate climate change. She became famous both because of her youth (she was born in 2003) and for her fearlessness in confronting world leaders over their inaction on environmental issues. She has become one of the foremost figures in the ongoing attempt to raise public awareness about the danger climate change poses to people worldwide.

Thunberg first won international attention in the summer of 2018 when, at the age of fifteen, she began picketing the Swedish parliament, holding a sign that said "School Strike for Climate." She declared she would refuse to attend school on Fridays until the parliament took action to address the issue of climate change in accordance with the Paris Agreement signed three years earlier. Thunberg consciously modeled her protest on the ongoing activism of young people in the United States who were protesting government inaction over school shootings at places like Marjory Stoneman Douglas High School in Parkland, Florida, and who refused to attend school until their concerns were addressed.

Soon Thunberg was joined by fellow students across Europe who likewise refused to attend classes one day a week and instead participated in protests. In December of 2018, only a few months after her protests had begun, she was invited to speak before the plenary session of the 2018 United Nations Climate Change Conference, or COP24. The following month, on January 25, she gave the speech known as "Our House Is on Fire" before the World Economic Forum at its annual meeting in Davos, Switzerland.

Swedish environmental activist Greta Thunberg
(Wikimedia Commons)

Document Text

Our house is on fire. I am here to say, our house is on fire.

According to the IPCC, we are less than 12 years away from not being able to undo our mistakes. In that time, unprecedented changes in all aspects of society need to have taken place, including a reduction of our CO2 emissions by at least 50 percent.

And please note that those numbers do not include the aspect of equity, which is absolutely necessary to make the Paris Agreement work on a global scale. Nor does it include tipping points or feedback loops like the extremely powerful methane gas being released from the thawing Arctic permafrost.

At places like Davos, people like to tell success stories. But their financial success has come with an unthinkable price tag. And on climate change, we have to acknowledge we have failed. All political movements in their present form have done so, and the media has failed to create broad public awareness.

But *Homo sapiens* have not yet failed.

Yes, we are failing, but there is still time to turn everything around. We can still fix this. We still have everything in our own hands. But unless we recognise the overall failures of our current systems, we most probably don't stand a chance.

We are facing a disaster of unspoken sufferings for enormous amounts of people. And now is not the time for speaking politely or focusing on what we can or cannot say. Now is the time to speak clearly.

Solving the climate crisis is the greatest and most complex challenge that *Homo sapiens* have ever faced. The main solution, however, is so simple that even a small child can understand it. We have to stop our emissions of greenhouse gases.

Either we do that or we don't.

You say nothing in life is black or white. But that is a lie. A very dangerous lie. Either we prevent 1.5 degree [Celsius] of warming or we don't. Either we avoid setting off that irreversible chain reaction beyond human control or we don't. Either we choose to go on as a civilisation or we don't. That is as black or white as it gets. There are no grey areas when it comes to survival.

Now we all have a choice. We can create transformational action that will safeguard the future living conditions for humankind. Or we can continue with our business as usual and fail.

That is up to you and me.

Some say we should not engage in activism. Instead we should leave everything to our politicians and just vote for a change instead. But what do we do when there is no political will? What do we do when the politics needed are nowhere in sight?

Here in Davos—just like everywhere else—everyone is talking about money. It seems that money and growth are our only main concerns.

And since the climate crisis has never once been treated as a crisis, people are simply not aware of the full consequences on our everyday life. People are not aware that there is such a thing as a carbon budget, and just how incredibly small that remaining carbon budget is. And that needs to change today.

No other current challenge can match the importance of establishing a wide, public awareness and understanding of our rapidly disappearing carbon budget, that should and must become our new global currency and the very heart of future and present economics.

We are now at a time in history where everyone with any insight of the climate crisis that threatens our civilisation—and the entire biosphere—must speak out in clear language, no matter how uncomfortable and unprofitable that may be.

We must change almost everything in our current societies. The bigger your carbon footprint is, the bigger your moral duty. The bigger your platform, the bigger your responsibility.

Adults keep saying: "We owe it to the young people to give them hope." But I don't want your hope. I don't want you to be hopeful. I want you to panic. I want you to feel the fear I feel every day. And then I want you to act.

I want you to act as you would in a crisis. I want you to act as if the house is on fire. Because it is.

Glossary

carbon budget: a way to try to slow the creation of carbon dioxide by spreading the economic costs of slowing CO2 emissions fairly among the nations worldwide

CO2: a scientific abbreviation for carbon dioxide, which is produced through the combustion of fossil fuels and is a major factor in global warming

Davos: a reference to the World Economic Forum, which has been hosted in the Swiss resort town of Davos since its founding (under the name European Management Forum) in 1971

IPCC: the Intergovernmental Panel on Climate Change, set up by the United Nations in 1988 to inform governments about human-caused climate change

Paris Agreement: also known as the Paris Climate Accords, an international treaty signed by 195 state members of a group called the United Nations Framework Convention on Climate Change in which the countries agreed to reduce emissions of greenhouse gasses to zero by the middle of the twenty-first century

Short-Answer Questions

1. When Thunberg says "Our house is on fire," does she mean it literally, figuratively, or both? Please explain.

2. How does Thunberg try to evoke feelings of responsibility for climate change in her audience?

3. Davos is the site where the World Economic Forum meets each year. Its members are made up of executives from corporations rather than elected officials. What does Thunberg think they can do about climate change?

Josina Machel:
"Male Violence against Women: The Next Frontier in Humanity"

Author	Significance
Josina Machel	Established the need to oppose all kinds of violence directed against women worldwide
Date	
2020	
Document Type	
Speeches/Addresses	

Overview

Josina Z. Machel (1976–) is the daughter of two prominent African politicians and the stepdaughter of another. She was born to the late president of Mozambique Samora Machel, who died (possibly murdered) in a plane crash in 1986. Her mother, Machel's second wife Graça Simbine Machel, a prominent Mozambican activist, later married Nelson Mandela. Renowned for his opposition to apartheid, Mandela became the first Black head of state in South African history. Machel attended the University of Cape Town, majoring in sociology and political science. She went on to study at the London School of Economics and earned a master of science degree in the same fields.

Machel had always had an interest in women's rights and women's health. Her master's dissertation examined the impact of AIDS on poverty-stricken young women in Mozambique. But it was not until October 1915, when her then-partner Rofino Licuco assaulted her, that Machel brought her personal experience to the issue of women's rights. Licuco beat Machel so badly that she lost sight in one eye. The organ later had to be removed. Licuco was tried and convicted, but despite his threats and intimidation addressed to Machel, the conviction was later overturned on the grounds that the abuse had not been witnessed. Machel has drawn on her personal experience with gender-based abuse to create the Kuhluka movement, which challenges rules that protect perpetrators of violence against women in South Africa. She delivered this TEDx Talk on February 21, 2020, identifying men's violence against women as a war against women and calling for a deep transformation of self and society.

Document Text

In the early hours of October 17, 2015, in a very small space . . . I was brutally and savagely abused and attacked by a man that professed to love me.

You know, I was born and raised by parents who were prepared to lay down their lives for breaching frontiers of colonial, of apartheid oppression—of exploitation and violence. Fate bestowed upon my life a different struggle, a struggle against violence against women, a struggle that I take proudly. And my face represents the socially weakened, the ever vulnerable. . . .

In a matter of thirty seconds—thirty seconds—it did not matter that I'd been raised as a daughter to two presidents, to a woman who is widely respected as a woman's rights advocate throughout the world. The security I grew up with, that guarded me, did not matter. The education that I received and the master's degree in sociology and gender studies that I had gotten from one of the best schools in the world, did not protect me at all. In a matter of thirty seconds all the struggles and the wins of . . . colonial independence, of work systems, of apartheid and women's emancipation were completely and utterly shattered. . . .

My first scream . . . of utter, utter panic and helplessness was really about the breaking—the shattering, rather—of my existence, and it was a cry for help. I decided then to use my voice from then onwards in order to ensure that . . . no other women go through what I did, screaming in the middle of the night and no single human being was able to help. The only reaction that I got were actually of dogs barking.

The days, the months, and the weeks that followed represented . . . the battle that we as humankind face at this point. As I took a few days to recover . . . there was a confirmation that, because of this thirty seconds, I was never ever going to be able to see again.

I decided that something needed to be done. . . . The power of men had conquered so much. . . . The colonial exploitation [and] . . . emancipation of women—everything was completely shattered, and all those wins disappeared actually as ashes as we realized that we were not immune to evil . . . and the shackles of violence against women are all about us.

. . . Most important [it] became very, very clear that [this is] not about the power of one man to beat you, but it's about the power that is behind it in terms of the institutions and the society that we allow to continue . . . and to continue doing all these things. That's where the power of men is. . . .

I've spoken about the perpetrators . . . but also it's very important to recognize perhaps as the survivors of violence have not been given the voice right now, because . . . every single day thousands of women [join] our ranks. Every single day they don't choose to, but that is the reality. So if today, if yesterday, we were nine hundred thousand, we [are] probably nine hundred and fifty thousand today. And these numbers will just increase if we continue doing that.

The issue that is also important for us to understand is that trauma doesn't disappear. . . . The fact that you were abused two months ago or two years ago, perhaps twenty years ago, does not mean that your life is all of a sudden rosy. We deal with the issues and the consequences of this abuse, of this wall in which we are—in which we become actually every day—veterans of war. . . . We learn to live with all these consequences. Every time our door shuts, we jump. Every time someone screams . . . it takes us to that point of pain. . . .

How to End the War

So we are in a war. How are we going to end this one? One of the first things that we have to think . . . is that in spite of all the victories, . . . we as human beings have [not] actually evolved as well. Because the way men behave right now . . . is primitive . . . in ways . . . in which there is no rationality. . . .

Women, you know, at birth . . . sign unwillingly what I would want to call a contract with death. . . . You know that your life is in the hands of this man . . . but more than that it's also pleasing your mother-in-law, so it's about adapting and killing your individuality in order to serve other people. . . . We want to defend our daughters and say no, not in our lifetime, but then when our very boys . . . beat them we start to . . . say, well no, perhaps the punishment shouldn't be that hard. . . .

I created the Kuhluka movement a few years ago after the abuse and all the degradation that I went through in order to ensure that the rights and the needs of women are recognized, and the way women are treated and the way women are recognized in our community is different. But also to make sure that we all know that this is not a fight that we can opt not to get involved with. You need to choose your side. . . . Are you of a perpetrator are you a victim? and do you choose to remain a victim? Do you choose to remain a victim? or you can pick up yourself and you can hold on to other women and in strength and giving voice you also become part of the numbers that say no more. . . .

Being an accomplice at this point is standing in the wrong side of history. To be an accomplice at this time really signifies standing on the side of the enemy, and it does mean that you continuously and in a conscious way . . . decide that we're not breaking into a new frontier of humanity. Thank you.

Glossary

apartheid: a system of racist oppression, and a governmental policy in South Africa throughout most of the twentieth century

colonial oppression: actions taken by colonizers (in this case, colonizers in Africa) that act against the interests of indigenous people

Kuhluka movement: an international organization founded by Josina Machel in Johannesburg, South Africa, designed to fight gender-based violence by advocating for policies that protect women from violence and providing social services for abused women

perpetrators: people who are responsible for a crime or injustice

Short-Answer Questions

1. What does Machel see as the greatest threat to women in the modern age?

2. How, according to Machel, can the resistance she advocates help end gender-based violence?

3. What does Machel think needs to be done to protect women against gender-based violence?

Kamala Harris: "The Status of Women Is the Status of Democracy"

Author
Kamala Harris

Date
2021

Document Type
Speeches/Addresses

Significance
Linked the worldwide rise of fascism and authoritarianism with a decline in the status of women, and pledged the support of the Biden administration for women's issues worldwide

Overview

In 2021 Kamala Devi Harris (1964–) became the forty-ninth vice president of the United States, serving with President Joe Biden. The former district attorney of Alameda County, California, Harris is the first African American, the first Asian American, and the first woman to hold the office of U.S. vice president.

Harris ran for the seat of retiring U.S. senator Barbara Boxer in 2016 after Boxer announced her retirement. In the election of that year, Harris handily defeated her rival, Representative Loretta Sanchez, and took her seat the following January. She quickly established a reputation as a strong critic of the methods of the Trump administration. In 2019 Harris declared her candidacy for the presidential election of the following year, but she withdrew before the primaries began. In March 2020 she accepted Joe Biden's offer to serve as his running mate.

The "defense of democracy" theme of this speech, delivered March 15, 2021, refers indirectly to the January 6, 2021, assault on the U.S. Capitol. The assault was an attempt to overturn the results of the presidential election, prevent the inauguration of Joe Biden, and reestablish Donald Trump, the loser of the election, as president. In her speech Harris directly links the worldwide rise of fascism and authoritarianism with a decline in the status of women, and she pledges the support of the Biden administration for women's issues worldwide.

Document Text

This year, in considering the status of women—especially as it pertains to the participation of women in decision making—we must also consider the status of democracy. At its best, democracy protects human rights; promotes human dignity; and upholds the rule of law. It is a means to establish peace and shared prosperity. It should ensure every citizen, regardless of gender, has an equal voice; and free and fair elections that will respect the will of the people. At the same time, democracy requires constant vigilance, constant improvement—it is a work in progress. And today we know that democracy is increasingly under great strain. For 15 consecutive years, we have seen a troubling decline in freedom around the globe. In fact, experts believe that this past year was the worst, on record, for the global deterioration of democracy and freedom.

The status of democracy also depends, fundamentally, on the empowerment of women. Not only because the exclusion of women in decision-making is a marker of a flawed democracy, but because the participation of women strengthens democracy. COVID-19 has threated the economic security; the physical security; and the health of women everywhere. As women struggle to get the healthcare they need, the pandemic appears to be reversing the global gains we've made in the fight against HIV, AIDS, tuberculosis, malaria, malnutrition, and maternal and child mortality. That's why, on the first day of our administration, the United States reengaged as a member-state and leader in the World Health Organization; and we are revitalizing our partnership with UN Women, to help empower women worldwide.

Eleanor Roosevelt, who shaped the Universal Declaration on Human Rights, once said, "Without equality there can be no democracy." In other words, the status of women is the status of democracy. For our part, the United States will work to improve both.

Official portrait of Vice President Kamala Harris (Library of Congress)

Glossary

Eleanor Roosevelt: First Lady of the United States from 1933 to 1945, a prominent civil rights and human rights activist, the first U.S. delegate to the United Nations General Assembly, and as chair of the UN Commission on Human Rights, responsible for the drafting of the Universal Declaration of Human Rights

UN Women: reference to the United Nations Entity for Gender Equality and the Empowerment of Women, an international organization that advocates for women's rights and the rights of LGBTQ+ individuals World Health Organization: also known as the WHO, an agency of the United Nations responsible for issues relating to public health

Short-Answer Questions

1. What is the main reason Vice President Harris is delivering this speech?

2. Why does Harris believe that improving the situation of women worldwide is so important?

3. What does Vice President Harris say is the relationship between the status of women and the status of democracy?

Sustainable Development Goal 5: Achieve Gender Equality and Empower All Women and Girls

Author
United Nations

Date
2022

Document Type
Cartoons, Images, Artwork

Significance
Called attention to the global disparities between men's and women's situations in political representation, allocation of funding, employment, protection from violence, and reproductive health care

Overview

The United Nations' Sustainable Development Goal 5, "Achieve Gender Equality and Empower All Women and Girls," is one of seventeen declared objectives adopted by the UN's member states in 2015. Together, the seventeen goals are known as the 2030 Agenda for Sustainable Development. The agenda is intended to bring together developed and underdeveloped countries in a shared vision for peace and prosperity in the twenty-first century. Among these goals are reducing the effects of climate change, ending poverty and hunger, assuring affordable health care and quality education, and supplying affordable and clean energy to people worldwide. The agenda also assures the development of institutions that support peace and justice and that reduce inequality—including inequalities that affect women worldwide.

The United Nations has always held the issue of gender equality as one of its most important goals. One of the earliest commissions founded after the establishment of the UN was the Commission on the Status of Women, created on June 21, 1946. In 1979, the UN's General Assembly adopted the Convention on the Elimination of All Forms of Discrimination against Women (CEDAW), a treaty that serves as a sort of international women's bill of rights. The 1995 Beijing Declaration was also adopted by the UN and serves as an international statement of the principles of women's equality. The Sustainable Development Goal 5 draws on the extensive work done to support women's rights and women's equality, and it shows what still needs to be accomplished. Among the facts cited on this infographic about the development goal is that one in four women is subjected to intimate partner violence at least once in their lifetime, and among its goals is to strengthen gender-responsive budgeting.

Document Text

5 GENDER EQUALITY: ACHIEVE GENDER EQUALITY AND EMPOWER ALL WOMEN AND GIRLS

THE WORLD IS NOT ON TRACK TO ACHIEVE GENDER EQUALITY BY 2030

OUT OF GOAL 5 INDICATORS:
- 15.4 "ON TRACK"
- 61.5 AT A MODERATE DISTANCE
- 23.1 FAR OR VERY FAR OFF TRACK

AT THE CURRENT RATE, IT WILL TAKE

300 YEARS TO END CHILD MARRIAGE

286 YEARS TO CLOSE GAPS IN LEGAL PROTECTION AND REMOVE DISCRIMINATORY LAWS

140 YEARS TO ACHIEVE EQUAL REPRESENTATION IN LEADERSHIP IN THE WORKPLACE

LEGISLATED GENDER QUOTAS ARE EFFECTIVE TO ACHIEVE EQUALITY IN POLITICS

WOMEN'S REPRESENTATION IN PARLIAMENT (2022)

 30.9% COUNTRIES APPLYING QUOTAS

 21.2% COUNTRIES WITHOUT QUOTAS

NEARLY HALF OF MARRIED WOMEN LACK DECISION-MAKING POWER OVER THEIR SEXUAL AND REPRODUCTIVE HEALTH AND RIGHTS

1 IN 5 YOUNG WOMEN ARE MARRIED BEFORE THEIR 18TH BIRTHDAY

THE SUSTAINABLE DEVELOPMENT GOALS REPORT 2023: SPECIAL EDITION- UNSTATS.UN.ORG/SDGS/REPORT/2023/

Glossary

gender-responsive budgeting: an attempt to redress the disparity in governmental and institutional funding so that all genders are represented equally when funding priorities are set

intimate partner violence: violence, especially sexual violence, from spouses, domestic partners, or roommates

Short-Answer Questions

1. What are the different general areas where gender equality is lacking that the UN considers to be vital? Why would these areas in particular be significant?

2. The UN's goal includes not only gender equality but empowerment of women and girls. How do the areas they highlight empower girls in particular?

3. By placing equal representation between men and women in national political leadership first, the UN suggests that it is the most important goal. Why might that be the case?

List of Documents by Category

Advertisements
Segregated Employment Ads

Cartoons, Images, Artwork
Sustainable Development Goal 5: Achieve Gender Equality and Empower All Women and Girls

Essays, Reports, Manifestos
Adrienne Rich: "Compulsory Heterosexuality and Lesbian Experience"
"African American Women in Defense of Ourselves"
Alice Moore Dunbar-Nelson: "The Negro Woman and the Ballot"
Alicia Garza: "A Herstory of the #BlackLivesMatter Movement"
Ama Ata Aidoo: "Ghana: To Be a Woman"
Audre Lorde: "Poetry Is Not a Luxury"
Audre Lorde: "The Master's Tools Will Never Dismantle the Master's House"
Ban Zhao: *Lessons for a Woman*
bell hooks: *Feminist Theory: From Margin to Center*
Betty Friedan: *The Feminine Mystique*
Caroline Norton: *Letter to the Queen on Lord Chancellor Cranworth's Marriage and Divorce Bill*
Casey Hayden and Mary King: "Sex and Caste"
Catherine E. Beecher: *Treatise on Domestic Economy*
Catherine Sawbridge Macaulay Graham: *Letters on Education*
Chandra Talpade Mohanty: "Under Western Eyes"
Christine de Pisan: *The Treasure of the City of Ladies*
Christine Jorgensen: "The Story of My Life"
Clara Barton: *The Red Cross in Peace and War*
Clara Lemlich: "Life in the Shop"
Clara Zetkin: "Women's Work and the Trade Unions"
Combahee River Collective Statement
Denise Harmon: "Stonewall Means Fight Back!"
Deodat Lawson: "A Further Account of the Tryals of the New England Witches, Sent in a Letter from Thence, to a Gentleman in London"
Edith M. Stern: "Women Are Household Slaves"
Eleanor Roosevelt: "Women Must Learn to Play the Game as Men Do"
"Elena's Story"
Elizabeth Cady Stanton: Seneca Falls Convention Declaration of Sentiments
Emma Goldman: "Marriage and Love"
"Fabienne's Story"
Frances Anne Kemble: *Journal of a Residence on a Georgian Plantation in 1838–1839*
Francis Parkman: *Some of the Reasons against Woman Suffrage*
Gloria Anzaldúa: *Borderlands/La Frontera: The New Mestiza*

Harriet Jacobs: *Incidents in the Life of a Slave Girl*
Hazel V. Carby: "White Woman Listen! Black Feminism and the Boundaries of Sisterhood"
Helena Swanwick: *The War in Its Effect upon Women*
Henrich Kramer: *Malleus Maleficarum*
Herodotus: *The History of the Persian Wars*
Ida B. Wells: "Lynching: Our National Crime"
Ida B. Wells: *Southern Horrors*
International Campaign for Abortion Rights: International Day of Action
Isabella Beeton: *Mrs. Beeton's Book of Household Management*
Jack London: *The People of the Abyss*
Jane Addams: "Why Women Should Vote"
Jessie Redmon Fauset: "Some Notes on Color"
Jo Ann Gibson Robinson: *The Montgomery Bus Boycott and the Women Who Started It*
Juana Inés de la Cruz: "The Poet's Answer to Sor Filotea de la Cruz"
Julian of Norwich: *Revelations of Divine Love*
June Jordan: "A New Politics of Sexuality"
Kelly Miller: "The Economic Handicap of the Negro in the North"
Kimberlé Williams Crenshaw: "Say Her Name"
Lady Hong: "Diary of Lady Hong," Queen of Korea
Luce Irigaray: "Women on the Market"
Lydia Maria Child: *An Appeal in Favor of That Class of Americans Called Africans*
Margaret Cerullo: "Hidden History: An Illegal Abortion in 1968"
Margaret Fuller: *Woman in the Nineteenth Century*
Margaret Sanger: "Birth Control and Racial Betterment"
Margery Kempe: *The Book of Margery Kempe*
Maria Eugenia Echenique: "The Emancipation of Women"
María Lugones: "Toward a Decolonial Feminism"
Marita O. Bonner: "On Being Young—A Woman—And Colored"
Mary Astell: *A Serious Proposal to the Ladies for the Advancement of Their True and Greatest Interest*
Mary Hays: Appeal to the Men of Great Britain in Behalf of Women
Mary Wollstonecraft: *A Vindication of the Rights of Woman*
"A Mother's Life in Rural Pernambuco, Brazil"
National Organization for Women Statement of Purpose
National Women's Trade Union League: Women's Work and War
Nellie Bly: *Ten Days in a Mad-House*
Olympe de Gouges: *Declaration of the Rights of Woman and of the Female Citizen*
Pauli Murray and Mary O. Eastwood: "Jane Crow and the Law: Sex Discrimination and Title VII"
Pauline Newman: A Worker Recalls Her Time at the Triangle Shirtwaist Factory
Phyllis Schlafly: "What's Wrong with 'Equal Rights' for Women?"
Plutarch: *Moralia*: "On the Bravery of Women"
President's Commission on the Status of Women: "American Women"
Priscilla Bell Wakefield: *Reflections on the Present Condition of the Female Sex; with Suggestions for Its Improvement*
Rachel Carson: *Silent Spring*
Robin Morgan: "No More Miss America!"
Sarah M. Grimké: Reply to the Pastoral Letter the General Association of Congregational Ministers of Massachusetts
Sarah Winnemucca Hopkins: *Life among the Piutes*
Say Her Name: Resisting Police Brutality against Black Women
Simone de Beauvoir: *The Second Sex*
Soranus: *Gynaecology*

Susan B. Anthony: "The Status of Woman, Past, Present, and Future"
Ursula de Jesus: "Visions of the World to Come"
Vibia Perpetua: *The Passion of Saints Perpetua and Felicity*
Victoria Woodhull: *Lecture on Constitutional Equality*
Virginia Woolf: *A Room of One's Own*
William Blackstone: *Commentaries on the Laws of England*: "Of Husband and Wife"
William Pickens: "The Woman Voter Hits the Color Line"
Xiao Lu: "China: Feudal Attitudes, Party Control, and Half the Sky"
Zitkala-Ša: "The Cutting of My Long Hair"
Zora Neale Hurston: "How It Feels to Be Colored Me"

Legal
Bradwell v. the State of Illinois
Buck v. Bell
Code of Assura
Dobbs v. Jackson Women's Health Organization
Frontiero v. Richardson
Griswold v. Connecticut
Henrich Kramer: *Malleus Maleficarum*
Hoyt v. Florida
Lawrence v. Texas
Mackenzie v. Hare
Margaret Brent's Request for Voting Rights
Massachusetts Bay Colony Trial against Anne Hutchinson
Meritor Savings Bank v. Vinson
Minor v. Happersett
Muller v. Oregon
Obergefell v. Hodges
Planned Parenthood v. Casey
Relf v. Weinberger
Roe v. Wade
Ruth Bader Ginsburg: Concurrence in Stenberg, Attorney General of Nebraska, et al. v. Carhart
Taylor v. Louisiana
United States v. Virginia
Virginia's Act XII: Negro Women's Children to Serve according to the Condition of the Mother
Webster v. Reproductive Health Services

Legislative
Comstock Act
Equal Pay Act
Equal Rights Amendment
Executive Order 11246: Equal Employment Opportunity
Mann Act
Margaret Brent's Request for Voting Rights

Nineteenth Amendment to the U.S. Constitution
Page Act of 1875
Shirley Chisholm: "For the Equal Rights Amendment"
Title IX Education Act of 1972
Title VII of the Civil Rights Act of 1964
Violence Against Women Act
Virginia's Act XII: Negro Women's Children to Serve according to the Condition of the Mother

Letters/Correspondence
Abigail Adams: Remember the Ladies Letter to John Adams
Caroline Norton: *Letter to the Queen on Lord Chancellor Cranworth's Marriage and Divorce Bill*
Casey Hayden and Mary King: "Sex and Caste"
Catherine Sawbridge Macaulay Graham: *Letters on Education*
Cherokee Women: Letter to Governor Benjamin Franklin
Deodat Lawson: "A Further Account of the Tryals of the New England Witches, Sent in a Letter from Thence, to a Gentleman in London"
Elinore Pruitt Stewart: *Letters of a Woman Homesteader*
Frances Anne Kemble: *Journal of a Residence on a Georgian Plantation in 1838–1839*
Joan of Arc: Letter to King Henry VI of England
Juana Inés de la Cruz: "The Poet's Answer to Sor Filotea de la Cruz"
Lady Mary Wortley Montagu: Smallpox Vaccination in Turkey
Letter from Elizabeth Sprigs to Her Father
Lucy Parsons: "The Negro: Let Him Leave Politics to the Politician and Prayers to the Preacher"
Mary S. Paul: Letters from Lowell Mills
Sarah M. Grimké: Reply to the Pastoral Letter the General Association of Congregational Ministers of Massachusetts
St. Jerome: Letter CVII to Laeta
Veronica Franco: A Warning to a Mother Considering Turning Her Daughter into a Courtesan

Poems, Plays, Fiction
Anne Bradstreet: "Before the Birth of One of Her Children"
Enheduanna: *Hymns to Inana*
Geoffrey Chaucer: "The Wife of Bath"
Juvenal: *The Satires*
Lucretia Mott: "Discourse on Women"
Phillis Wheatley: "His Excellency General Washington"
Sappho: Poems and Fragments
Savitribai Phule: "Go, Get Education"

Presidential/Executive
Benazir Bhutto: Address at the Fourth World Conference on Women
Indira Gandhi: "What Educated Women Can Do"
President's Commission on the Status of Women: "American Women"
Queen Noor of Jordan: Remarks at the National Organization for Arab-American Women Banquet

Speeches/Addresses

Alice Paul: Testimony before the House Judiciary Committee
Amelia Jenks Bloomer: "Alas! Poor Adam"
Anita Hill: Opening Statement at the Senate Confirmation Hearing of Clarence Thomas
Anna Howard Shaw: Address on the Place of Women in Society
Atifete Jahjaga: Support of Women's Property Rights in Kosovo
Audre Lorde: "The Master's Tools Will Never Dismantle the Master's House"
Autumn Peltier: Address at the UN World Water Day
Bella Abzug: "Women and the Fate of the Earth"
Benazir Bhutto: Address at the Fourth World Conference on Women
Benjamin Rush: "Thoughts upon Female Education"
Betty Williams: "Peace in the World Is Everybody's Business"
Billie Jean King: Commencement Address for University of Massachusetts, Amherst
Carmen Perez: Address at the Women's March on Washington
Carrie Chapman Catt: "Equal Suffrage"
Charlotte Bunch: "Through Women's Eyes: Global Forces Facing Women in the 21st Century"
Charlotte Perkins Gilman: "The Humanness of Women"
Chimamanda Ngozi Adichie: "We Should All Be Feminists"
Dolores Huerta: Statement to the Senate Subcommittee on Migratory Labor
Elizabeth Cady Stanton: Address to the New York Legislature
Elizabeth Gurley Flynn: "The Truth about the Paterson Strike"
Ella Baker: "The Black Woman in the Civil Rights Struggle"
Ellen Johnson Sirleaf: "A Voice for Freedom"
Emma Watson: "HeForShe" Speech to the United Nations
Emmeline Pankhurst: "Freedom or Death"
Fannie Lou Hamer: Testimony at the Democratic National Convention
Florence Kelley: "Child Labor and Women's Suffrage"
Frances Willard: Address before the Woman's Christian Temperance Union
Frances Wright: "Of Free Enquiry"
Gloria Steinem: "Living the Revolution"
Greta Thunberg: "Our House Is on Fire"
Hillary Rodham Clinton: "Women's Rights Are Human Rights"
Ida Husted Harper: Statement before the U.S. Senate Select Committee on Woman Suffrage
Indira Gandhi: "What Educated Women Can Do"
International Campaign for Abortion Rights: International Day of Action
Jane Addams: "The Subjective Necessity for Social Settlements"
Josephine St. Pierre Ruffin: "Address to the First National Conference of Colored Women"
Josina Machel: "Male Violence against Women: The Next Frontier in Humanity"
Joyce Banda: Wheelock College Commencement Address
Judith Heumann: "Our Fight for Disability Rights—And Why We're Not Done Yet"
June Jordan: "A New Politics of Sexuality"
Kamala Harris: "The Status of Women Is the Status of Democracy"
Leonora O'Reilly: Statement to the U.S. House Judiciary Committee
Luisa D. Diogo: "Women for a Better World"
Mabel Ping-Hua Lee: "The Submerged Half"
Malala Yousafzai: Nobel Peace Prize Acceptance Speech
Margaret Cerullo: "Hidden History: An Illegal Abortion in 1968"

Mary Church Terrell: "The Progress of Colored Women"
Mary McLeod Bethune: "What Does American Democracy Mean to Me?"
Michelle Bachelet: "Time to Make the Promise of Equality a Reality"
Michelle Obama: Remarks at the 2012 International Women of Courage Awards
Oprah Winfrey: Cecil B. DeMille Award Acceptance Speech
Patsy Mink: Speech on the 25th Anniversary of Title IX
Phyllis Schlafly: "What's Wrong with 'Equal Rights' for Women?"
Queen Elizabeth I: Speech to the Troops at Tilbury
Queen Noor of Jordan: Remarks at the National Organization for Arab-American Women Banquet
Rigoberta Menchú Tum: Nobel Peace Prize Lecture
Robin Morgan: "No More Miss America!"
Rose Schneiderman: Speech on the Triangle Shirtwaist Fire
Sandra Day O'Connor: "Portia's Progress"
Shirin Ebadi: "Iran Awakening: Human Rights, Women, and Islam"
Shirley Chisholm: "The Black Woman in Contemporary America"
Shirley Chisholm: "For the Equal Rights Amendment"
Sojourner Truth: "Ain't I a Woman?"
Sylvia Rivera: "Y'All Better Quiet Down"
Tarana Burke: "Full Power of Women"
Wangari Maathai: Nobel Peace Prize Acceptance Speech
X González: "We Call BS"

Index

Volume Page Key
Volume 1: 1–288
Volume 2: 289–562
Volume 3: 565–832

A

Abigail Adams: "Remember the Ladies" Letter to John Adams 98, 120–121
Abolition movement 175–176, 289–290
Abzug, Bella
    "Women and the Fate of the Earth" 491–494
Achebe, Chinua 764
Adams, Abigail 135
    "Remember the Ladies" Letter to John Adams 98, 120–121
Adams, John 98, 120–121, 135
Adam Smith: *The Wealth of Nations* 150
Addams, Jane 214, 290
    "The Subjective Necessity for Social Settlements" 307–309
    Twenty Years at Hull-House 307
    "Why Women Should Vote" 260–263
Adichie, Chimamanda Ngozi 747
    Purple Hibiscus 765
    "We Should All Be Feminists" 764–767
Adrienne Rich: "Compulsory Heterosexuality and Lesbian Experience" 590–594
African American Policy Forum (AAPF) 678, 682
"African American Women in Defense of Ourselves" 672–674
Aidoo, Ama Ata 608
    Dilemma of the Ghost 627
    "Ghana: To Be a Woman" 627–629
Albert Parsons: *The Alarm* 342
Alcott, Bronson 182
Alice Moore Dunbar-Nelson: "The Negro Woman and the Ballot" 281–283
Alice Paul: Testimony before the House Judiciary Committee 264–267
Alicia Garza: "A Herstory of the #BlackLivesMatter Movement" 644, 675–677
Alito, Samuel 559
Allen, Pam 439
Ama Ata Aidoo: "Ghana: To Be a Woman" 627–629
Ama Ata Aidoo: *The Dilemma of the Ghost* 627
Amelia Jenks Bloomer: "Alas! Poor Adam" Speech 191–195
Amelia Jenks Bloomer: *The Lily* 191
American Birth Control League 515
American Civil Liberties Union (ACLU) 261, 503, 555
American Equal Rights Association 224
American Revolution 97–98, 117, 131–132, 165, 289, 462
"American Women." *See* President's Commission on the Status of Women: "American Women"
American Woman Suffrage Association (AWSA) 214
Anita Hill: Opening Statement at the Senate Confirmation Hearing of Clarence Thomas 644, 668–671
Anna Howard Shaw: Address on the Place of Women in Society 249–251
Anne Bradstreet: "Before the Birth of One of Her Children" 98, 108–110
Anne Bradstreet: *The Tenth Muse Lately Sprung Up in America, By a Gentlewoman in Those Parts* 108
Anne Hutchinson: Massachusetts Bay Colony Trial 97, 100–103
Anspach, Rachel 678
Anthony Amendment 264
Anthony, Susan B. 275, 643
    "The Status of Woman, Past, Present, and Future" 176, 206–209
Anzaldúa, Gloria E.
    Borderlands/La Frontera: The New Mestiza 608, 634–637
Aristotle 4, 5, 25
Astell, Mary
    A Serious Proposal to the Ladies for the Advancement of Their True and Greatest Interest 46, 83–86
Athletics Disclosure Act of 1994 464
Atifete Jahjaga: Support of Women's Property Rights in Kosovo 780–783
Audre Lorde: "Poetry Is Not a Luxury" 479–482
Audre Lorde: *Sister Outsider: Essays and Speeches* 479, 630

Audre Lorde: "The Master's Tools Will Never Dismantle the Master's House" 608, 630–633
Augustine of Hippo 41
Aung, Zin Mar 768
Autumn Peltier: Address at the UN World Water Day 796–798

B

Bachelet, Michelle 747
    "Time to Make the Promise of Equality a Reality" 760–763
Baker, Ella
    "The Black Woman in the Civil Rights Struggle" 397, 447–449
Baker v. Nelson 602
Banda, Joyce Hilda 747
    Wheelock College Commencement Address 784–787
Ban Zhao: *History of the Han* 21
Ban Zhao: *Lessons for a Woman* 21–24
Barrett, Amy Coney 559
Barton, Clara
    The Red Cross in War and Peace 290, 316–318
Beecher, Catharine E.
    Treatise on Domestic Economy 176, 178–181
Beeton, Isabella
    Mrs. Beeton's Book of Household Management 326, 334–337
Beeton, Samuel Orchart 334
Begum, Shad 768
Beijing Declaration 809
Bella Abzug: "Women and the Fate of the Earth" 491–494
bell hooks: *Feminist Theory: From Margin to Center* 644, 664–667
Benazir Bhutto: Address at the Fourth World Conference on Women 718–721
Benjamin Rush: "Thoughts upon Female Education" 98, 125–129
Berkeley, William 106
Bethune, Mary McLeod
    "What Does American Democracy Mean to Me?" 644, 658–660
Betty Friedan: *The Feminine Mystique* 396–397, 408–411, 431
Betty Friedan: "The Problem That Has No Name" 408
Betty Williams: "Peace in the World Is Everybody's Business" 700, 734–739
Bhutto, Benazir 700
    Address at the Fourth World Conference on Women 718–721
Bhutto, Zulfikar 718
Biden, Joe 747, 806
Billie Jean King: Commencement Address for University of Massachusetts, Amherst 511–513
Bill of Rights 131
Bin-Laden, Osama 746
Black, Hugo 528
#BlackLivesMatter (BLM) 644–645, 675–677, 746
Blackstone, William
    Commentaries on the Laws of England: "Of Husband and Wife" 47, 93–96
Bloomer, Amelia Jenks
    "Alas! Poor Adam" Speech 176, 191–195
    The Lily 191
Bloomer, Dexter 191
Bly, Nellie
    Ten Days in a Mad-House 290, 303–306
Boccaccio, Giovanni 45
Bonner, Marita O.
    "On Being Young—A Woman—And Colored" 644, 652–654
Bonnin, Gertrude Simmons. *See* Zitkala-Ša: "The Cutting of My Long Hair"
Bowers v. Hardwick 598
Bradley, Joseph P. 339
Bradstreet, Anne
    "Before the Birth of One of Her Children" 98, 108–110
    The Tenth Muse Lately Sprung Up in America, By a Gentlewoman in Those Parts 108
Bradstreet, Simon 108
Bradwell, Myra 338
Bradwell v. the State of Illinois 326, 338–341
Brent, Linda 300
Brent, Margaret: Request for Voting Rights 97, 104–105
Breyer, Stephen 555
Britain's Prisoner Act of 1913 165
Brooks, Jack 499
Brown, Elsa Barkley 672
Brown v. Board of Education of Topeka 435, 672
Buck, Carrie 515, 524
Buck v. Bell 515, 524–527
Bunch, Charlotte 700

"Through Women's Eyes: Global Forces Facing Women in the 21st Century" 722–725
Bureau of Indian Affairs 646
Burke, Edmund
 Reflections on the French Revolution 142
Burke, Tarana 644–645
 "Full Power of Women" 645, 695–698
Bush, George H.W. 644, 746
Bush v. Gore 746
Butler, Benjamin 196
Butler, Pierce 175, 187
Buxton, C. Lee 515, 528

C

Callixtus III (Pope) 59
Calvert, George 104
Calvert, Leonard 104
Carby, Hazel V. 608
 "White Woman Listen! Black Feminism and the Boundaries of Sisterhood" 616–619
Carmen Perez: Address at the Women's March on Washington 788–791
Caroline Norton: *Letter to the Queen on Lord Chancellor Cranworth's Marriage and Divorce Bill* 157–161
Carrie Chapman Catt: "Equal Suffrage" 272–274
Carson, Rachel
 Silent Spring 290, 322–325
Casey Hayden: "Sex and Caste" 427–430
Cat and Mouse Law. *See* Britain's Prisoner Act of 1913
Catharine Sawbridge Macauley Graham: *History of England* 135
Catharine Sawbridge Macauley Graham: *Letters on Education* 132, 135–138
Catherine E. Beecher: *Treatise on Domestic Economy* 176, 178–181
Catt, Carrie Chapman 215
 "Equal Suffrage" 272–274
Celler, Emanuel 419
Center for Women's Global Leadership 722
Cerullo, Margaret
 "Hidden History: An Illegal Abortion in 1968" 515, 548–550
Chadwick, Sarah 792
Chandra Talpade Mohanty: "Under Western Eyes" 620–622
Charles VI (King) 59

Charlotte Bunch: "Through Women's Eyes: Global Forces Facing Women in the 21st Century" 722–725
Charlotte Perkins Gilman: "The Humanness of Women" 256–259
Charlotte Perkins Gilman: "The Yellow Wallpaper" 256
Chaucer, Geoffrey
 The Canterbury Tales 51–53
 "The Wife of Bath" 45, 51–54
Chauvin, Derek 746
Chavez, Cesar 388
Cherokee Women: Letter to Governor Benjamin Franklin 122–124
Child, Lydia Maria
An Appeal in Favor of That Class of Americans Called Africans 290, 297–299
Chimamanda Ngozi Adichie: *Purple Hibiscus* 765
Chimamanda Ngozi Adichie: "We Should All Be Feminists" 764–767
Chinese Exclusion Act of 1882 176, 200
Chinese Revolution 268
Chisholm, Shirley 397, 431
 "Black Woman in Contemporary America" 472–475
 "For the Equal Rights Amendment" 454–457
Christine de Pisan: *The Treasure of the City of Ladies* 45, 55–58
Christine Jorgensen: "The Story of My Life" 580–583
Civil Rights Act of 1875 310
Civil Rights Act of 1964 265, 384, 396, 419–422, 423, 431, 435, 443, 462, 464, 483, 506
Civil Rights Act of 1965 644
Clara Barton: *The Red Cross in War and Peace* 290, 316–318
Clara Lemlich: "Life in the Shop" 362–364
Clara Lemlich: *New York Evening Journal* 362
Clara Zetkin: *Gleichhheit (Equality)* 345
Clara Zetkin: "Women's Work and the Trade Unions" 327, 345–347
Clarke, Cheryl 661
Clinton, Bill 499, 555, 713
Clinton, Hillary Rodham 699–700
 "Women's Rights Are Human Rights" 713–717
Code of Assura 11–13
Combahee River Collective Statement 644, 661–663
Comstock Act 514, 517–519
Comstock, Anthony 514
Congressional Union for Woman Suffrage 264
Constantine 37
Convention on the Elimination of All Forms of

Discrimination against Women (CEDAW) 809
Convention on the Rights of Persons with Disabilities (CRPD) 687, 689
Copeny, Mari 747
COVID-19 pandemic 746
Crenshaw, Kimberlé Williams 643, 644
    "Say Her Name" 678–681, 682–686
Cruz, Nikolas 792

Douglass, Frederick 213
Douglas, William O. 528
Du Bois, W. E. B. 355
Dudley, Robert 73
Dudley, Thomas 108
Dunbar-Nelson, Alice Moore 215
    "The Negro Woman and the Ballot" 281–283
Dyer Anti-Lynching Bill 215, 281

D

de Beauvoir, Simone 608
    The Second Sex 607, 610–612
Declaration of Independence 131, 220, 228
Defense of Marriage Act of 1996 566
de Gouges, Olympe 610
Declaration of the Rights of Woman and of the Female Citizen 131, 139–141
de Jesus, Ursula
    "Visions of the World to Come" 46, 76–78
de la Cruz, Juana Inés
    "The Poet's Answer to Sor Filotea de La Cruz" 46, 79–82
de Meun, Jean
    Romance of the Rose 55
Denise Harmon: "Stonewall Means Fight Back!" 566, 584–586
Deodat Lawson: *A Brief and True Narrative* 112
Deodat Lawson: "A Further Account of the Tryals of the New England Witches, Sent in a Letter from Thence, to a Gentleman in London" 98, 111–114
de Oliveira Azevedo, Pricilla 768
Department of Defense (DOD) 388
de Pisan, Christine
    The Treasure of the City of Ladies 45, 55–58
de Santa Cruz, Manuel Fernández 80
de Sigüenza y Góngora, Don Carlos 79
Dichloro-diphenyl-trichloroethane (DDT) 322
Diogo, Luisa D. 747
    "Women for a Better World" 753–756
Dobbs, Thomas 516
Dobbs v. Jackson Women's Health Organization 516, 518, 532, 549, 558–562
Dolores Huerta: "Migrant and Seasonal Farmworker Powerlessness" 388
Dolores Huerta: Statement to the Senate Subcommittee on Migratory Labor 388–391

E

Eastwood, Mary O.
    "Jane Crow and the Law: Sex Discrimination and Title VII" 423–426
Ebadi, Shirin 747
    "Iran Awakening: Human Rights, Women, and Islam" 749–752
Echenique, Maria Eugenia 132
    "The Emancipation of Women" 162–164
Edith M. Stern: "Women Are Household Slaves" 400–403
Edmund Burke: *Reflections on the French Revolution* 142
Education Act of 1972 464–467
Educational Amendments Act 397
Eleanor Roosevelt: *Red Book* 284
Eleanor Roosevelt: "Women Must Learn to Play the Game as Men Do" 215, 284–287
"Elena's Story" 738–741
Elinore Pruitt Stewart: *Letters of a Woman Homesteader* 177, 210–212
Elinore Pruitt Stewart: *Letters on an Elk Hunt* 210
Elizabeth Cady Stanton: Address to the New York Legislature 214, 231–234
Elizabeth Cady Stanton: Seneca Falls Convention Declaration of Sentiments 139, 213, 220–222, 228
Elizabeth Gurley Flynn: "The Truth about the Paterson Strike" 371–374
Elizabeth I (Queen): Speech to the Troops at Tilbury 46–47, 73–75
Elizabeth II (Queen) 784
Ella Baker: "The Black Woman in the Civil Rights Struggle" 397, 447–449
Ellen Johnson Sirleaf: "A Voice for Freedom" 757–759
Emerson, Ralph Waldo 182
Emma Goldman: *Anarchism and Other Essays* 569
Emma Goldman: "Marriage and Love" 565, 569–572
Emma Watson: "HeForShe" Speech to the United

Nations 776–779
Emmeline Pankhurst: "Freedom or Death" `132, 165–169
Enheduanna: *Hymns to Inana* 7–10
Environmental Protection Agency (EPA) 290, 323
Equal Employment Opportunity Commission (EEOC) 396, 397, 420, 443
Equal Opportunity in Education Act 507
Equal Pay Act 327, 381–383, 396–397, 412, 431, 462
Equal Rights Amendment (ERA) 265, 396, 397, 450, 454, 458, 462–463
Eusebius 41
Evers, Medgar 419
Executive Order 9981 435
Executive Order 10980 412
Executive Order 11246: Equal Employment Opportunity 384–387
Expatriation Act of 1907 577
Extradition Act of 1907 565

F

"Fabienne's Story" 742–745
Fair Labor Standards Act of 1938 381
Family Act 2004 753
Fannie Lou Hamer: Testimony at the Democratic National Convention 416–418
Fauset, Jessie Redmon
    "Some Notes on Color" 644, 649–651
Federal Council on Negro Affairs 658
Female genital mutilation (FGM) 743
Fifteenth Amendment 176, 191, 196, 214, 275, 310, 462
Fifth Amendment 602
Firestone, Shulmath 439
First Amendment 528
Florence Kelley: "Child Labor and Women's Suffrage" 352–354
Floyd, George 746
Flynn, Elizabeth Gurley 327
    "The Truth about the Paterson Strike" 371–374
Fourteenth Amendment 176, 196, 214, 235, 338, 339, 397, 404, 423, 435, 503, 524, 551, 598, 602, 643
France Revolution 131–132
Frances Anne Kemble: *Journal of a Residence on a Georgian Plantation in 1838-1839* 175, 187–190
Frances Gage: *Anti-Slavery Bugle* 229

Frances Willard: Address before the Woman's Christian Temperance Union 313–315
Frances Willard: "Do Everything Policy" 313
Frances Wright: *Course of Public Lectures* 293
Frances Wright: "Of Free Enquiry" 289, 293–296
Francis Parkman: *England and France in North America* 239
Francis Parkman: *Oregon Trail: Sketches of Prairie and Rocky-Mountain Life* 239
Francis Parkman: *Some of the Reasons against Woman Suffrage* 214, 239–242
Franco, Veronica
    A Warning to a Mother Considering Turning Her Daughter into a Courtesan 46, 70–71
Franklin, Benjamin 98, 122–123, 135, 559
Frazier, Demita 661
Freedom Summer project 416
Freedom Trash Can. *See* Miss America Pageant protest
Friedan, Betty
    Feminine Mystique 396–397, 408–411, 431
    "The Problem That Has No Name" 408
Frontiero, Sharron 468
Frontiero v. Richardson 468–471
Fuller, Margaret
    "The Great Lawsuit" 182
    Woman in the Nineteenth Century 176, 182–186

G

Gage, Frances
    Anti-Slavery Bugle 229
Gandhi, Indira
    "What Educated Women Can Do" 699, 702–705
Garrison, William Lloyd 297
Garza, Alicia
    "A Herstory of the #BlackLivesMatter Movement" 644, 675–677
Gbowee, Leymah 747
Gender Equality Architecture Reform 722
Geoffrey Chaucer: *The Canterbury Tales* 51–53
Geoffrey Chaucer: "The Wife of Bath" 45, 51–54
George III (King) 117
Gesell, Gerhard 536
Gestational Age Act 532
Gilman, Charlotte Perkins 214
    "The Humanness of Women" 256–259
    "The Yellow Wallpaper" 256

Ginsburg, Ruth Bader 503, 555–557, 558
    Concurrence in *Stenberg, Attorney General of Nebraska, et al. v. Carhart* 555–557
Glimer, Rachel 678
Gloria E. Anzaldúa: *Borderlands/La Frontera: The New Mestiza* 608, 634–637
Gloria Steinem: "A Bunny's Tale" 450
Gloria Steinem: "Living the Revolution" 450–453
Godwin, William 142, 147
Goldman, Emma
    Anarchism and Other Essays 569
    "Marriage and Love" 565, 569–572
González, X
    "We Call BS" 747, 792–795
Gough, Kathleen 590
Gouze, Marie. *See* Olympe de Gouges: *Declaration of the Rights of Man and of the Citizen*
Graham, Catharine Sawbridge Macauley
    History of England 135
    Letters on Education 132, 135–137
Great Depression 658
Great Migration 355
Greeley, Horace 300
Green Belt Movement 700, 730
Greene, Harold 419
Greta Thunberg: "Our House Is on Fire" 799–802
Grimké, Sarah M. 213
    Reply to the Pastoral Letter the General Association of Congregational Ministers of Massachusetts 216–219
Griswold, Estelle 515, 528
Griswold v. Connecticut 431–432, 515, 518, 528–531

H

Hadrian 29, 33
Hamer, Fannie Lou
    Testimony at the Democratic National Convention 416–418
"Hammer of the Witches" *See* Heinrich Kramer: *Malleus Maleficarum*
Han Dynasty 21
Hanisch, Carol 439
Happersett, Reese 235
Harlem Renaissance 644, 649, 652
Harmon, Denise
    "Stonewall Means Fight Back!" 566, 584–586

Harper, Ida Husted
    Statement before the U.S. Senate Select Committee on Woman Suffrage 214–215, 252–255
Harriet Beecher Stowe: *Boys' Own* 335
Harriet Beecher Stowe: *Uncle Tom's Cabin* 334
Harriet Jacobs: *Incidents in the Life of a Slave Girl* 290, 300–302
Harris, Kamala 747
    "The Status of Women Is the Status of Democracy" 806–808
Harris, Luke 678
Hatshepsut 3
Hayden, Casey
    "Sex and Caste" 427–430
Hays, Mary
    Appeal to the Men of Great Britain in Behalf of Women 147–149
    Female Biography 147
    Memoirs of Emma Courtney 147
    The Victim of Prejudice 147
Hazel V. Carby: "White Woman Listen! Black Feminism and the Boundaries of Sisterhood" 616–619
Heinrich Kramer: *Malleus Maleficarum* 46, 66–69
Helena Swanwick: *The Common Cause* 375
Helena Swanwick: *The War in Its Effect upon Women* 375–377
Helena Swanwick: *Women and War* 375
Henry, Patrick
    "Give me liberty or give me death" 165
Henry VI (King) 59
Hepburn, Katharine Houghton 165
Herodotus: *The History of the Persian Wars* 18–20
Heumann, Judith
    "Our Fight for Disability Rights and Why We're Not Done Yet" 643–644, 687–690
Higher Education Act of 1965 507
Hill, Anita 672
    Opening Statement at the Senate Confirmation Hearing of Clarence Thomas 644, 668–771
Hillary Rodham Clinton
    "Women's Rights Are Human Rights" 713–717
Hogg, David 792
Holmes, Oliver Wendell, Jr. 515
hooks, bell
    Feminist Theory: From Margin to Center 644, 664–667
Hoyt, Gwendolyn 404
Hoyt v. Florida 404–407
Huerta, Dolores 327

"Migrant and Seasonal Farmworker Powerlessness," 388
  Statement to the Senate Subcommittee on Migratory Labor 388–391
Hughes, Langston 649
Hull, Gloria Akasha 661
Hunt, Jane 220
Hurston, Zora Neale
  "How It Feels to Be Colored Me" 644, 655–657
Hussein (King) 726
Hutchinson, Anne
  Massachusetts Bay Colony Trial 97, 100–103

I

Ida B. Wells: "Lynching: Our National Crime" 290, 319–321
Ida B. Wells: *Southern Horrors* 290, 310–312
Ida Husted Harper: Statement before the U.S. Senate Select Committee on Woman Suffrage 214–215, 252–255
Indian Removal Act (1830) 178
Indira Gandhi: "What Educated Women Can Do" 699, 702–705
Industrial Revolution 326–327, 348
Industrial Workers of the World (IWW) 371
International Campaign for Abortion Rights (ICAR): International Day of Action 515, 540–543
International Council of Women (ICW) 252
International Ladies' Garment Workers' Union 379, 392
Iranian Revolution 749
Irigaray, Luce 607
  This Sex Which Is Not One 613
  "Women on the Market" 613–615
Irish Republican Army 700
Isabella Beeton: *Mrs. Beeton's Book of Household Management* 326, 334–337

J

Jack London: *The Call of the Wild and White Fang* 348
Jack London: *The People of the Abyss* 348–351
Jackson, Andrew 178
Jackson Women's Health Organization 516, 558
Jacobs, Harriet
  Incidents in the Life of a Slave Girl 290, 300–302
Jahjaga, Atifete 747
  Support of Women's Property Rights in Kosovo 780–783
Jane Addams: "The Subjective Necessity for Social Settlements" 307–309
Jane Addams: *Twenty Years at Hull-House* 307
Jane Addams: "Why Women Should Vote" 260–263
Jean de Meun: *Romance of the Rose* 55
Jenner, Edward 88
Jessie Redmon Fauset: "Some Notes on Color" 644, 649–651
Jeter, Mildred 435
Jim Crow laws 310, 423, 435, 693
Jo Ann Gibson Robinson: *The Montgomery Bus Boycott and the Women Who Started It* 487–490
Joan of Arc: Letter to King Henry VI of England 45, 59–61
Johnson, Georgia Douglas 649
Johnson, Jack 573
Johnson, Lyndon B. 327, 384, 419
Johnson, Marsha P. 587
Jordan, June
  "A New Politics of Sexuality" 566, 595–597
Jorgensen, Christine
  "The Story of My Life" 566, 580–583
Josephine St. Pierre Ruffin: "Address to the First National Conference of Colored Women" 243–245
Josina Machel: "Male Violence against Women: The Next Frontier in Humanity" 803–805
Joyce Hilda Banda: Wheelock College Commencement Address 784–787
Juana Inés de la Cruz: "The Poet's Answer to Sor Filotea de La Cruz" 46, 79–82
Judith Heumann: "Our Fight for Disability Rights and Why We're Not Done Yet" 643–644, 687–690
Julian of Norwich: *Revelations of Divine Love* 46, 48–50
June Jordan: "A New Politics of Sexuality" 566, 595–597
Juvenal: *Satires* 5, 33–35

K

Kamala Harris: "The Status of Women Is the Status of Democracy" 806–808
Kaskey, Cameron 792
Katzenbach, Nicholas 419

Kavanaugh, Brett 559
Kelley, Florence
    "Child Labor and Women's Suffrage" 352–354
Kelly Miller: "The Economic Handicap of the Negro in the North" 327, 355–357
Kemble, Frances Anne
    Journal of a Residence on a Georgian Plantation in 1838-1839 175, 187–190
Kempe, John 62
Kempe, Margery
    The Book of Margery Kempe 46, 62–65
Kennedy, Anthony M. 558, 598, 602
Kennedy, John F. 381, 396, 412, 419, 423, 431
Kennedy, Robert 419
Kimberlé Williams Crenshaw: "Say Her Name" 678–681, 682–686
King, Billie Jean
    Commencement Address for University of Massachusetts, Amherst 511–513
King, Deborah 672
King, Martin Luther, Jr. 427, 487
King, Mary
    "Sex and Caste" 427–430
Knights of Labor 368
Kramer, Heinrich
    Malleus Maleficarum 46, 66–69
Kuhluka movement 803

L

Lady Hong: "Diary of Lady Hong, Queen of Korea" 46, 90–92
Lady Mary Wortley Montagu: Smallpox Vaccination in Turkey 46, 87–89
La Maestra Community Health Centers 742
Lawrence v. Texas 566, 598–601
Lawson, Deodat
    A Brief and True Narrative 112
    "A Further Account of the Tryals of the New England Witches, Sent in a Letter from Thence, to a Gentleman in London" 98, 111–114
Lee, Mabel Ping-Hua 214
    "The Submerged Half" 268–271
Leiserson and the Rosen Brothers factories 392
Lemlich, Clara 326, 327
    "Life in the Shop" 362–364
    New York Evening Journal 362

Leonora O'Reilly: Statement to the U.S. House Judiciary Committee 368–370
Lesbian, gay, bisexual, transgender, and queer (LGBTQ+) community 566, 584
Letter from Elizabeth Sprigs to Her Father 115–116
Lévi-Strauss, Claude 613
Licuco, Rofino 803
Lima, Jineth Bedoya 768
Lindsey, Theophilus 147
London, Jack
    The Call of the Wild and White Fang 348
    The People of the Abyss 348–351
London Missionary Society 154
Lorde, Audre 661
    "Master's Tools Will Never Dismantle the Master's House" 608, 630–633
    "Poetry Is Not a Luxury" 479–482
    Sister Outsider: Essays and Speeches 479, 630
Loughridge, William 196
Loving, Richard 435
Loving v. Virginia 435–438
Lowell, Francis Cabot 330
Luce Irigaray: *This Sex Which Is Not One* 613
Luce Irigaray: "Women on the Market" 613–615
Lucretia Mott: "Discourse on Women" 224–227
Lucy Parsons: "The Negro: Let Him Leave Politics to the Politician and Prayers to the Preacher" 342–344
Lugones, María
    "Heterosexualism and the Colonial/Modern Gender System" 638
    "Toward a Decolonial Feminism" 608, 638–641
Luisa D. Diogo: "Women for a Better World" 753–756
Lu, Xiao 608
    "China: Feudal Attitudes, Party Control, and Half the Sky" 623–626
Lydia Maria Child: *An Appeal in Favor of That Class of Americans Called Africans* 290, 297–299

M

Maathai, Wangari 700
    Nobel Peace Prize Acceptance Speech 730–733
Mabel Ping-Hua Lee: "The Submerged Half" 268–271
Machel, Graça Simbine 803
Machel, Josina 747
    "Male Violence against Women: The Next Frontier in Humanity" 803–805

Machel, Samora 803
Mackenzie, Ethel 577
Mackenzie v. Hare 565, 577–579
Madrigal v. Quilligan 515
Maguire, Mairead Corrigan 700
Malala Yousafzai: *I Am Malala: The Girl Who Stood Up for Education and Was Shot by the Taliban* 747
Malala Yousafzai: Nobel Peace Prize Acceptance Speech 772–775
Mandamin, Josephine 796
Mandela, Nelson 803
Mann Act 565, 566, 573–576
Mann, James R. 573
Mao Zedong 608, 623
Marcus Aurelius 29
Margaret Brent's Request for Voting Rights 97, 104–105
Margaret Cerullo: "Hidden History: An Illegal Abortion in 1968" 515, 548–550
Margaret Fuller: "The Great Lawsuit" 182
Margaret Fuller: *Woman in the Nineteenth Century* 176, 182–186
Margaret Sanger: "Awakening and Revolt" 514
Margaret Sanger: "Birth Control and Racial Betterment" 514, 520–522
Margaret Sanger: *What Every Girl Should Know* 520
Margery Kempe: *The Book of Margery Kempe* 46, 62–65
Maria Eugenia Echenique: "The Emancipation of Women" 162–164
María Lugones: "Heterosexualism and the Colonial/Modern Gender System" 638
María Lugones: "Toward a Decolonial Feminism" 608, 638–641
Marie-Atoinette (Queen) 139
Marita O. Bonner: "On Being Young—A Woman—And Colored" 644, 652–654
Married Women's Property Act (1870) 157
Marselian, Zara 738–741, 742–745
Marshall, Burke 419
Martin, Trayvon 644, 675
Marxist-Leninist Liberation Front 608
Mary (Queen) 73
Mary Astell: *A Serious Proposal to the Ladies for the Advancement of Their True and Greatest Interest* 46, 83–86
Mary Church Terrell: "The Progress of Colored Women" 246–248
Mary Hays: *Appeal to the Men of Great Britain in Behalf of Women* 147–149
Mary Hays: *Female Biography* 147
Mary Hays: *Memoirs of Emma Courtney* 147
Mary Hays: *The Victim of Prejudice* 147
Mary King: "Sex and Caste" 427–430
Mary McLeod Bethune: "What Does American Democracy Mean to Me?" 644, 658–660
Mary O. Eastwood: "Jane Crow and the Law: Sex Discrimination and Title VII" 423–426
Mary S. Paul: Letters from Lowell Mills 330–333
Mary Wollstonecraft: *A Vindication of the Rights of Woman* 132, 139, 142–146, 147
Massachusetts Bay Colony Trial against Anne Hutchinson 97, 100–103
Matrimonial Causes Act (1857) 157
McClintock, Mary Ann 220
McCray, Chirlane 661
McCulloch, William 419
Menchú Tum, Rigoberta
    Nobel Peace Prize Lecture 699, 709–712
Meritor Savings Bank v. Vinson 483–486
#MeToo 644, 695
Michelle Bachelet: "Time to Make the Promise of Equality a Reality" 760–763
Michelle Obama: *Becoming* 768
Michelle Obama: Remarks at the 2012 International Women of Courage Awards 768–771
Michelle Obama: *The Light We Carry: Overcoming in Uncertain Times* 768
Michelle Obama: *The Story of the White House Kitchen Garden and Gardens across America* 768
Miller, Kelly
    "The Economic Handicap of the Negro in the North" 327, 355–357
Miller, Samuel Freeman 338
Mink, Patsy
    Speech on the 25th Anniversary of Title IX 507–510
Minor v. Happersett 214, 235–238
Minor, Virginia 235
Miss America Pageant protest 439
Mississippi Freedom Democratic Party (MFDP) 416
Mohanty, Chandra Talpade 608
    "Under Western Eyes" 620–622
Mondell, Franklin Wheeler 264
Montagu, Lady Mary Wortley 46
Morgan, Robin
    "No More Miss America!" 439–442
Morrison, Joan 392
Moss, Thomas 319

"Mother's Life in Rural Pernambuco, Brazil" 706–708
Mott, Lucretia 213, 220, 289
    "Discourse on Women" 224–227
Mulizi, Bakili 784
Muller v. Oregon 358–361
Murray, Pauli 431
    "Jane Crow and the Law: Sex Discrimination and Title VII" 423–426

N

National American Woman Suffrage Association (NAWSA) 214, 215, 246, 272, 275, 352
National Association for the Advancement of Colored People (NAACP) 278, 319, 447
National Association of Colored Women 658
National Association of Colored Women's Clubs (NACWC) 246
National Black Feminist Organization 661
National Collegiate Athletic Association (NCAA) 511
National Council of Negro Women 658
National Council of Women of Kenya 730
National Farm Workers Association 388
National Organization for Women (NOW) Statement of Purpose 397, 431–434, 443
National Union of Women's Suffrage Societies (NUWSS) 375
National Woman's Party (NWP) 214, 215, 462
National Women's Suffrage Association (NWSA) 214
National Women's Trade Union League: Women's Work and War 327, 378–380
Near Eastern legal codes 11
Nehru, Jawaharlal 702
Nellie Bly: *Ten Days in a Mad-House* 290, 303–306
Newman, Pauline
    A Worker Recalls Her Time at the Triangle Shirtwaist Factory 392–395
Nineteenth Amendment to the U.S. Constitution 214–215, 235, 252, 265, 275–277, 396, 458, 462, 643
Nixon, Richard 511
Noor of Jordan (Queen): Remarks at the National Organization for Arab-American Women Banquet 726–729
Norton, Caroline
    Letter to the Queen on Lord Chancellor Cranworth's Marriage and Divorce Bill 157–161
Norton, George 157
Norton v. Melbourne 157

O

Obama, Barack 691, 747, 768
Obama, Michelle 747
    Becoming 768
    The Light We Carry: Overcoming in Uncertain Times 768
    Remarks at the 2012 International Women of Courage Awards 768–771
    The Story of the White House Kitchen Garden and Gardens across America 768
Obergefell v. Hodges 435, 566, 602–605
O'Connor, Sandra Day
    "Portia's Progress" 495–498
Okazawa-Rey, Margo 661
Olympe de Gouges: *Declaration of the Rights of Woman and of the Female Citizen* 131, 139
Oprah Winfrey: Cecil B. DeMille Award Acceptance Speech 645, 691–694
O'Reilly, Leonora
    Statement to the U.S. House Judiciary Committee 368–370
Origen 41

P

Page Act of 1875 176, 200–202
Paine, Thomas 142
Pankhurst, Emmeline
    "Freedom or Death" 132, 165–169
Parkman, Francis
    England and France in North America 239
    Oregon Trail: Sketches of Prairie and Rocky-Mountain Life 239
    Some of the Reasons against Woman Suffrage 214, 239–242
Parsons, Albert
    The Alarm 342
Parsons, Lucy
    "The Negro: Let Him Leave Politics to the Politician and Prayers to the Preacher" 342–344
Patrick Henry: "Give me liberty or give me death" 165

Patriot Act of 2001 746
Patsy Mink: Speech on the 25th Anniversary of Title IX 507–510
Paul, Alice 215, 462
    Testimony before the House Judiciary Committee 264–267
Pauli Murray: "Jane Crow and the Law: Sex Discrimination and Title VII" 423–426
Pauline Newman: A Worker Recalls Her Time at the Triangle Shirtwaist Factory 392–395
Paul, Mary S. 326, 327
    Letters from Lowell Mills 330–333
Pavey, Safak 768
Pelosi, Nancy 747
Peltier, Autumn 747
    Address at the UN World Water Day 796–798
Perez, Carmen
    Address at the Women's March on Washington 788–791
Perpetua, Vibia
    The Passion of Saints Perpetua and Felicity 37–40
Peterson, Esther 381
Philip II (King) 73
Phillis Wheatley: "His Excellency General Washington" 98, 117–119
Phillis Wheatley: *Poems on Various Subjects, Religious and Moral* 117
Phips, William 111–112
Phule, Jyotiba 154
Phule, Savitribai
    "Go, Get Education" 132, 154–156
Phyllis Schlafly: "What's Wrong with 'Equal Rights' for Women?" 458–461
Pickens, William 215
    "The Woman Voter Hits the Color Line" 278–280
Pittsburgh Press v. Pittsburgh Human Relations Committee 444
Planned Parenthood v. Casey 397, 515, 532, 551–554
Plutarch: *Moralia*: "On the Bravery of Women" 5, 25–26
Pratt, Richard Henry 646
President's Commission on the Status of Women: "American Women" 412–415
Priestley, Joseph 147
Priscilla Bell Wakefield: *An Introduction to Botany* 150
Priscilla Bell Wakefield: *An Introduction to the Natural History and Classifications of Insects* 150
Priscilla Bell Wakefield: *Juvenile Anecdotes, Founded on Facts* 150
Priscilla Bell Wakefield: *The Juvenile Travellers* 150
Priscilla Bell Wakefield: *Reflection on the Present Condition of the Female Sex; with Suggestions for Improvement* 132, 150–153

R

Rachel Carson: *Silent Spring* 290, 322–325
Rankin, Jeannette 275
Ransby, Barbara 672
Rauh, Joseph L., Jr. 416
Rehnquist, William 544
Relf, Mary Alice 515
Relf, Minnie Lee 515
Relf v. Weinberger 515, 536–539
Representation of the People Act 166
Rich, Adrienne
    "Compulsory Heterosexuality and Lesbian Experience" 590–594
Richie, Andrea J. 678
Riggs, Bobby 511
Rigoberta Menchú Tum: Nobel Peace Prize Lecture 699, 709–712
Rivera, Sylvia 587–589
    "Y'all Better Quiet Down" 566
Robin Morgan: "No More Miss America!" 439–442
Robinson, Jo Ann Gibson
    The Montgomery Bus Boycott and the Women Who Started It 487–490
Robinson, Marius 229
Roe v. Wade 397, 511, 515, 518, 532–535, 540, 544, 549, 551, 558
Roosevelt, Eleanor 412, 431
    Red Book 284
    "Women Must Learn to Play the Game as Men Do" 215, 284–287
Roosevelt, Franklin D. 644, 658
Roosevelt, Theodore 275
Rose Schneiderman: Speech on the Triangle Shirtwaist Fire 365–367
Rousseau, Jean-Jacques 142
Ruffin, Josephine St. Pierre 214, "Address to the First National Conference of Colored Women" 243–245
Rush, Benjamin 135
    "Thoughts upon Female Education" 98, 125–129

S

St. Jerome: Letter CVII to Laeta 41–44
Sanchez, Loretta 806
Sandra Day O'Connor: "Portia's Progress" 495–498
Sanger, Margaret
    "Awakening and Revolt" 514
    "Birth Control and Racial Betterment" 514, 520–522
    What Every Girl Should Know 520
Sappho: Poems and Fragments 14–17
Sarah M. Grimké: Reply to the Pastoral Letter the General Association of Congregational Ministers of Massachusetts 216–219
Sarah Winnemucca Hopkins: *Life Among the Paiutes* 176–177, 203–205
Sargent, Aaron A. 275
Savitribai Phule: "Go, Get Education" 132, 154–156
Say Her Name: Resisting Police Brutality against Black Women 644, 678–681
Schlafly, Phyllis 397
    "What's Wrong with 'Equal Rights' for Women?" 458–461
Schneiderman, Rose
    Speech on the Triangle Shirtwaist Fire 327, 365–367
Scott, C. P. 375
Seaman, Elizabeth Cochran 290, 303
Segregated Employment Ads 443–446
Seneca Falls Convention Declaration of Sentiments 139, 213, 220–223, 228
Septimius Severus 38
Shakespeare, William
    The Merchant of Venice 495
Shammuramat 3
Shaw, Anna Howard 214
    Address on the Place of Women in Society 249–251
Sheridan, Richard 157
Shirin Ebadi: "Iran Awakening: Human Rights, Women, and Islam" 749–752
Shirley Chisholm: "The Black Woman in Contemporary America" 472–475
Shirley Chisholm: "For the Equal Rights Amendment" 454–457
Sickert, Oswald 375
Simango, Celina 608
Simone de Beauvoir: *The Second Sex* 607, 610–612
Sirleaf, Ellen Johnson 747
    "A Voice for Freedom" 757–759
Smith, Adam
    The Wealth of Nations 150
Smith, Barbara 661
Smith, Beverly 661
Smith, Howard W. 420
Sojourner Truth: "Ain't I a Woman?" 214, 228–230
Soranus: *Gynaecology* 29–32
Southern Christian Leadership Conference (SCLC) 447
Sprigs, Elizabeth 98
    Letter to Her Father 115–116
Sprigs, John 115–116
Stanton, Elizabeth Cady 191, 643
    Address to the New York Legislature 214, 231–234
    Seneca Falls Convention Declaration of Sentiments 139, 213, 220–223, 228
Steinem, Gloria
    "A Bunny's Tale" 450
    "Living the Revolution" 450–453
Stenberg, Attorney General of Nebraska, et al. v. Carhart 555–557
Stern, Edith M. 396
    "Women Are Household Slaves" 400–403
Stewart, Clyde 210
Stewart, Elinore Pruitt
    Letters of a Woman Homesteader 177, 210–212
    Letters on an Elk Hunt 210
Stewart, Helen L. 661
Stonewall Riots 566
STOP ERA (Stop Taking Our Privileges ERA) 458–459
Stowe, Harriet Beecher
    Boys' Own 335
    Uncle Tom's Cabin 334
Street Transvestite Action Revolutionaries (STAR) 587
Student Nonviolent Coordinating Committee (SNCC) 427, 447
Susan B. Anthony: "The Status of Woman, Past, Present, and Future" 176, 206–209
Sustainable Development Goal 5: Achieve Gender Equality and Empower All Women and Girls 809–811
Sutherland, George 264
Swanwick, Frederick Tertius 375
Swanwick, Helena
    The Common Cause 375
    The War in Its Effect upon Women 375–377
    Women and War 375
Sylvia Rivera: "Y'all Better Quiet Down" 566

T

Taft, William Howard 573
Tarana Burke: "Full Power of Women" 645, 695–698
Taylor, Billy Jean 476
Taylor, Sidney L. 483
Taylor v. Louisiana 476–478
Temperance Movement 214
Terrell, Mary Church 214
    "The Progress of Colored Women" 246–248
Theodosius I 37
Thirteenth Amendment 290, 644
Thomas, Clarence 644, 668, 672
Thoreau, Henry David 182
Thunberg, Greta 747
    "Our House Is on Fire" 799–802
TIME'S UP organization 692
Title IX Education Act of 1972
Title VII of the Civil Rights Act of 1964 419–422
Tower Amendment 464
Tower, John 464
Trajan 29, 33
Triangle Shirtwaist Factory Fire 327, 365–367, 392–395
Truman, Harry S. 435
Trump, Donald 747, 788, 806
Truth, Sojourner 661
    "Ain't I a Woman?" 214, 228–230
Tubman, Harriet 661
Twenty-first Amendment 290

U

United Farm Workers (UFW) 388
United Nations Entity for Gender Equality and the Empowerment of Women (UN Women) 722, 760, 776
United Nations Security Council 760
United Nations World Conference 700
United States v. Virginia 397, 503–506
Ursula de Jesus: "Visions of the World to Come" 46, 76–78

V

Veronica Franco: A Warning to a Mother Considering Turning Her Daughter into a Courtesan 46, 70–72
Vibia Perpetua: *The Passion of Saints Perpetua and Felicity* 37–40

Victoria (Queen) 157
Victoria Woodhull: *Lecture on Constitutional Equality* 196–199
Vieira, António 80
Vinson, Mechelle 483
Violence Against Women Act (VAWA) 397, 499–502
Violent Crime Control and Law Enforcement Act of 1994 499
Virginia's Act XII: Negro Women's Children to Serve according to the Condition of the Mother 106
Virginia Woolf: *A Room of One's Own* 170–173
Votes for Women: Suffrage in the United States 213–215
Voting Rights Act of 1965 435

W

Wage Earner's Suffrage League 368
Waite, Morrison 235
Wakefield, Priscilla Bell
    An Introduction to Botany 150
    An Introduction to the Natural History and Classifications of Insects 150
    Juvenile Anecdotes, Founded on Facts 150
    Juvenile Travellers 150
    Reflection on the Present Condition of the Female Sex; with Suggestions for Improvement 132, 150–153
Wangari Maathai: Nobel Peace Prize Acceptance Speech 730–733
Warren, Earl 435
Warren, Mercy Otis 98
Washington, Booker T. 355
Washington, George 120, 135
Watkins, Gloria Jean. See bell hooks: *Feminist Theory: From Margin to Center*
Watson, Emma 747
    "HeForShe" Speech to the United Nations 776–779
Webster v. Reproductive Health Services 515, 544–547
Weinstein, Harvey 645
Wells, Ida B. 661
    "Lynching: Our National Crime" 290, 319–321
    Southern Horrors 290, 310–312
Wheatley, Phillis 98
    "His Excellency General Washington" 98, 117–118
    Poems on Various Subjects, Religious and Moral 117

White-Slave Traffic Act 1910. *See* Mann Act 1910
Willard, Frances 290
    Address before the Woman's Christian Temperance Union 313–315
    "Do Everything Policy" 313
William Blackstone: *Commentaries on the Laws of England*: "Of Husband and Wife" 47, 93–96
William Pickens: "The Woman Voter Hits the Color Line" 278–280
Williams, Betty
    "Peace in the World Is Everybody's Business" 700, 734–739
William Shakespeare: *The Merchant of Venice* 495
Wilson, Woodrow 215, 275
Winfrey, Oprah
    Cecil B. DeMille Award Acceptance Speech 645, 691–694
Winnemucca Hopkins, Sarah
    Life among the Paiutes 176–177, 203–205
Winthrop, John 100
Wittenmyer, Annie 313
Wollstonecraft, Mary
    A Vindication of the Rights of Woman 132, 139, 142–146, 147
Woman's Christian Temperance Union (WCTU) 290, 313
Women of Liberia Mass Action for Peace movement 747
Women of the World (WOW) 682
Women's Educational Equity Act of 1974 507
Women's Environment and Development Organization (WEDO) 491
Women's March on Washington 788
Women's Rights Convention 228, 231
Women's Social and Political Union (WSPU) 165
Women's Suffrage Association 235
Woodhull, Victoria
    Lecture on Constitutional Equality 176, 196–199
Woolf, Virginia 132
    A Room of One's Own 170–173
Wordsworth, William 142
Wright, Frances
    Course of Public Lectures 293
    "Of Free Enquiry" 289, 293–296
Wright, Martha 220
Wynne, Robert 106

X

X González: "We Call BS" 747, 792–795
Xiao Lu: "China: Feudal Attitudes, Party Control, and Half the Sky" 623–626

Y

Yousafzai, Malala
    I Am Malala: The Girl Who Stood Up for Education and Was Shot by the Taliban 747
    Nobel Peace Prize Acceptance Speech 772–775

Z

Zara Marselian: *The Soul Speaks* 738–745
Zedong, Mao 608, 623
Zetkin, Clara
    Gleichhheit (Equality) 345
    "Women's Work and the Trade Unions" 327, 345–347
Zetkin, Ossip 345
Zhao, Ban
    History of the Han 21
    Lessons for a Woman 21–24
Zimmerman, George 675
Zitkala-Ša: *American Indian Stories* 646
Zitkala-Ša: "The Cutting of My Long Hair" 643, 646–648
Zora Neale Hurston: "How It Feels to Be Colored Me" 644, 655–657
Zundel, Georg Friedrich 345